DOGS IN THE WORKPLACE

unleashing the benefits of canine companionship

JACKIE RICHARDS

SUPPORTING

All Dogs Matter
Rescue and Rehoming

BYTHEBOOK.PRESS

First published in 2025

Typesetting: ByTheBook
Printed and bound in Europe through Xpedient Book Print

A CIP record for this book is available from the British Library

ISBN 978-1-917625-05-0

MIX
Paper | Supporting responsible forestry
FSC® C129413

To all the wonderful, loyal dogs I have met and to their equally wonderful owners. Canine presence in the workplace is invaluable – dogs bring joy, companionship, listening ears, wagging tails and love. They do this without complaint, tea breaks, or boardroom demands.

And to all my wonderful, supportive humans.

CONTENTS

FOREWORD

I'm a huge supporter and fan of dogs in the workplace. We are so lucky to have dogs in our lives and if the workplace is a suitable environment for the dog to be relaxed and happy it is a win-win for us all. Dogs are so completely members of our family and – unlike our human members – never seem to grow up. They always depend on us just as we depend on them. Our bond with dogs releases oxytocin, a bonding hormone which releases stress. Making the workplace a less stressful place helps us function better, in my opinion. But that aside... I just love having my dogs with me, so... I'm all for dogs in the workplace. Read and enjoy.

Peter Egan
Patron – All Dogs Matter

INTRODUCTION

I've been photographing dogs in workplaces since 2013. It's been a joyous, surprising, and transformative journey – and this book is the result. It pays tribute to a changing work culture: one that recognises the deep connection between wellbeing and productivity, and the powerful ways our environments shape how we feel.

In recent years, a quiet shift has taken place. Amid the click of keyboards and the hum of meetings, a new sound is being welcomed: the soft padding of paws. Increasingly, this is viewed as forward-thinking, humane, and grounded in both science and experience. Once seen as unprofessional or impractical, dogs in the workplace are now embraced by forward-thinking companies like Salesforce, Google, Ben & Jerry's and Uber. Their presence isn't just a quirk or a perk – it's part of a broader understanding that wellbeing matters. And dogs, it turns out, can make a measurable difference.

Research shows that dogs can reduce stress, lower blood pressure, boost morale and elevate levels of dopamine, serotonin and oxytocin – the neurochemicals behind happiness, bonding and calm. They spark conversations, foster connection, and lighten the emotional load of high-pressure environments. They help make workplaces feel more friendly.

Dogs model the qualities we aspire to in ourselves and hope for from our colleagues: loyalty, presence, empathy, and the ability to lift spirits with small, authentic gestures. Their quiet companionship reminds us that success isn't just about performance or productivity – it's also about how we feel while we work.

Of course, this cultural shift comes with challenges. Not every space can or should become a free-for-all of paws and play. Allergies, fears and practical concerns matter. That's why many organisations are crafting thoughtful policies – or partnering with groups like Cuddle Club UK or Canine Workplace Wellbeing – to integrate dogs in ways that are inclusive, respectful and sustainable.

This trend also reflects a generational shift. During the COVID-19 pandemic, dog ownership soared. Post-pandemic, many workers were reluctant to leave their canine companions behind – and for younger generations, pet-friendly policies are now a serious factor in job decisions. Some surveys suggest up to 50% of employees would consider changing jobs to work in an environment where they could bring their dog.

That may sound surprising – unless you've experienced it. Once you've shared your workday with a dog curled up under your desk or greeting your team at the door, it's hard to go back. They don't just change how we work – they change the nature of the work itself.

This book documents that shift across the world. My hope is that, beyond the delightful faces and wagging tails, you'll see a new philosophy of work emerging: one that embraces care, connection and community.

As you turn these pages, you may be reminded of a dog you know – or wish you did. You might imagine what your own workday would feel like with a Golden Retriever at your feet, or a snoozing Dachshund snuggled in the seat behind you.

Most of all, I hope this book invites you to pause and reflect on what it means to feel at ease – not just at work, but in life. And to remember that sometimes, the smallest changes – like opening the door to a dog – can have the biggest impact.

Welcome to the evolving world of work.

Jackie Richards
August 2025

Publishers' Note:
Jackie is donating 50% of the royalties for this book to All Dogs Matter, a dog rescue charity working in and around London to transform the lives of unwanted and abandoned dogs.

alldogsmatter.co.uk

SHOP DOGS

How it all began:
a stroll through cities, towns and villages with my camera, on the lookout for dogs in shops, searching for telltale signs of a dog's presence: a soft toy, a treat, a lead or a dog's bed near the counter. Days in shops can be long;
dogs help break the monotony – and also charm customers.
The owners I meet are equally charming and happy to take part when I explain the purpose of my project. Often, they say, 'I'm not looking my best today,' and I reassure them that they are fine as they are, and remind them that, after all, it's not really about them – it's mainly about the dogs.

CHARLIE Hammersmith, London, UK

Young Jackapoo Charlie sulks if his owner, Bill, doesn't take him to work – and won't make eye contact when Bill comes back in the evening. Charlie likes to watch the world go by, perched on the counter of the key cutting and cobbler's shop in the entrance hall of a London tube station. When not attracting customers, he spends time under a desk, chewing on a leather sole.

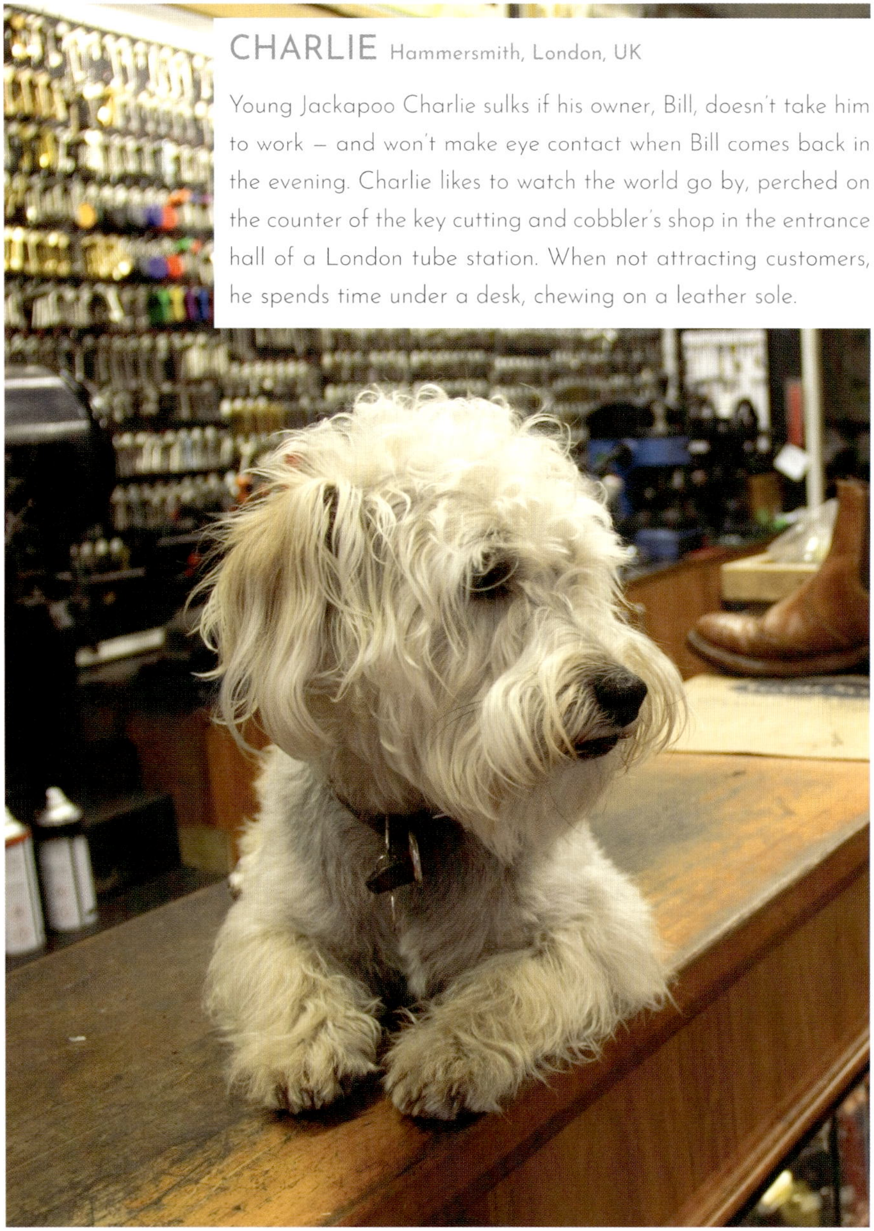

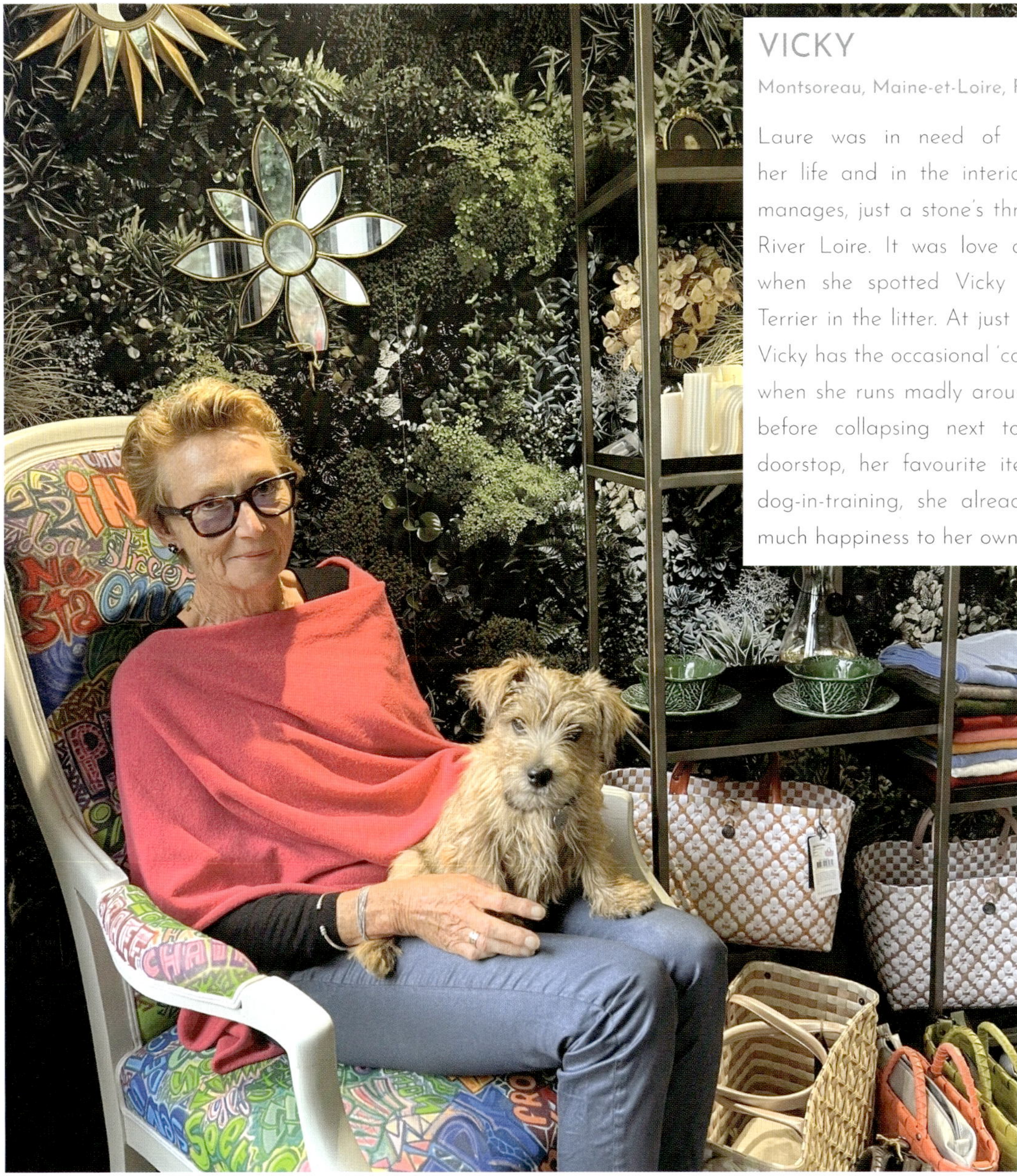

VICKY

Montsoreau, Maine-et-Loire, France

Laure was in need of company in her life and in the interiors shop she manages, just a stone's throw from the River Loire. It was love at first sight when she spotted Vicky the Norfolk Terrier in the litter. At just four months, Vicky has the occasional 'coupe de folie' when she runs madly around the store, before collapsing next to the sheep doorstop, her favourite item. A shop-dog-in-training, she already brings so much happiness to her owner.

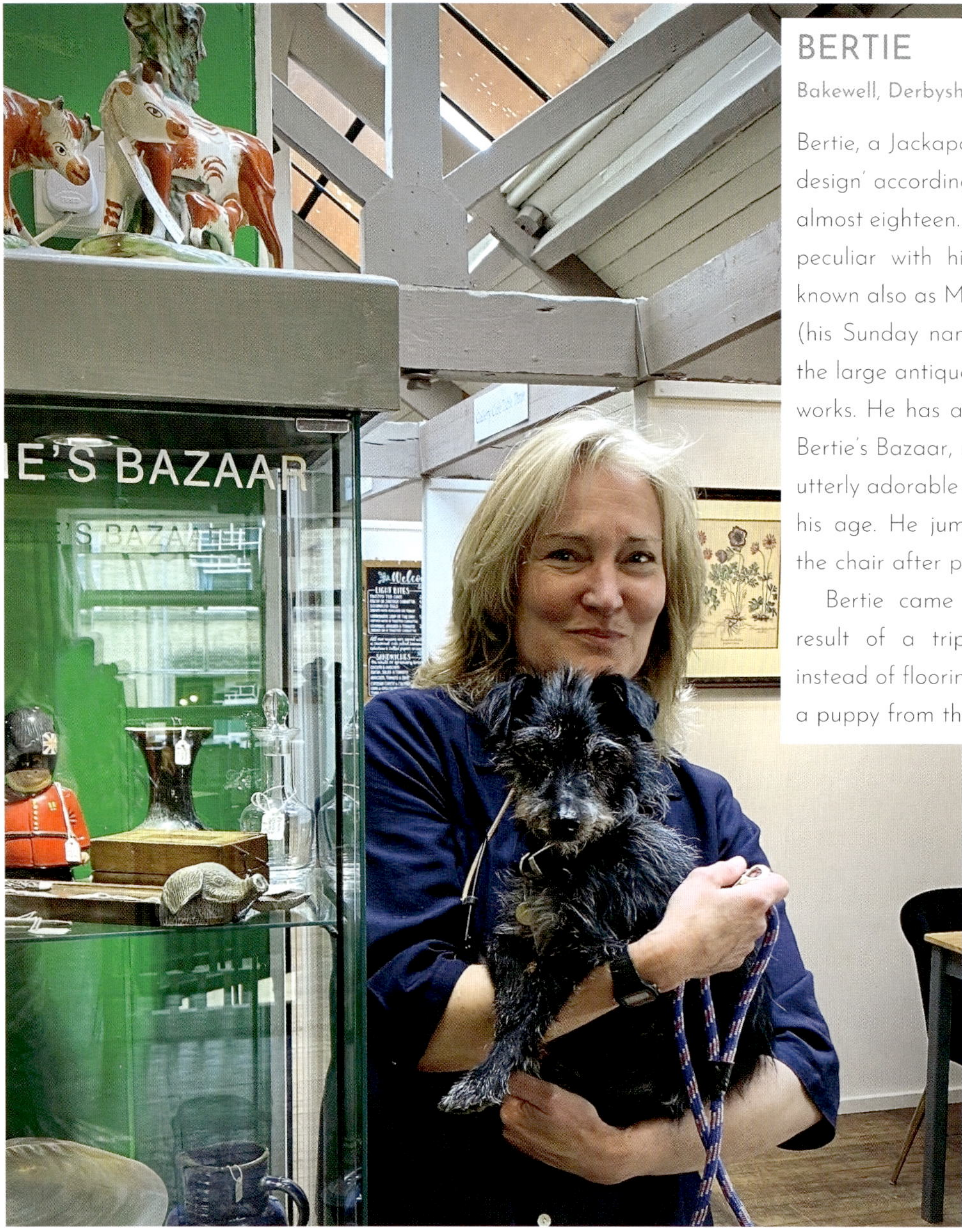

BERTIE

Bakewell, Derbyshire, UK

Bertie, a Jackapoo – 'by crime and not design' according to his owner, Liz – is almost eighteen. Delightful with people, peculiar with his own kind, Bertie – known also as Mr B, Berts and Bertram (his Sunday name) – loves coming to the large antiques emporium where Liz works. He has a glass display cabinet, Bertie's Bazaar, named after him. He is utterly adorable and very agile, despite his age. He jumped quite happily off the chair after posing.

Bertie came into Liz's life as the result of a trip to buy floorboards; instead of flooring, Liz came home with a puppy from the showroom litter.

PAGAY

La Garde-Freinet, Var, France

Pagay, the butcher's Chihuahua, lives with Mickael above the shop. Pagay knows when it's Sunday, as it's the only day she is allowed a treat, and she waits patiently beneath the butcher's block for her weekly morsel of steak haché.

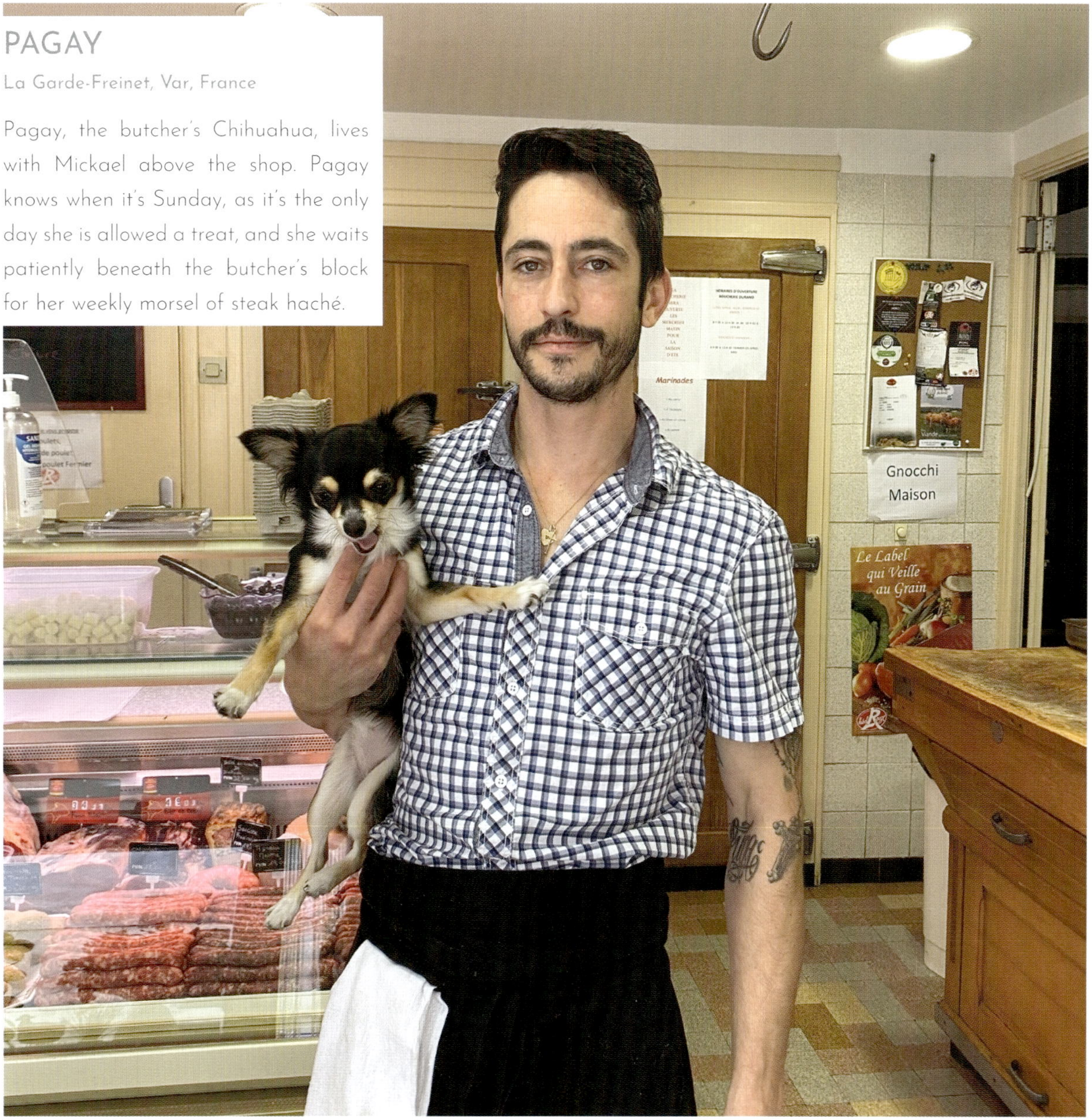

MURPHY Frome, Somerset, UK

Murphy is a gentle giant who loves sitting in the window of the gift shop named after his owner Ben's mum, Jude, who had been battling cancer. When the Golden Retriever isn't watching the world go by from the front window, he will be in the office upstairs, lying on his bed next to Ben's desk. As soon as Murphy hears the shop service bell go, he will be the first to charge downstairs to greet the customers.

He is beautifully behaved and knows not to touch the soft toys on display. He has his own dinosaur toy – Steggy – to play with. His best friend, Otis, works his own magic in the stationery store across the way.

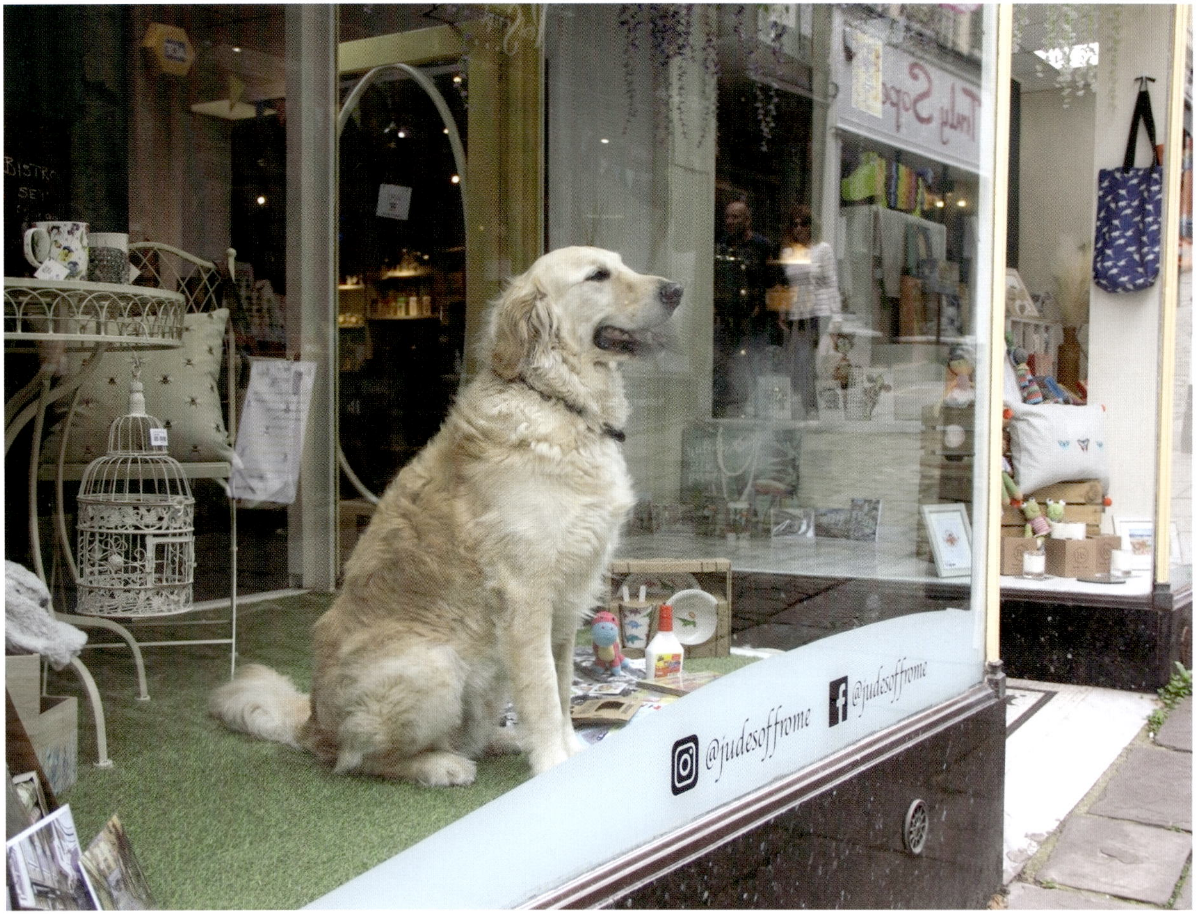

YUNA Sainte Maxime, Var, France

'I am not a fox. I am a Shiba Inu. Photo in exchange for treats,' reads a sticker outside Marion's boutique, where Yuna often lies. She loves her life in the shop and is happy with any form of verbal appreciation, although she has a tag requesting visitors not to touch her.

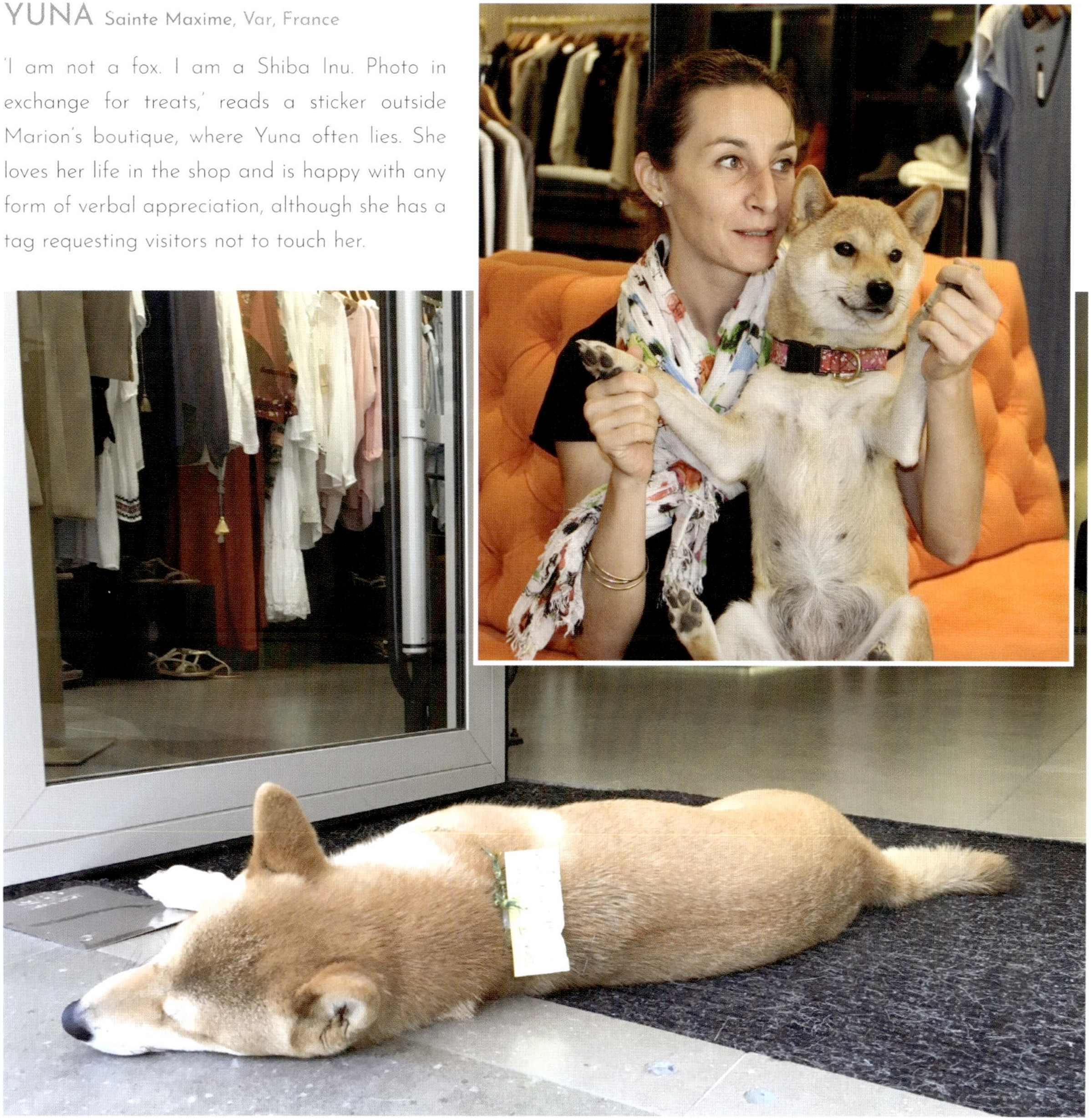

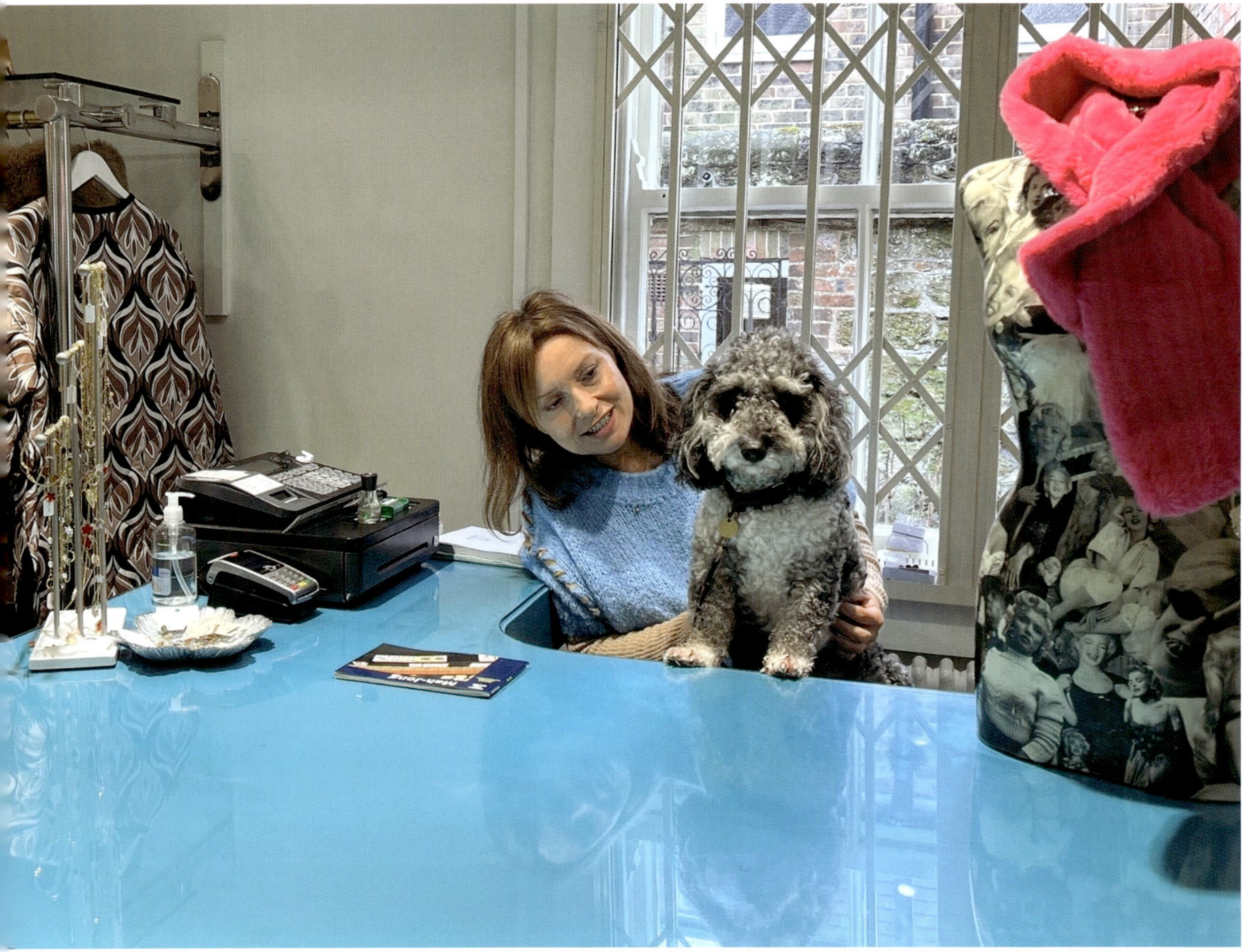

ERNIE Petworth, West Sussex, UK

Kathy lost her previous dog to an adder, and wanted a new dog to keep her company in lockdown. She bought a Cockapoo and called him Ernie, because she had worked hard to earn him. Now he is a decorative addition to the clothes boutique where she works, with a bed by the radiator next to the counter. When Kathy works late, Ernie will drag his bed out and chew on it until she gets the message that it is time to shut up shop.

STELLA & TATO Breuil-Cervinia, Valle d'Aosta, Italy

Stella and Tato are Galgos Españoles – Spanish hunting dogs – two of ten rescue dogs Marco brings to his ski shop. Since he was young, Marco has always wanted to rescue abandoned dogs. Tato is still afraid of people and remains quietly on her bed behind the till. Stella sleeps close by.

Both dogs go out skiing with Marco; Tato runs alongside him, and Stella sits in a special rucksack, as she has difficulties running.

Marco says he needs to have his dogs around him all the time; although they keep him busy, they cheer him up and raise his oxytocin levels.

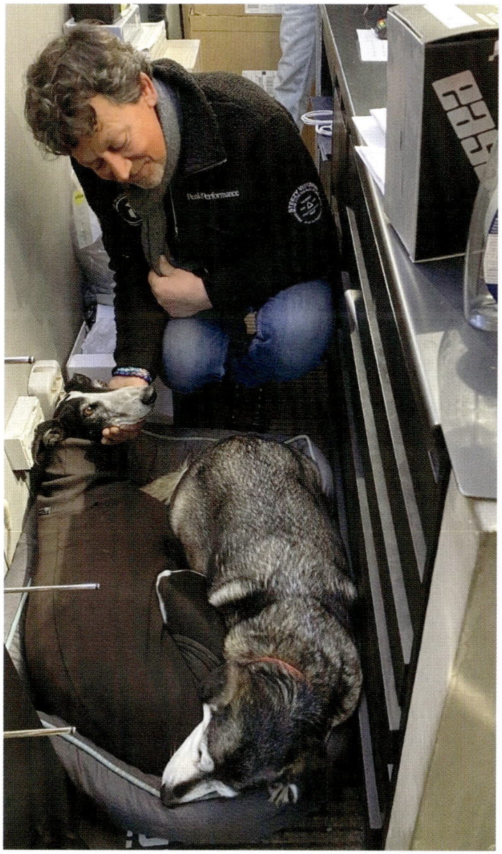

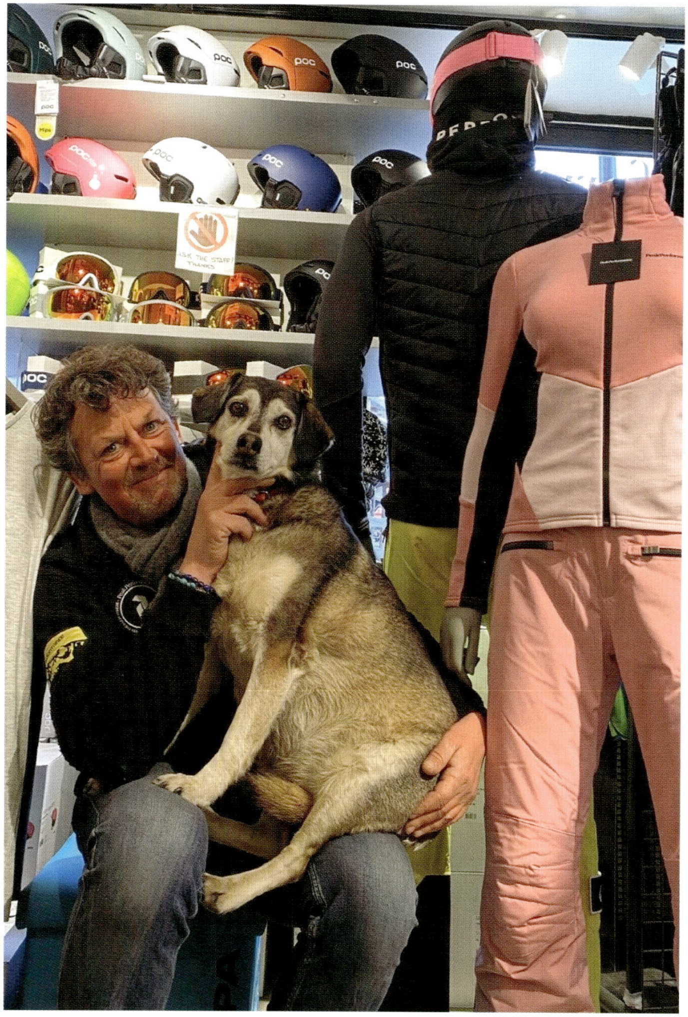

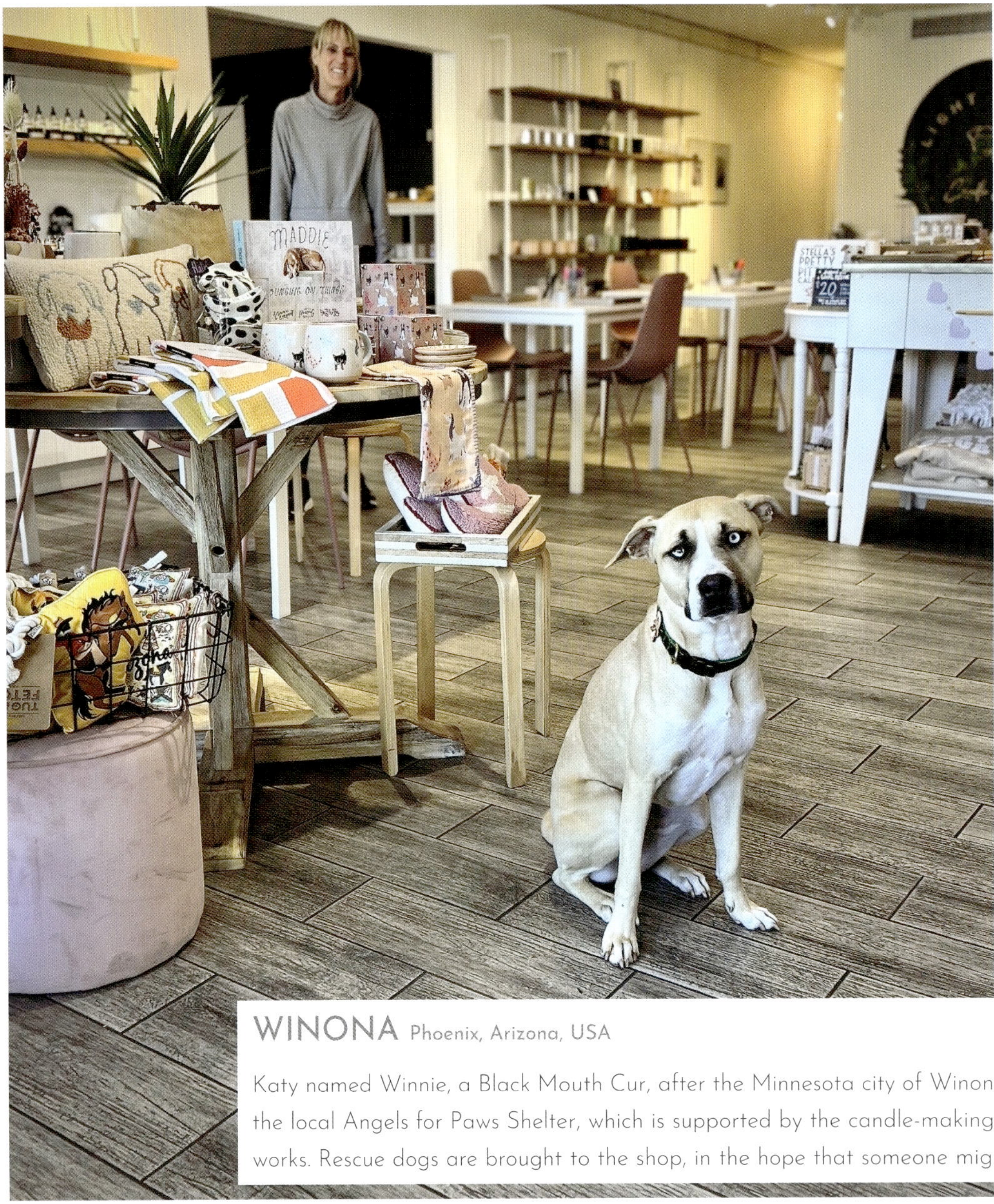

WINONA Phoenix, Arizona, USA

Katy named Winnie, a Black Mouth Cur, after the Minnesota city of Winona. She came from the local Angels for Paws Shelter, which is supported by the candle-making store where Katy works. Rescue dogs are brought to the shop, in the hope that someone might adopt them.

JOEY Brighton, East Sussex, UK

Joey the Welsh Terrier is one of three dogs that bring entertainment to the cycle shop managed by Jamie. The others are Bill (who is female) and Joy (who, despite her name, is permanently grumpy).

Joey is the most expensive, having been operated on and cared for by a celebrity supervet.

Bruno, who repairs the bikes, enjoys throwing balls for the dogs to retrieve, allowing them to create mayhem between the rows of bikes and stands.

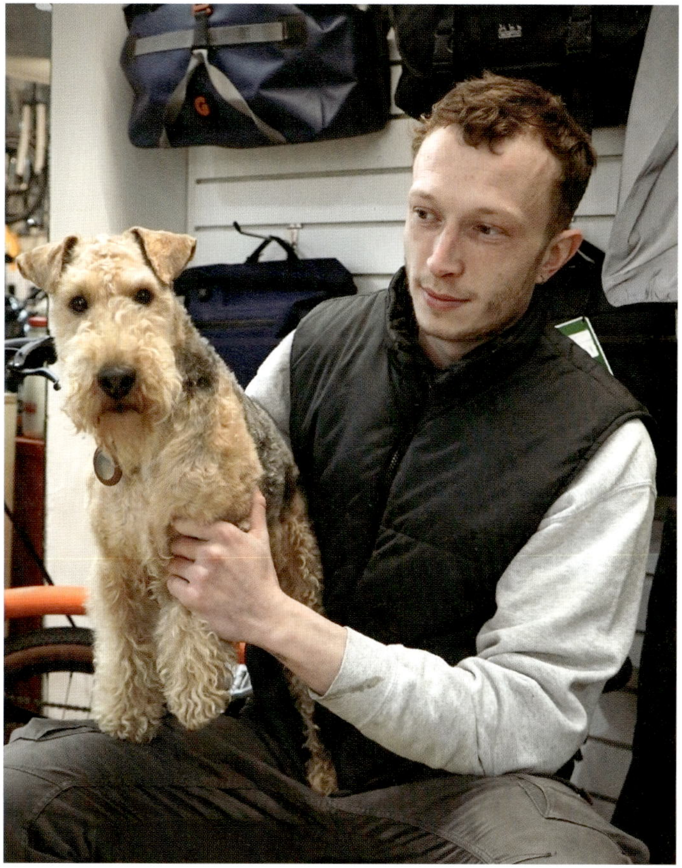

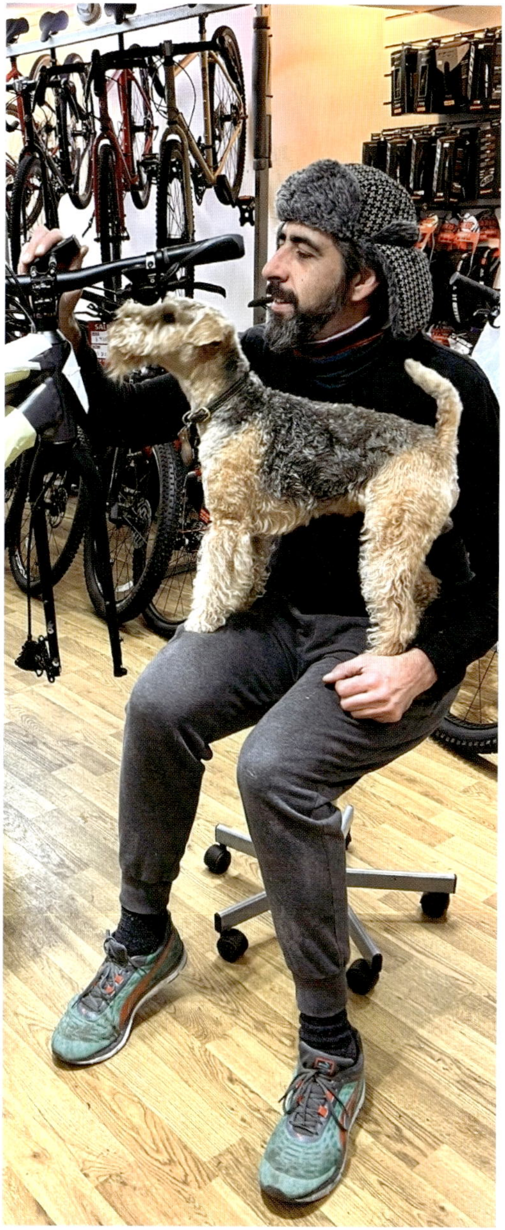

HELIOS Paris, France

Helios the Akita arrives in style at the men's boutique where his owner, Nathan, works. Nathan transports Helios all over Paris in his tricycle. According to Nathan's father, his son has a closer bond with his dog than his girlfriend.

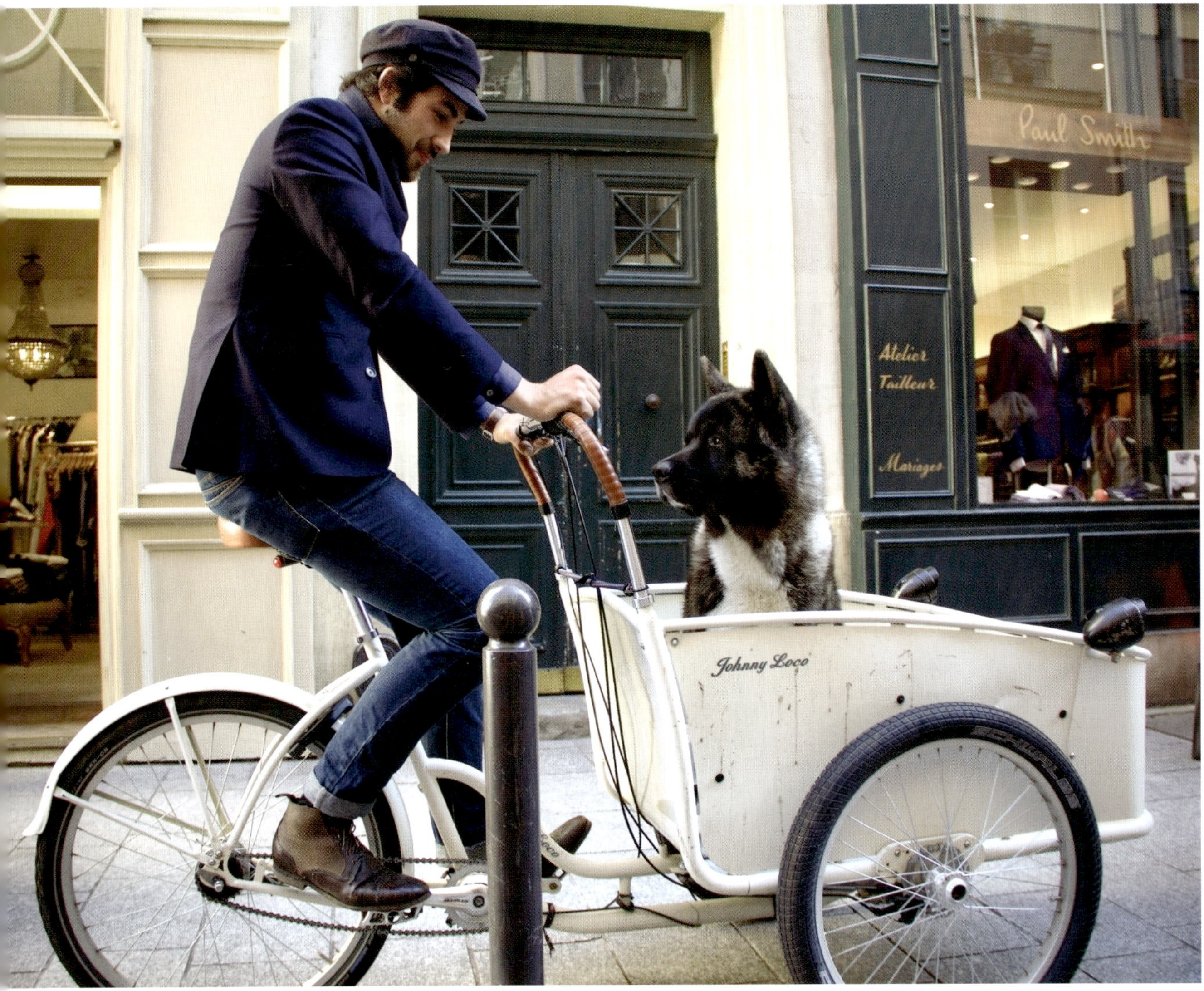

KHALEESI

Tallinn, Estonia

Khaleesi, named after the famed *Game of Thrones* character who raises dragons, is a celebrity in Tallinn. She lives with her owner, Anastasia, in the oldest house in the Baltic and above the doll shop Anastasia runs for her parents. The house is steeped in history and was once inhabited by Dominican priests who called themselves godhounds.

Khaleesi sits on the front step of the shop, drawing admiring glances from the many tourists, and tempting them in to purchase the famous Russian dolls made by Anastasia's mother.

Khaleesi is a Samoyed, one of the oldest breeds. Anastasia calls Khaleesi her 'fluffy angel, made out of clouds. She's my happiness, she listens to me.'

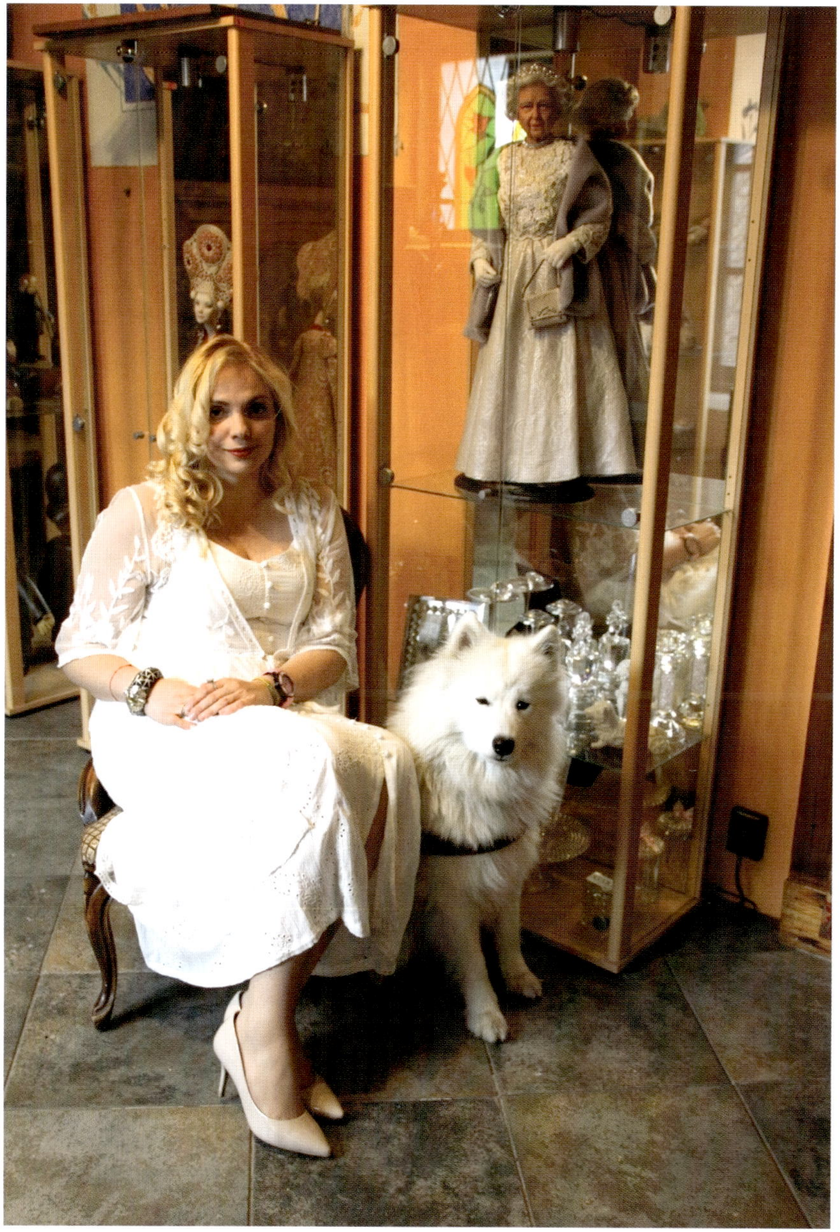

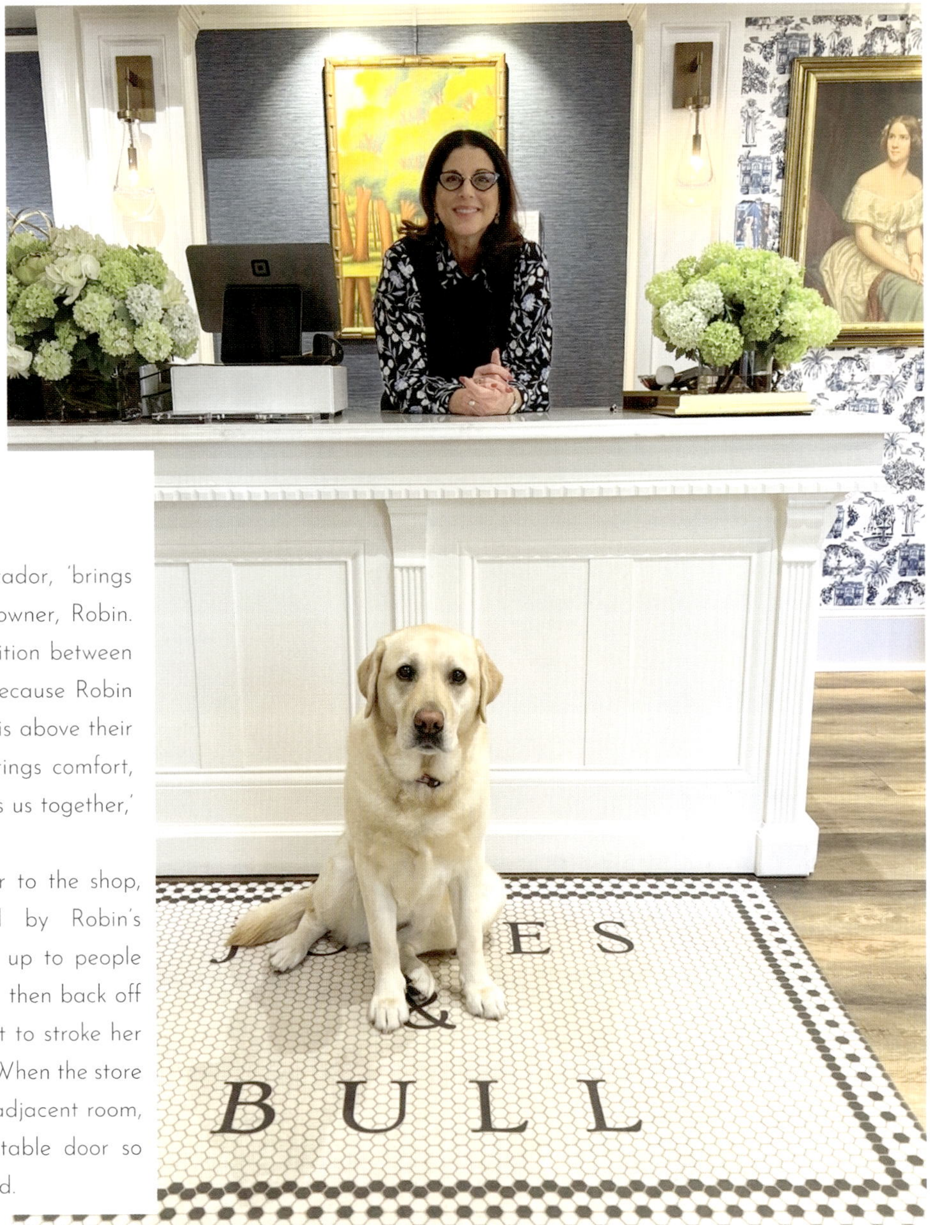

MURPHY

Savannah, Georgia, USA

Murphy, a Golden Labrador, 'brings home to work' says her owner, Robin. There is a seamless transition between home and work, partly because Robin and her husband's home is above their antique shop. 'Murphy brings comfort, and is the glue that keeps us together,' adds Robin.

She also adds humour to the shop, and has been trained by Robin's husband, Andy, to come up to people who want to pat her, and then back off as soon as they reach out to stroke her – like a missed high five. When the store is busy, Murphy is in an adjacent room, separated by a Dutch stable door so she can still feel connected.

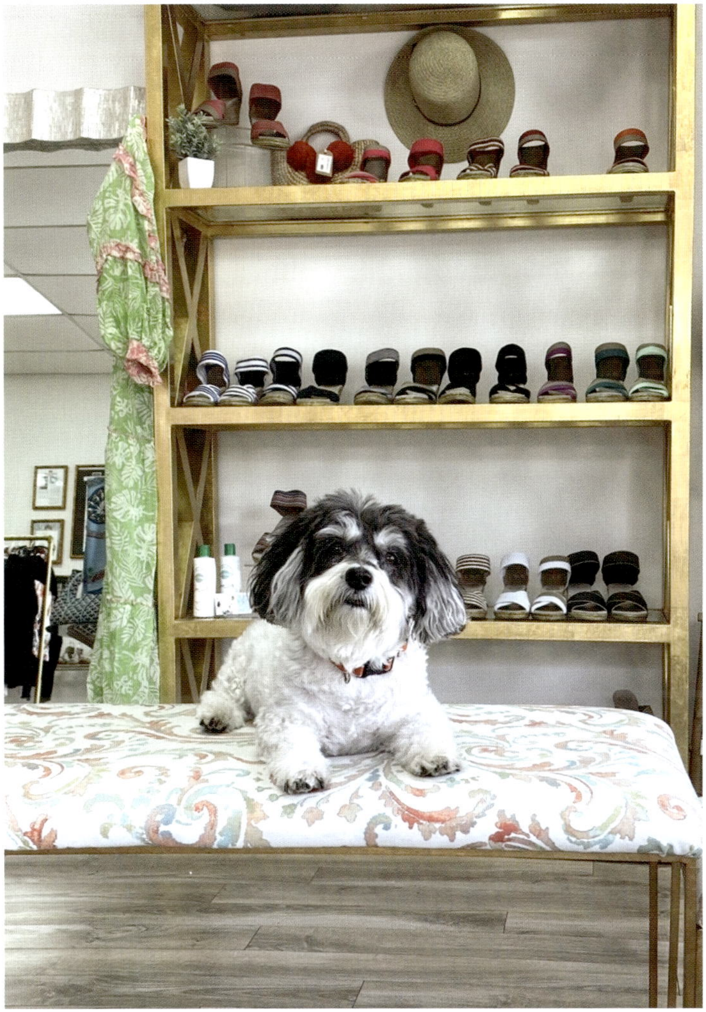

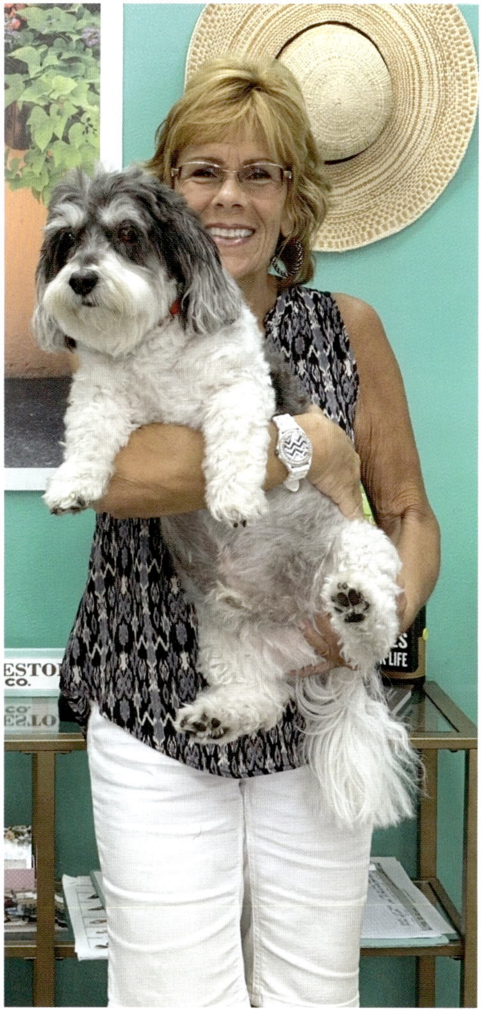

RAFA Naples, Florida, USA

This little Havanese – named after the tennis player, Rafa Nadal, and the archangel, Raphael – soothes customers and creates a peaceful shopping environment inside the smart shoe store where he assists his owner, Sara. The store owner is dog-mad and has created a shoe called the Chewie. Rafa does not chew shoes.

PIP

Margate, Kent, UK

I came across Pip fast asleep on a Biba low armchair, outside the antiques shop run by her owner, Roxana.

Pip, a (mostly) very chilled King Charles Spaniel, came into Roxana's life quite by chance. One day, Roxana found a bronze sculpture of a Greyhound that had been discarded into a skip. Sensing it was worth something, she took it to be valued and it fetched a tidy sum at auction. With the money, Roxana bought Pip, originally as a gift for her daughter, although the dog now spends most of her time with Roxana.

Pip's life is in and around antiques and she is often found asleep in or on different pieces – from a wok to a Victorian pram – in or outside the shop. She has good road sense, and does not wander off.

Roxana takes her for walks by the sea, where her unchilled side comes through and she runs round and round in circles.

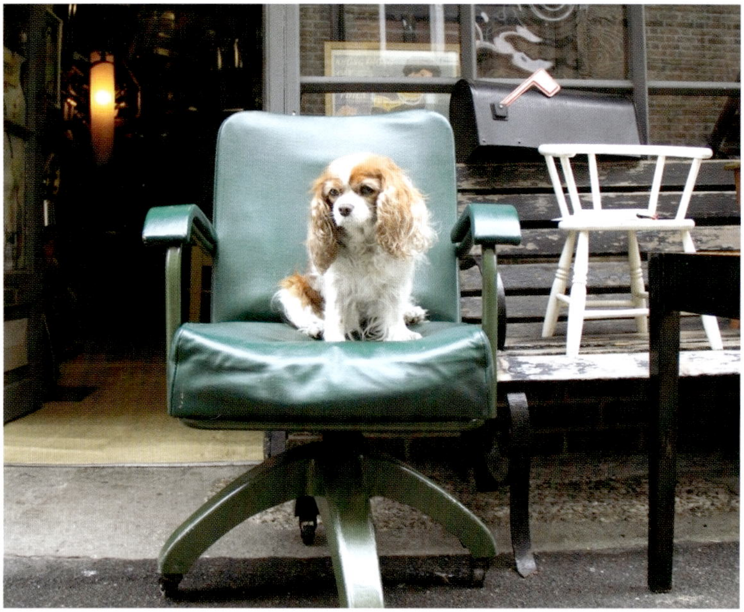

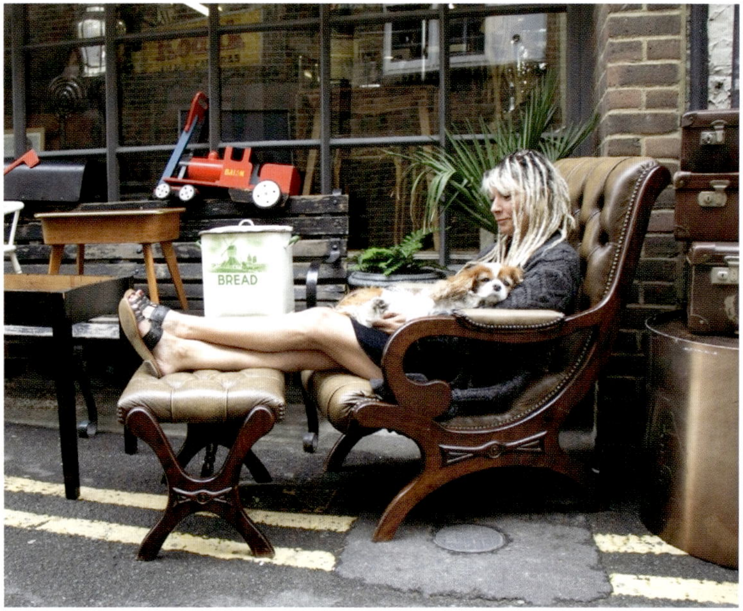

TWIGLET & BEA Yarmouth, Isle of Wight, UK

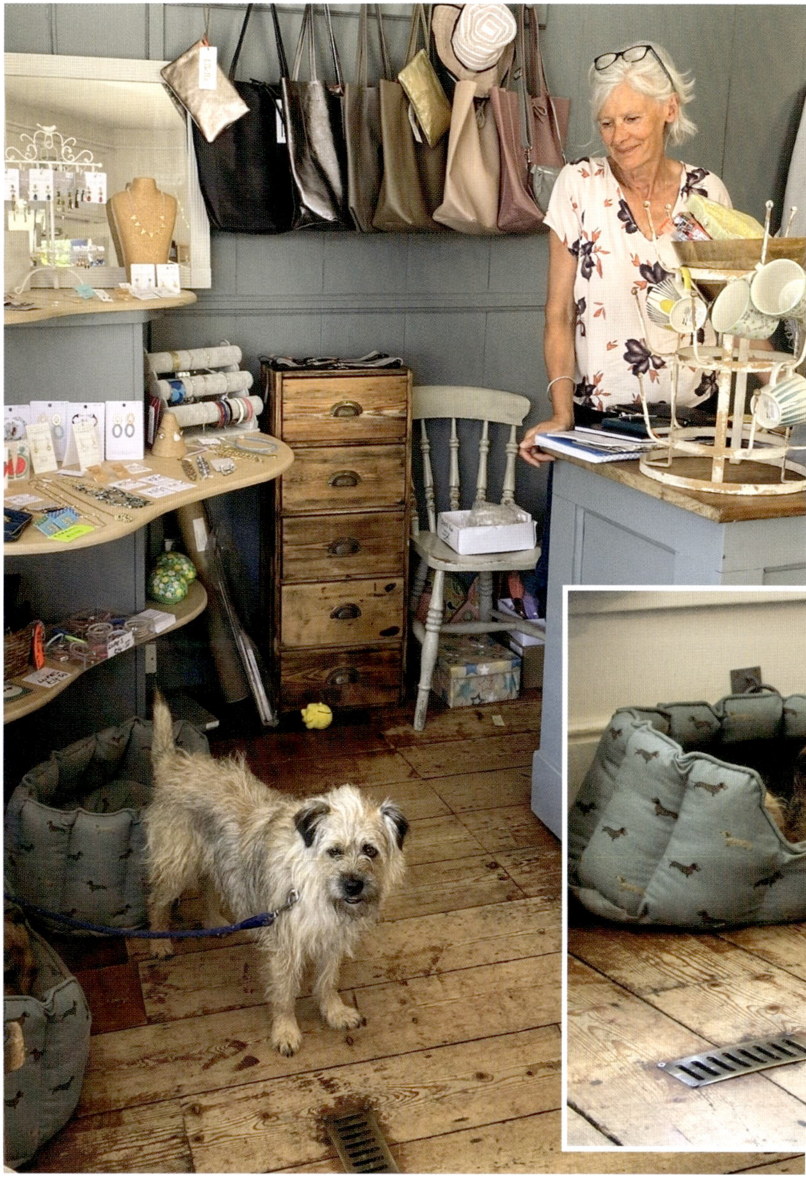

Twiglet, a Wire-haired Terrier mix, belongs to Alison, who runs a gift shop on the Isle of Wight. Before she died, Alison's best friend convinced her she should get a dog, and Twiglet was acquired from a vet who had had several terriers dumped on his practice. Twiglet's son, Bea, was conceived at a Christmas party.

Both dogs are very well-behaved. Alison says that they are wonderful company in the shop – in fact, they are just wonderful company: full stop.

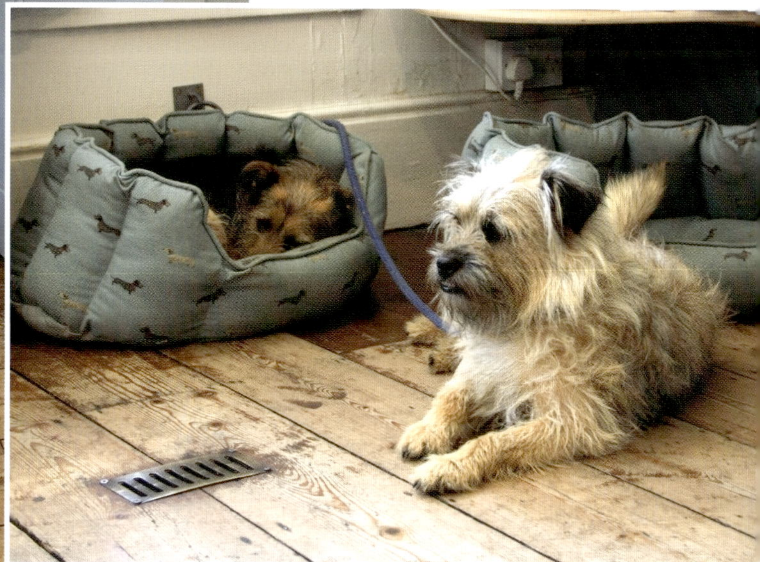

BRISKET Chiswick, London, UK

Brisket, a Red Fox Lab, knows he's coming to work when his owner, Philippa, takes him on the bus. He is reluctant to get off, but speeds up as soon as they are near the shop. Philippa is a florist and works in a basement below a bakery: hot upstairs, cool below – perfect for loaves and flowers. As soon as they arrive, Raluca, the baker, leaves her sourdough prepping and greets Brisket with floury hands. Then Brisket heads downstairs and straight to his bed.

His favourite toys are the twigs that Philippa occasionally drops when preparing her floral arrangements. He loves to play in the nearby dog park on his break-time. Often, when he returns from his mid-day walk, Brisket will slurp water from the bowl, flop down on his bed, and maintain that he is too exhausted to get up.

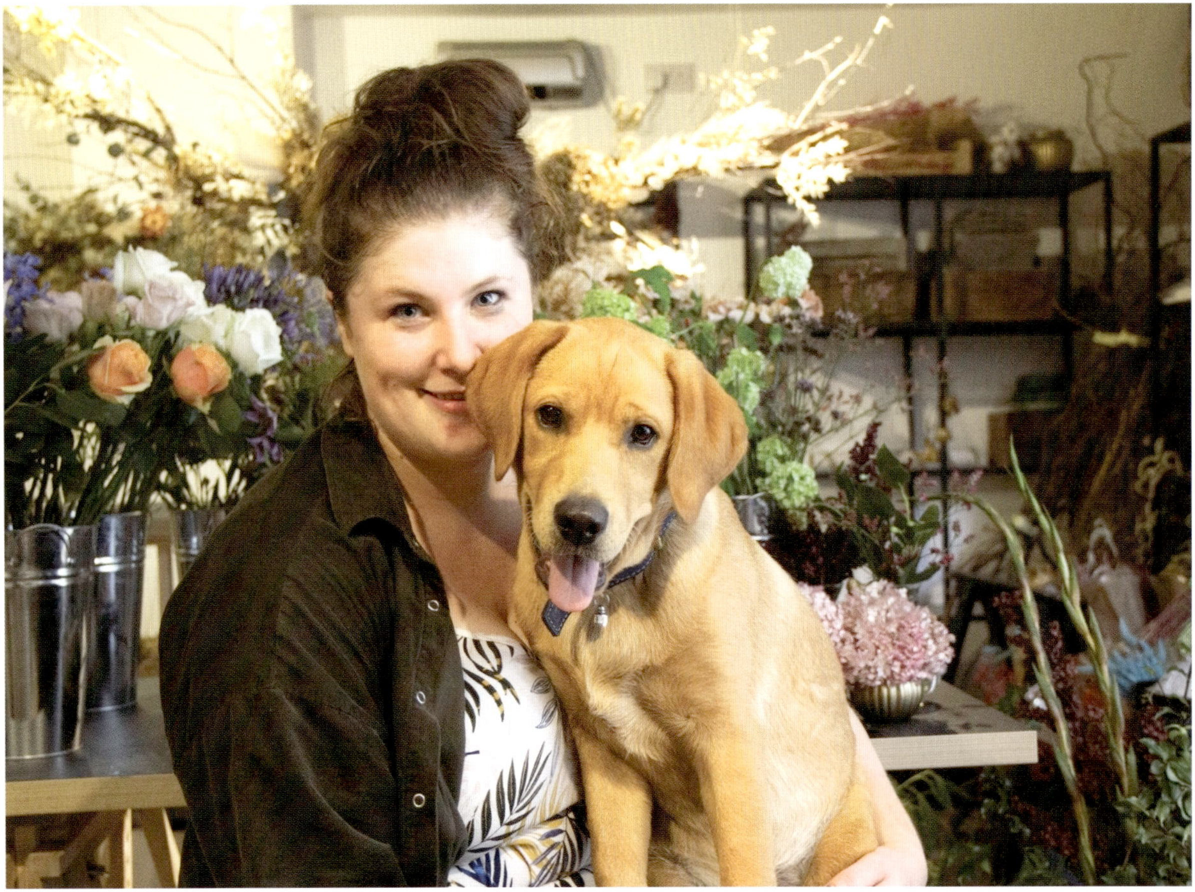

BIJOU

Naples, Florida, USA

'The absolute joy that wasn't there before' is how Cindy describes her dog, Bijou, named after the jewellery store she owns and runs. Bijou, now six, was a happy accident – Cindy wasn't thinking of having a dog, but when she met a friend's new litter of Bernedoodle puppies, it was Bijou who picked Cindy, by jumping into her arms. And now Bijou, French for jewel, is part of the business, and one of its employees.

According to Cindy, Bijou is 'eye spy' – she sits under the counter and jumps up to greet and sniff everybody, hoping for a belly rub. She was shy of customers at first and preferred to spend her time stretched out in the back office – until a visiting dog had the audacity to lie in her bed. Bijou has refused to use it ever since.

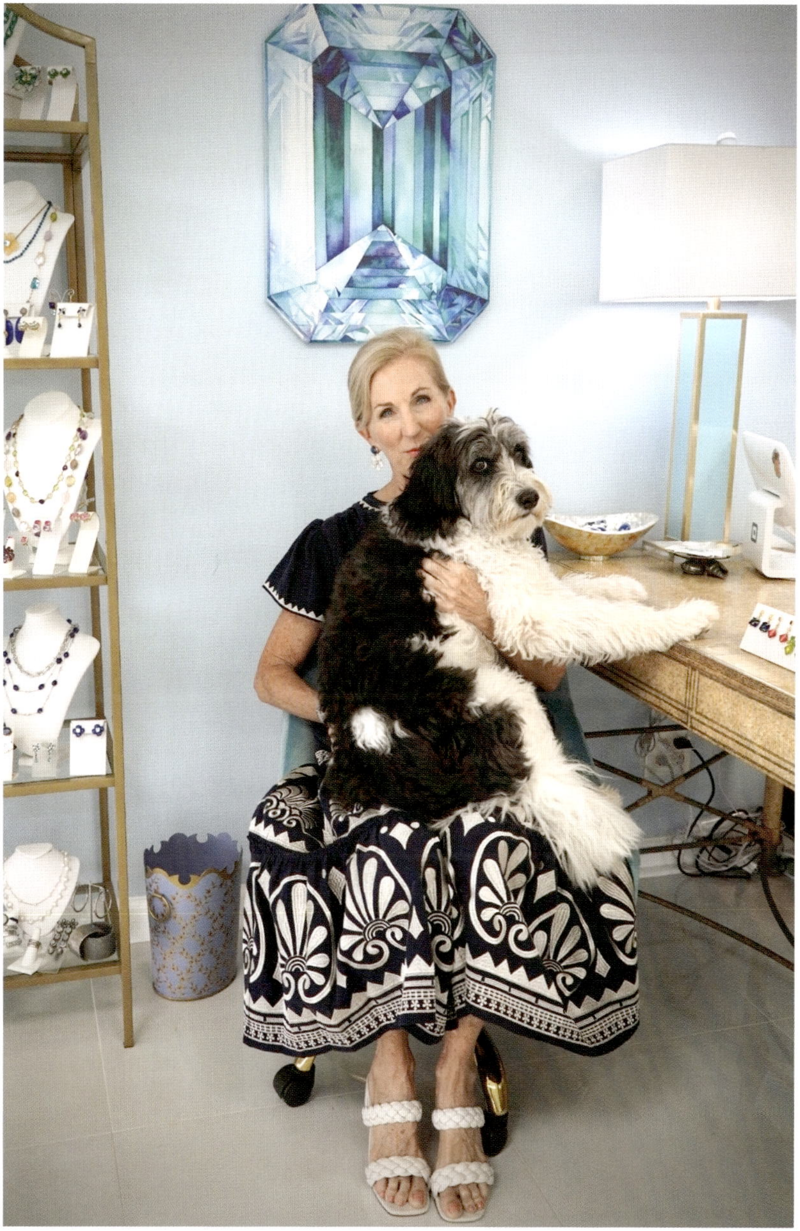

DORA & HETTIE Salisbury, Wiltshire, UK

Dora and Hettie, both Labradoodles, spend their days with Gemma, a florist, in her garage workshop. Dora, seven, likes to sleep on a cushion indoors, but is happy to sit on the concrete floor while Gemma assembles her bouquets. As a puppy, Dora used to bite the flower heads off, and her favourite drink remains flower water.

Hettie, just a year old, came along when Gemma and her husband chose a second dog over a third child. She is sociable and vocal, but Dora remains top dog.

'I love having them around,' says Gemma, 'and they love having me around.'

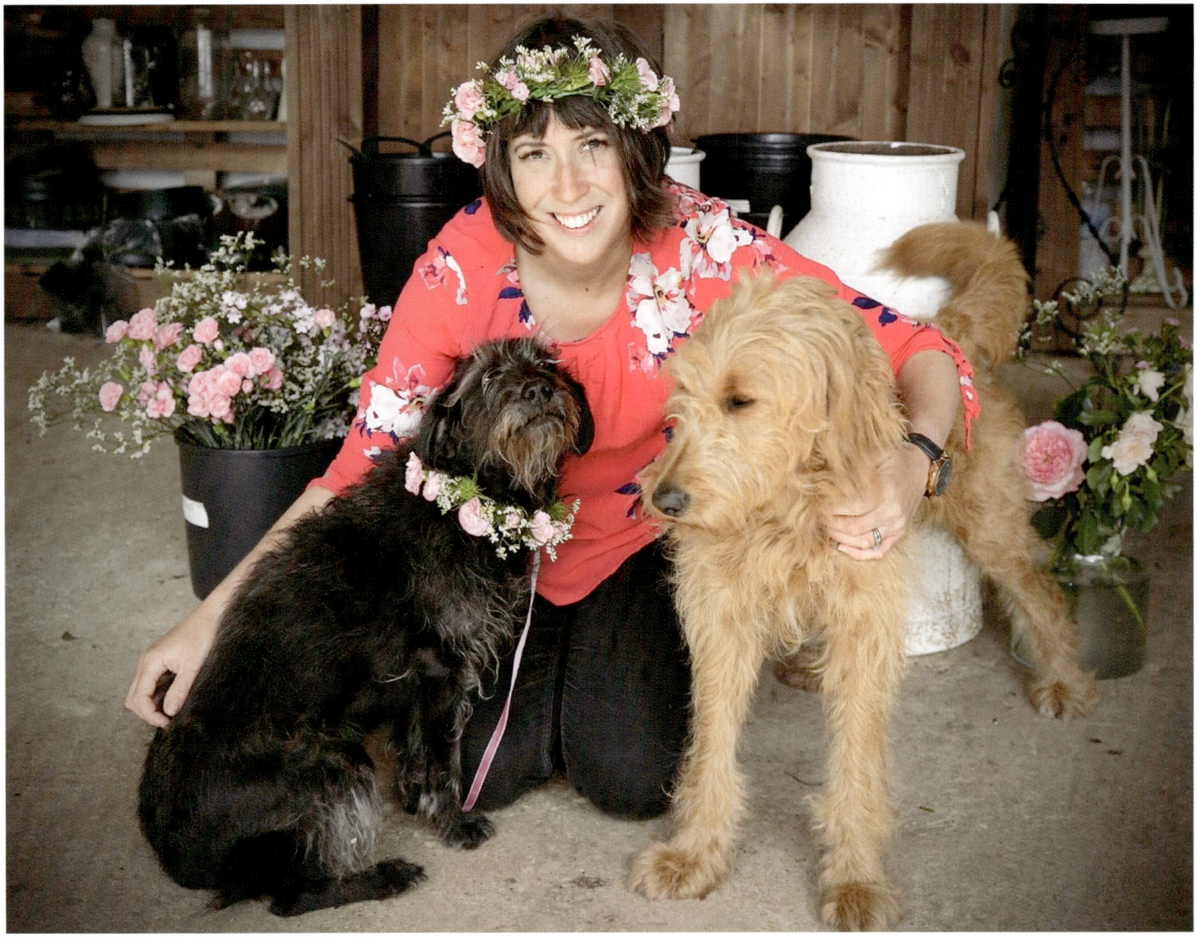

KING LOUIS

Chelsea, London, UK

King Louis the blind Chow Chow reigns supreme at the dog-boarding house managed by Charlie and Nick, who adopted him after a client dropped him off one weekend and never returned.

His original name was Prince, but the couple upgraded it to King, and added Louis after Louis Armstrong.

According to Charlie, King Louis is the shop bear – a gentle giant who flicks his ears and listens out for visiting dogs.

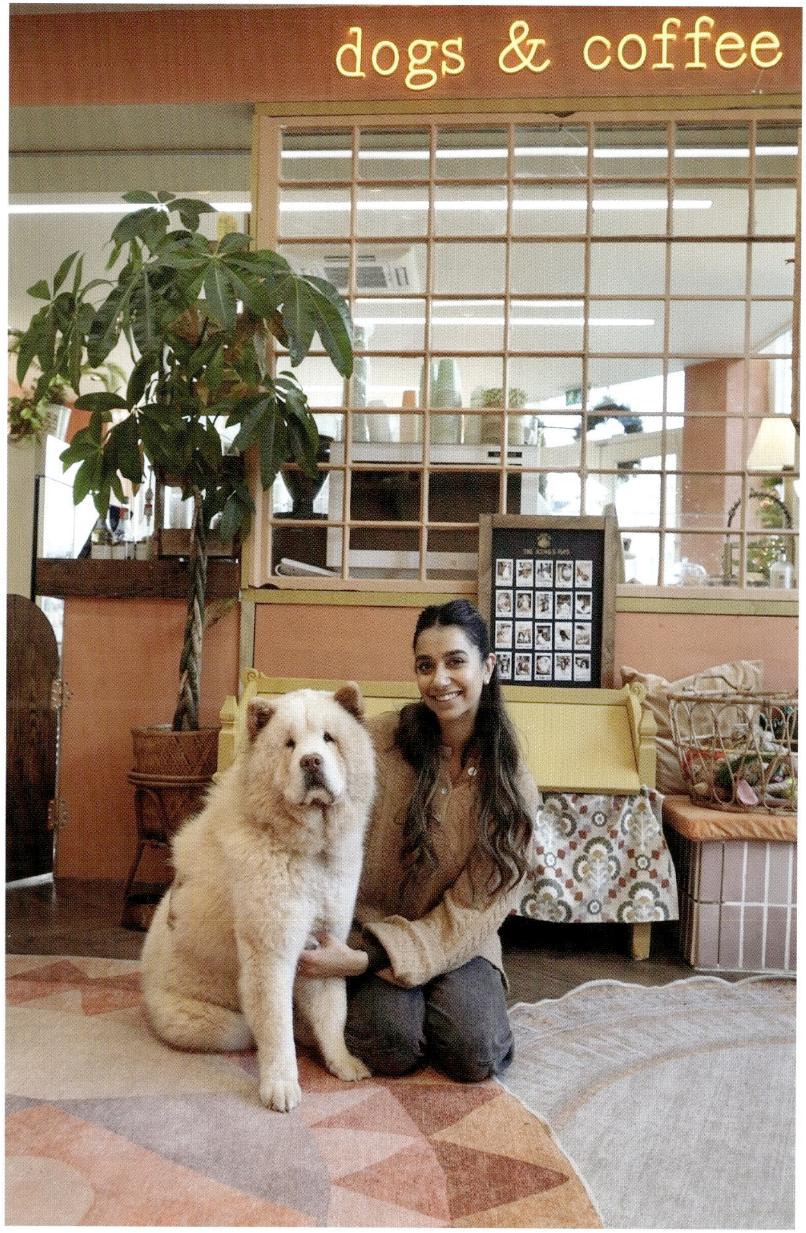

CLAUDE Wandsworth, London, UK

Claude, a French Bulldog, comes to work with florist Freddie, who set up Freddie's Flowers. Confusingly, she is not the only female with that name in the office they share in the old station master's house at Wandsworth Station.

Claude is definitely top dog. According to Freddie, she runs the place. She has been known to jump up onto people's desks and eat their lunch. She is apt to knock things over in the cramped office, but is well-behaved when they travel to the warehouse to sort out deliveries.

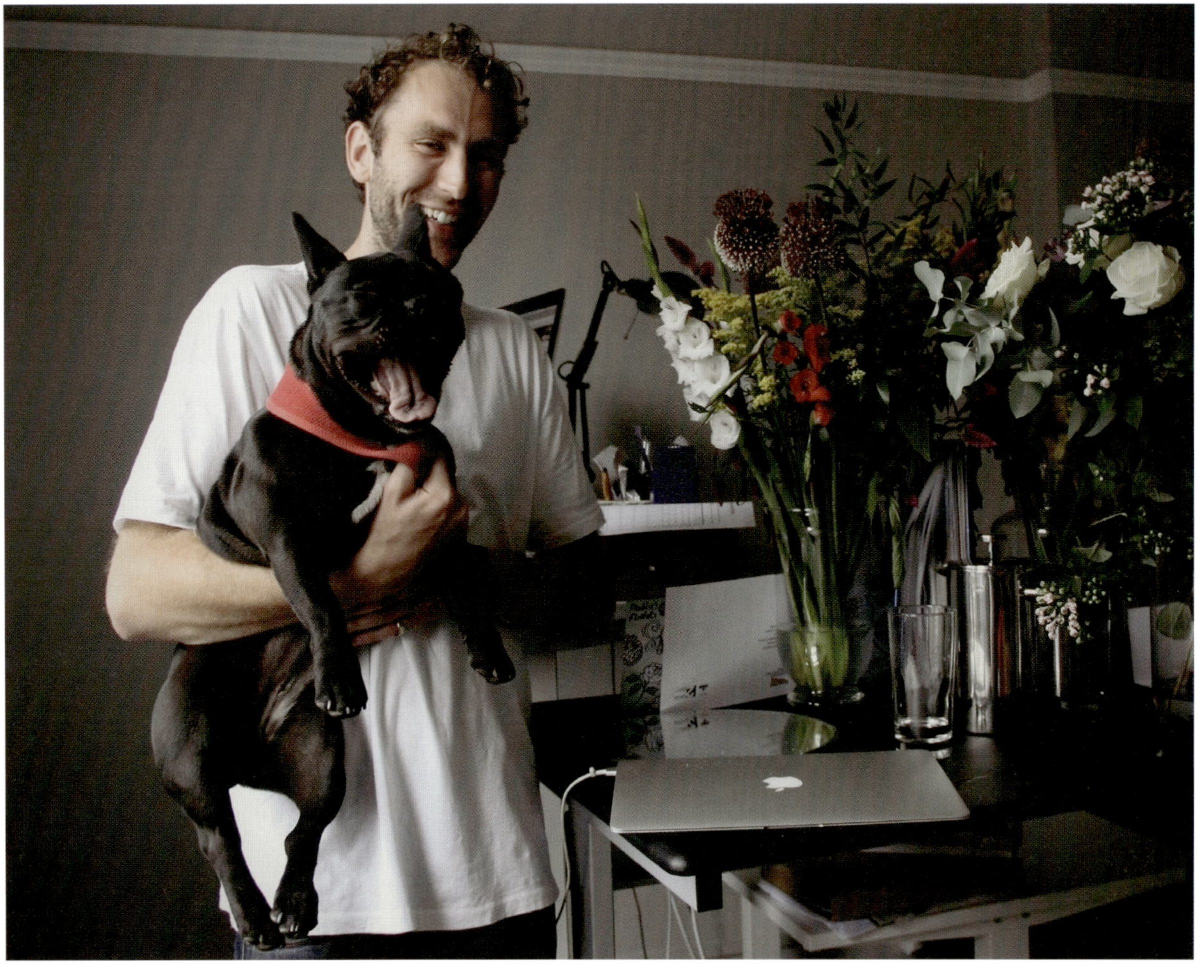

MISS LILY Fremantle, Western Australia

Miss Lily – or Tiger Lily – is a Jack Russell/Staffie/Beagle/Kelpie crossbreed rescue dog. According to her owner, Adriana, a fashion boutique manager, Lily had been severely beaten and is scared of people in glasses, hats, black clothes or uniforms. If scared, she shakes so much that the floorboards rattle.

She loves coming to the shop with Adriana, where she naps on her bed under the display table. At home, she has a bed in every room and eats only organic food.

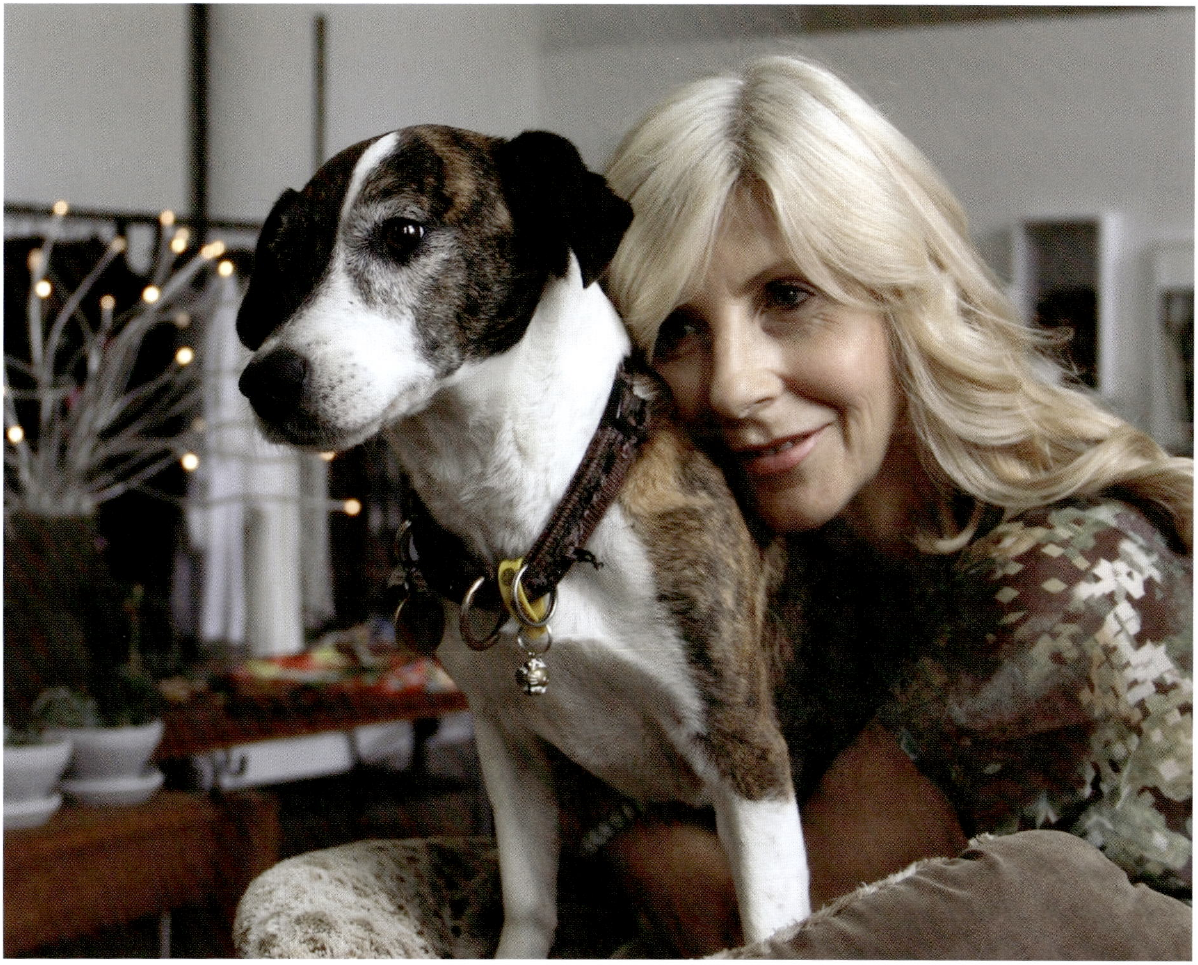

GOOSE Exmouth Market, London, UK

Diabetic and blind, Goose leads a happy life. 'He's my little sidekick,' says his owner, Alice, who runs a florist in London's East End. Until quite recently, Goose would arrive at the shop and take himself off to a neighbouring café, where he was fed titbits by a group of men who met in the morning for coffee. He would then wander off to a different café after lunch, to hang out with another group for the afternoon treats.

Thanks to Goose, Alice feels she has connected with other shopkeepers on the street. In spite of his failing health, Goose loves nothing more than to lie on his cushion near the pots of flowers, listening to the world go by.

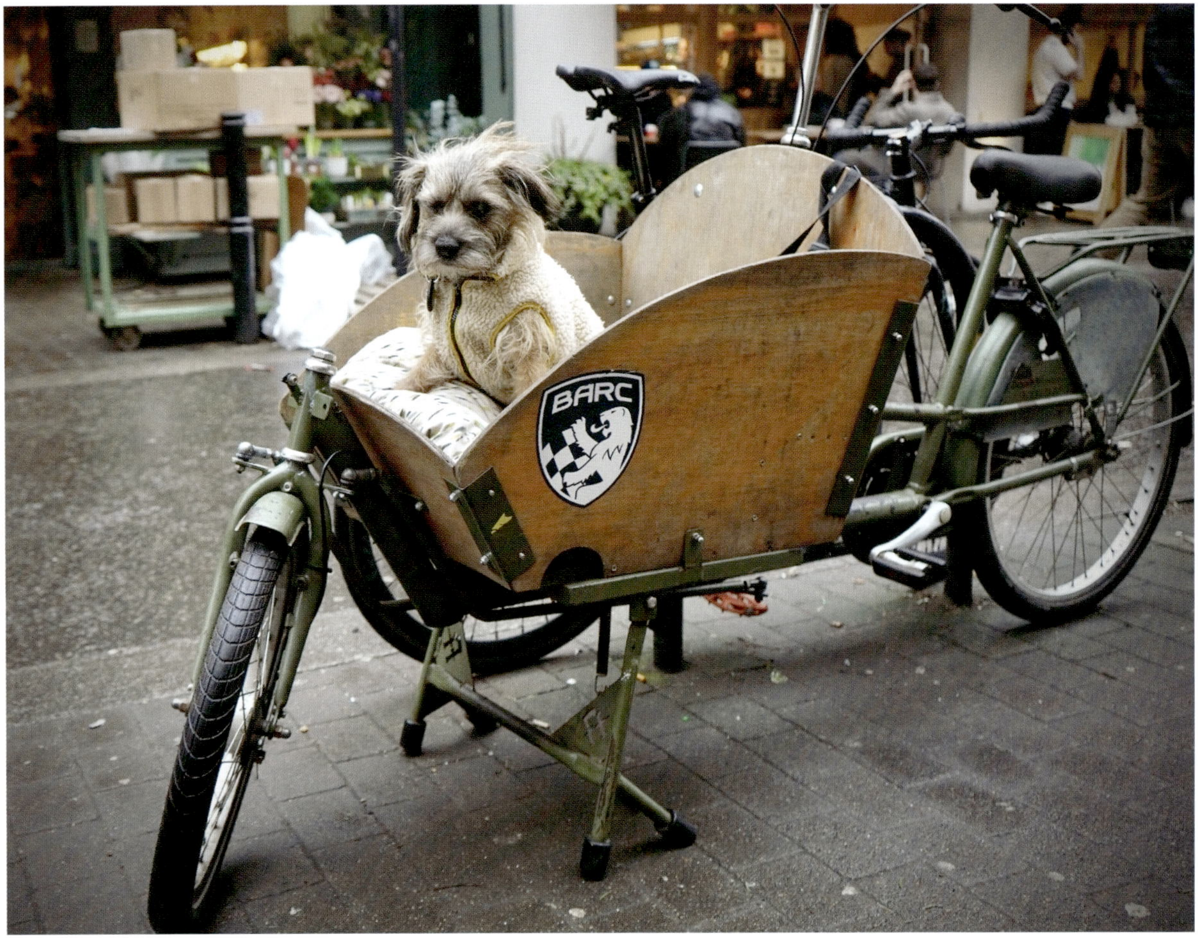

FRANKIE Tunbridge Wells, Kent, UK

Frankie, thirteen, a Miniature Wire-haired Dachshund, is something of a bionic dog, having survived a number of accidents, several of which required surgery. Frankie has seen Sabine through thick and thin, and Sabine says she gives 'joy and companionship beyond belief'.

Sabine's boss, Paula, is happy for her to bring the dog in and there is no doubt she is the sweetest meet-and-greet. She will greet with a wag of her tail, and sometimes too vocally. Frankie's ears used to be down, until two years ago when they started standing up – she looks a very different dog these days, more like a gremlin than a Dachshund.

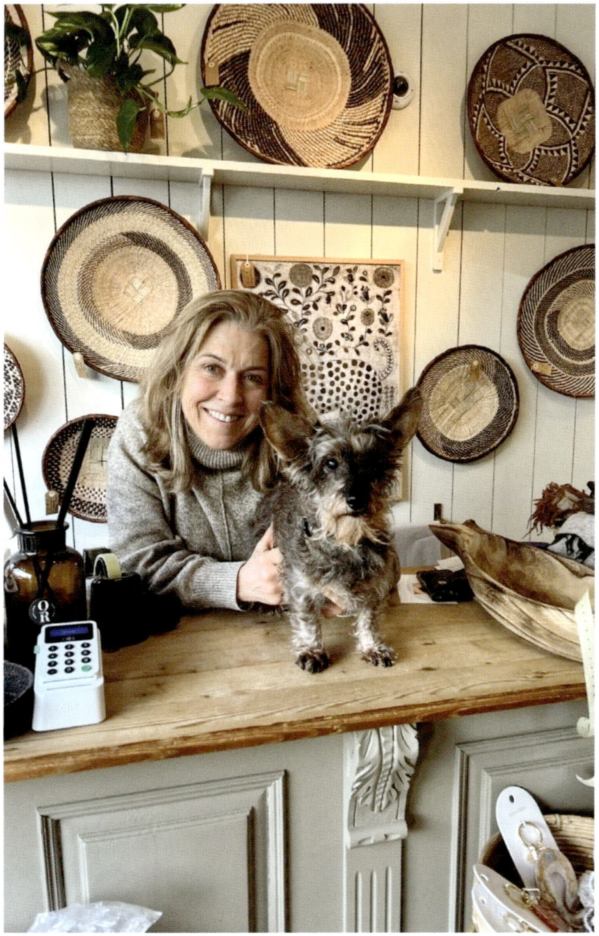

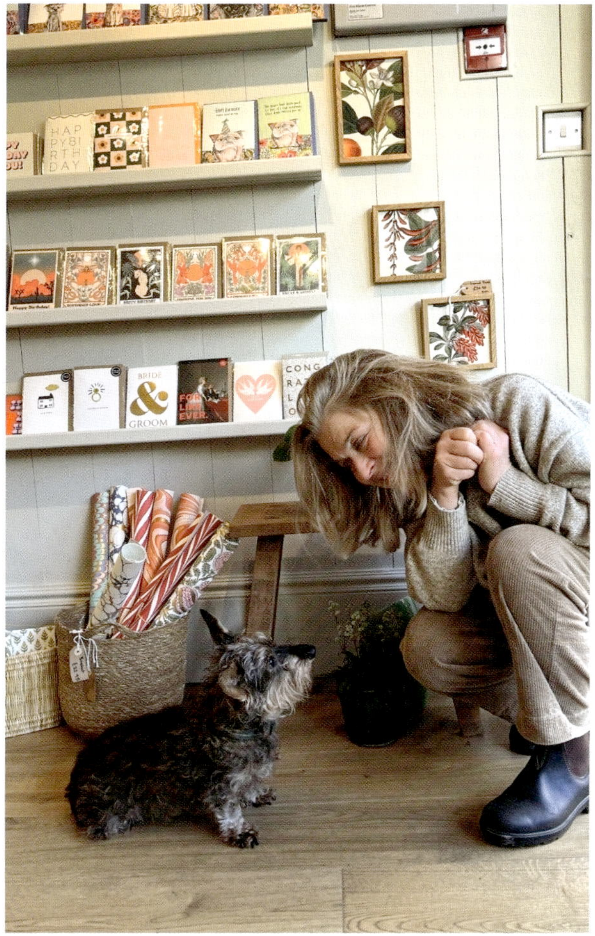

SALON DOGS

Salon dogs are a special 'breed' of dog in the workplace, in that they are there not only for their owner's convenience and pleasure, but also for the customers' distraction. More than just a meet-and-greet service, they help time pass in the waiting room, and provide cuddles by sitting on laps while hair is cut or feet are massaged. Mostly though they are decorative, and just lie somewhere where they can be easily seen in the hope of a belly rub.

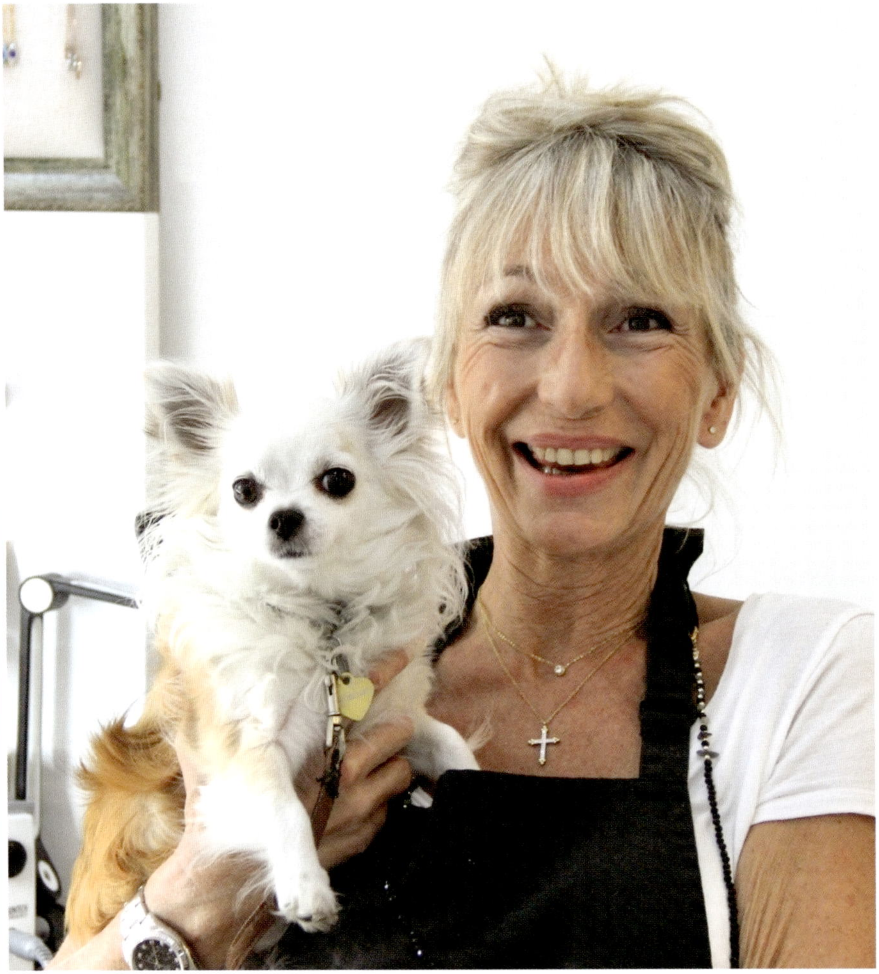

NIKKI Sainte-Maxime, Var, France

Nathalie chose Nikki, a long-haired Chihuahua, because she thinks long-haired dogs are elegant. Nikki has been coming to work in the nail bar with Nathalie since she was a pup. She prefers humans to dogs, although she is picky about which clients she will approach for a cuddle. She is also very territorial, and makes sure no visiting dogs go beyond the front treatment table.

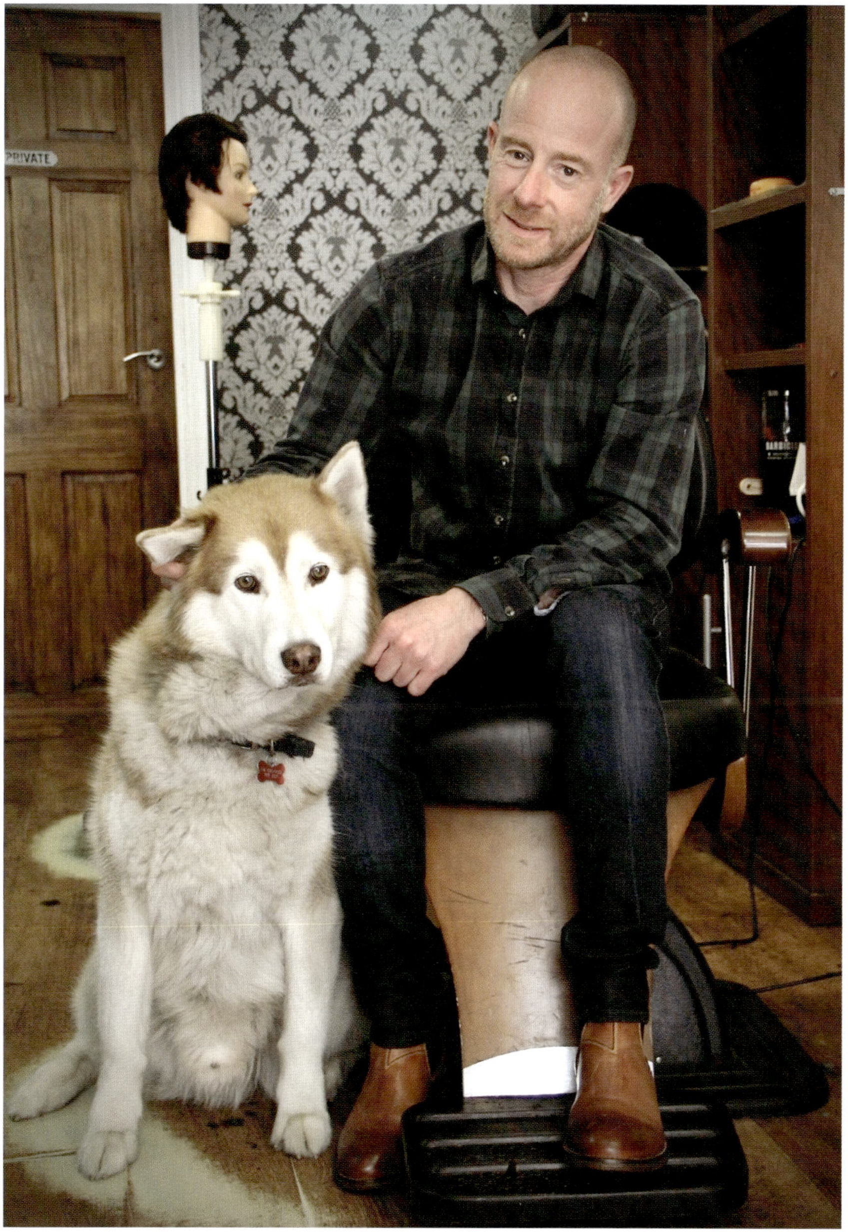

WOODY

Bristol, UK

Eight-year-old Woody is a Husky (apparently, the second most rescued breed of dog in the UK). Andrew, his owner, works at one of the many barbershops in Bristol.

Woody generally lies on the pavement just outside, although he will seek out the bed set up at the back of the shop when he wants some peace and quiet. He does less in the heat and becomes livelier in cold weather.

He has been known to pull Andrew round Bristol on his pedal bike.

HARVEY

Devizes, Wiltshire, UK

For all his size, Harvey the Great Dane puppy is only twelve weeks old, so still too young to have a responsible role at Mel's beauty salon. He does not bother yet to get up from his bed or his favourite place on the landing to greet clients. He playfully removes towels from the shelves or takes one tissue from the box upstairs, brings it down to his bed, chews it up then goes back for another.

Harvey has already become well known in Devizes and has his own Instagram page. He is frightened of rain and refuses to get out of the shop or car when the weather is wet.

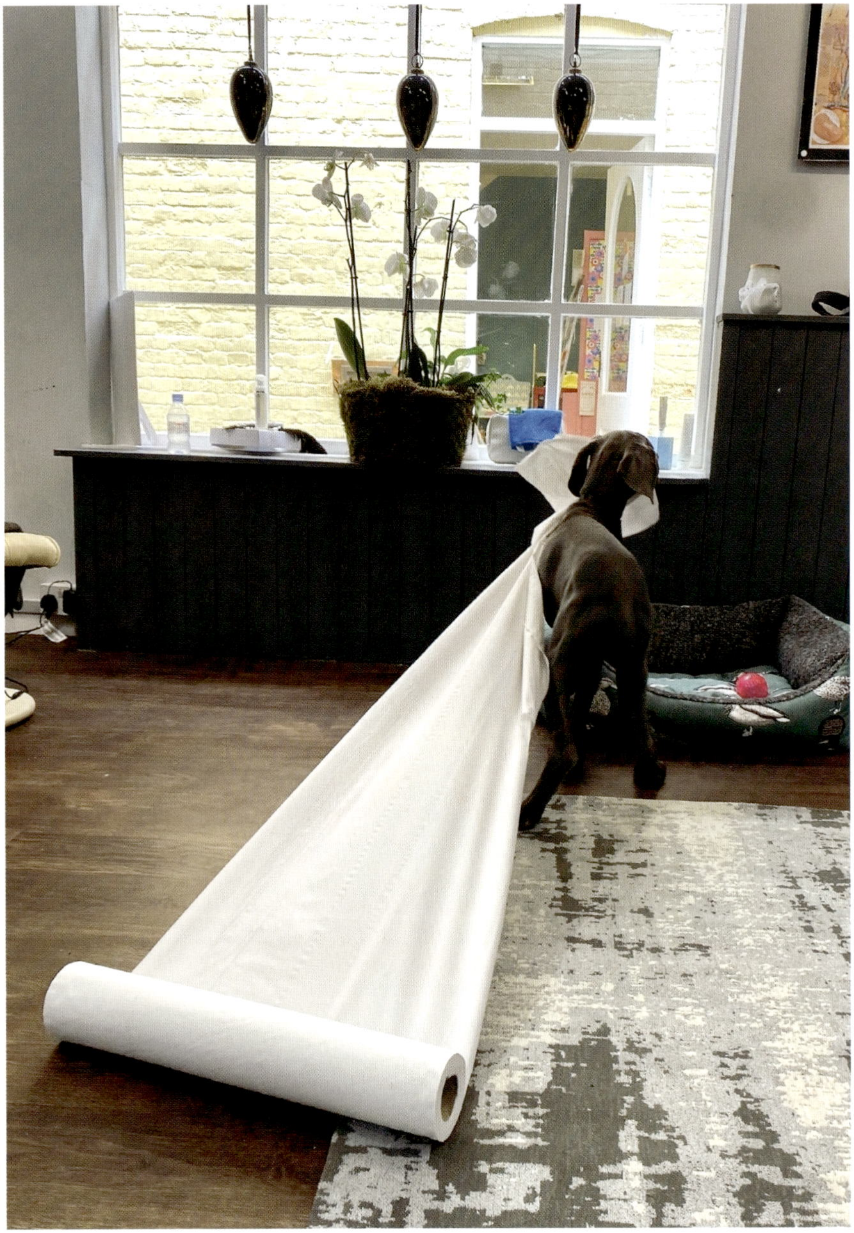

CHANELLE Naples, Florida, USA

Chanelle is a fifteen-month-old French Bulldog, who comes to the glamorous Florida hair salon owned by Sashy and Stephanie. The German couple had been married for ten years when Stephanie threatened that they either 'divorce, have a baby or a dog'. Their 'baby' now goes everywhere with them: first-class travel. Sashy and Stephanie are so obsessed with Chanelle that they have had her image painted on the front of their house. Photos and artwork of their 'chunky monster' adorn the salon, including the restroom. She is a celebrity locally in Naples, and the pink car parked opposite the salon has her signature crown emblazoned on the paintwork.

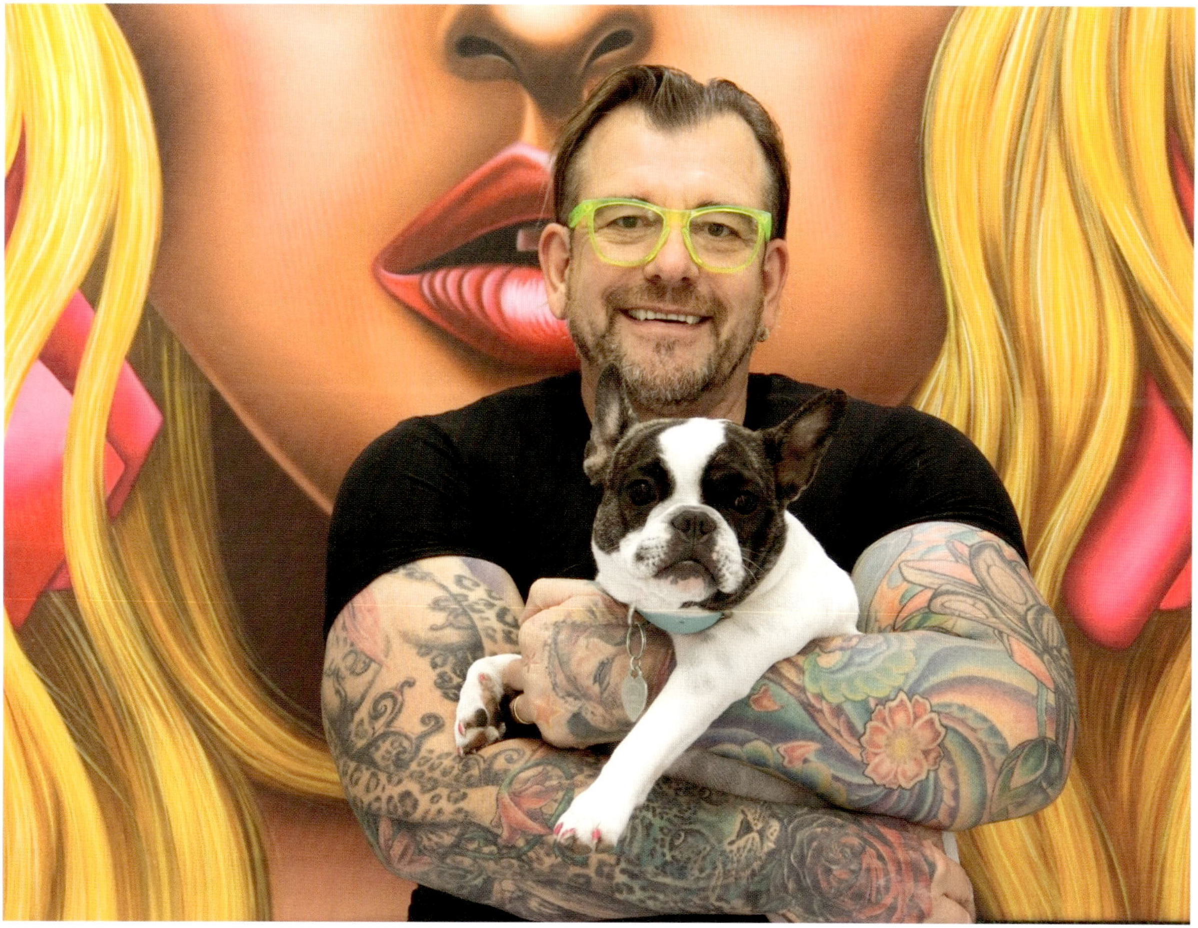

SERVICE DOGS

Service dogs are highly in tune with their owners. They are trained to do an investigative job, sometimes with life-changing results. Like any emergency service, they are always ready for action. It is an honour to meet these hard-working dogs and their owners. Service dogs can switch on to commands during the day and switch off in the evening. They too know that work is work and home is home.

DAVEY & team Chorley, Lancashire, UK

Davey, Rue, Murphy and Louie are casualty search dogs, whose speed and acute sense of smell mean they can give information that no other current technology is able to deliver. During one incident, Davey was able to find a victim buried under rubble in only five minutes, after a detector machine had been unsuccessfully used for six hours.

All Lindsay's dogs know that they are going to work when she gets the van keys at home. They are excited at the prospect, and love their jobs. Once home, though, they switch off and revert to being pets.

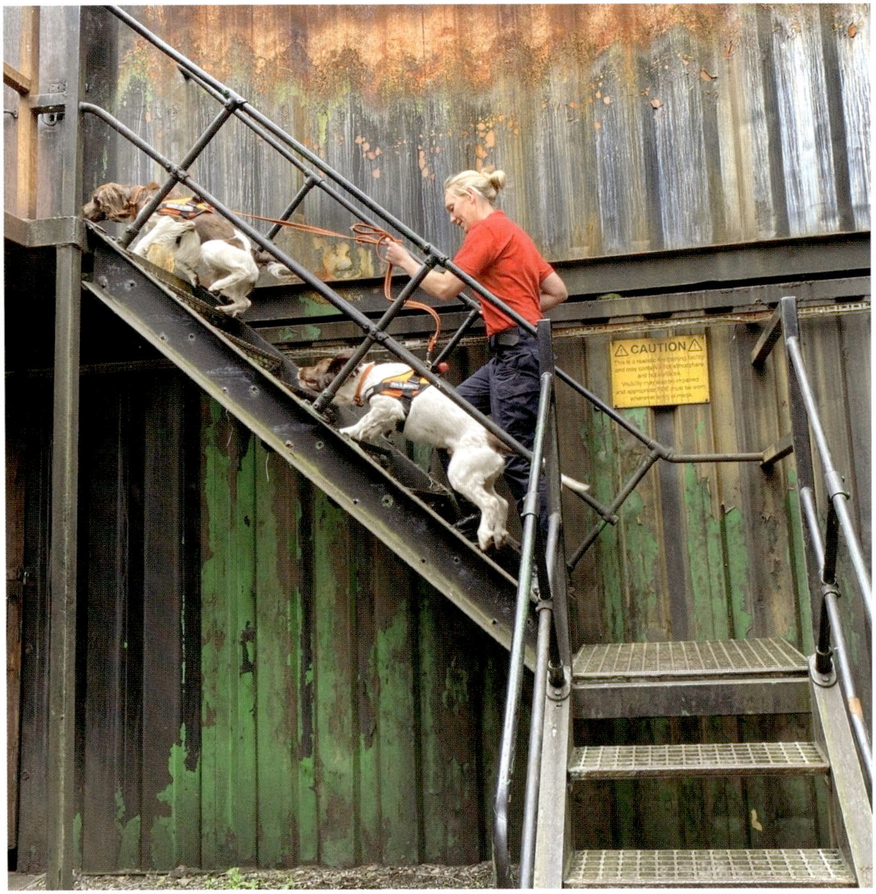

ROSIE

Barnes, London, UK

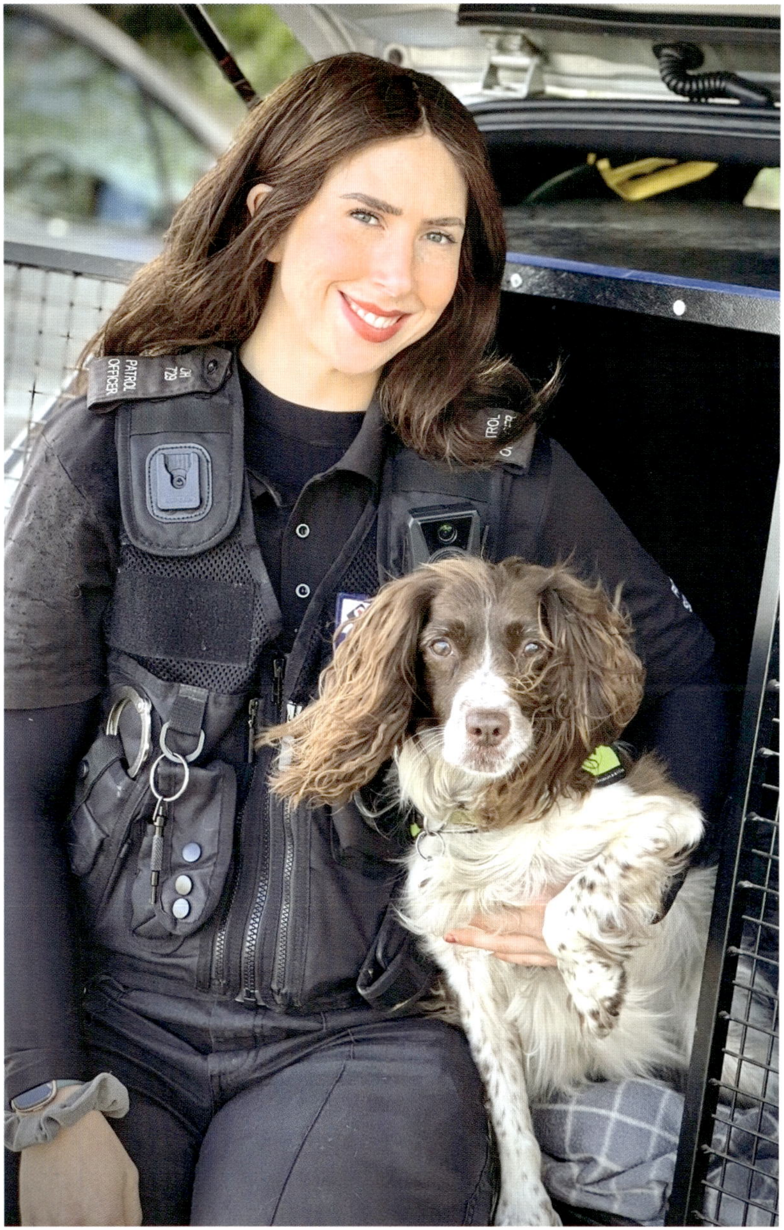

Rosie, a Springer Spaniel, was dumped outside a training centre for sniffer dogs. Patrol officer Zoë fell in love with her, adopted her and trained her up. Rosie was initially very anxious and Zoë was concerned she wouldn't pass the course. However, she did, and she is now a regular on Zoë's beat round the parks and playgrounds of South West London.

Sniffer dogs and drug detection dogs tend to lose some of their sense of smell when they reach the age of seven, so Rosie, at the grand age of nine, should be retiring soon. She still loves going in the patrol car, and her motivation and reward when out detecting is a ball; even the word 'ball' will sometimes do.

Zoë says Rosie brings her lots of energy – 'she will light up your day.'

BLUE

Hammersmith & Fulham, London, UK

'Blue is my buffer and my bridge,' says Borough Commander and firefighter Lucy of her miniature Australian Shepherd dog, who has been featured on the BBC, highlighting the important work he does supporting London Fire Brigade crews after tough incidents.

Blue is one of the trauma and well-being volunteer dogs for firefighters in need of emotional support after witnessing catastrophic events. Blue helps Lucy when she faces difficult conversations, and reduces stress not only for her but for her colleagues by being on hand for cuddles.

Lucy brings Blue into work once a week and will take him to other local fire stations under her command. He chills in her office and sits under her desk with a fan when it's hot. At home, he relaxes and watches 'Fox-TV' all night through her French doors.

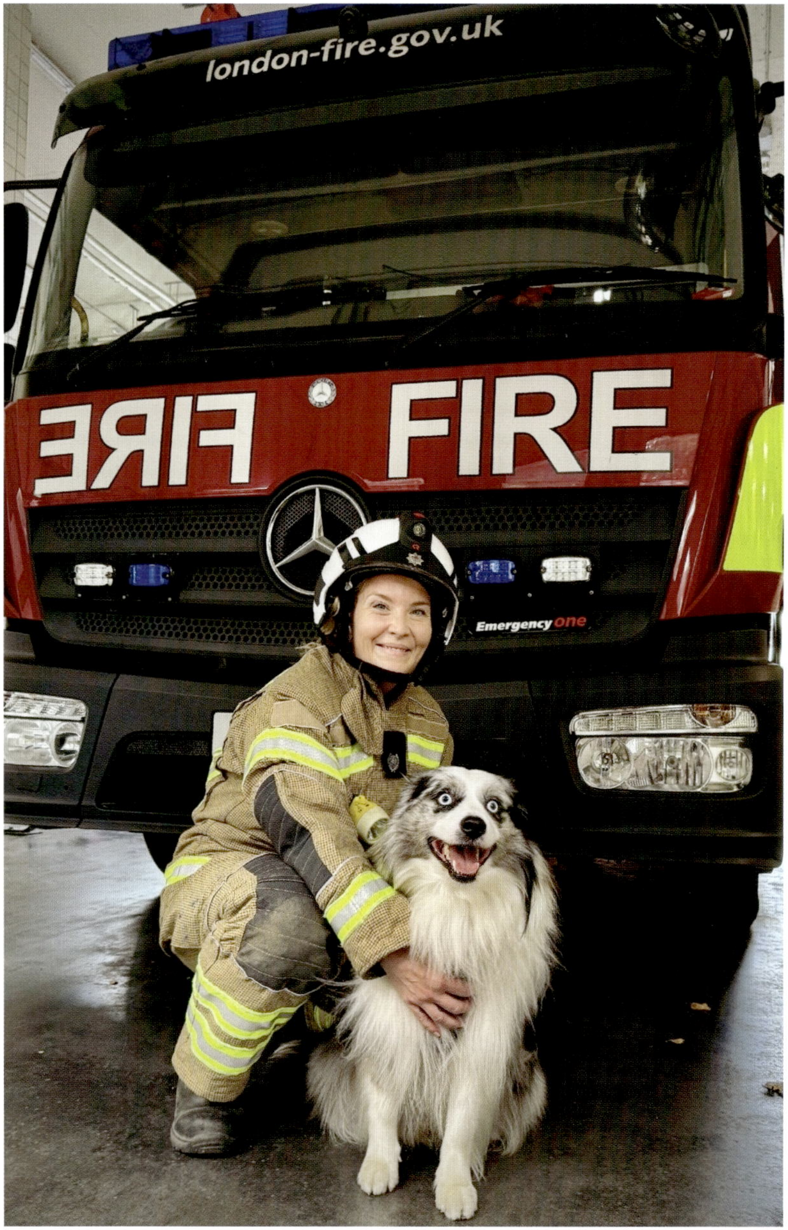

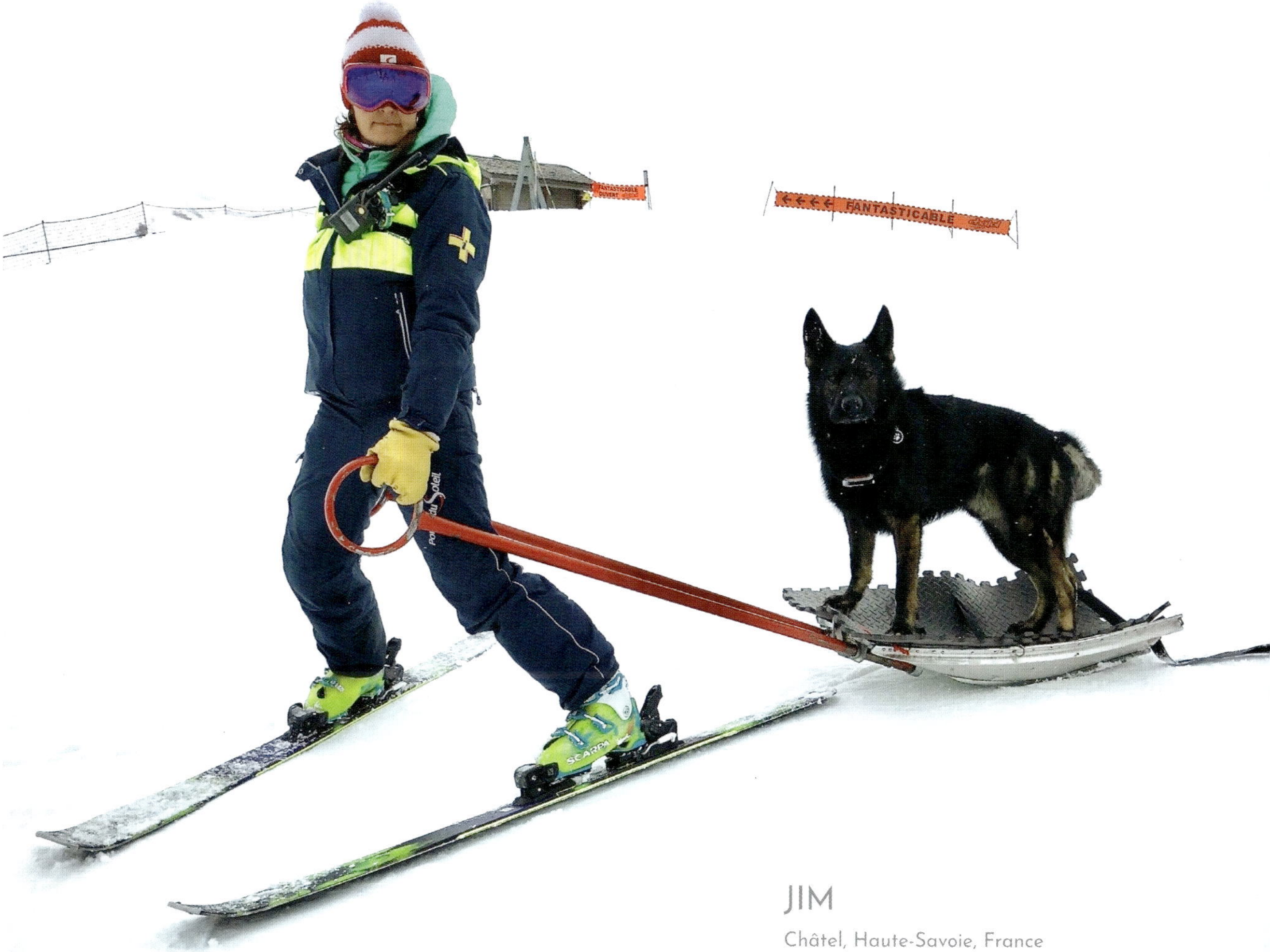

JIM

Châtel, Haute-Savoie, France

As an avalanche sniffer patrol dog, Jim works hard throughout the day, expending huge amounts of energy When it's time to knock off, he enjoys a free ride down the slopes, courtesy of his owner, Nicole.

OUTDOOR DOGS

Some of the outdoor dogs I come across are companions, simply enjoying the fresh air with their owners. Others are working dogs, intelligent and alert, at their happiest doing the job they have been trained to do, rewarded by a pat on the head or a 'good dog'.

All the outdoor dogs I meet have two things in common: they are loyal to the core, and they are totally in tune with their owner's commands. Neither can do without the other.

AUTUMN Shoreditch, London, UK

Autumn is a Staff/Lab/Pitbull Terrier. Mother of sixteen. Sings for her dinner. Sits on people's feet so they can't run away. Her owner, Darren, who is homeless, sells the figures he makes out of coloured wire, and is known locally as 'the wire man'.

Autumn's best feeling in the world? To roll on a carpet when they are able to pay for a hostel room.

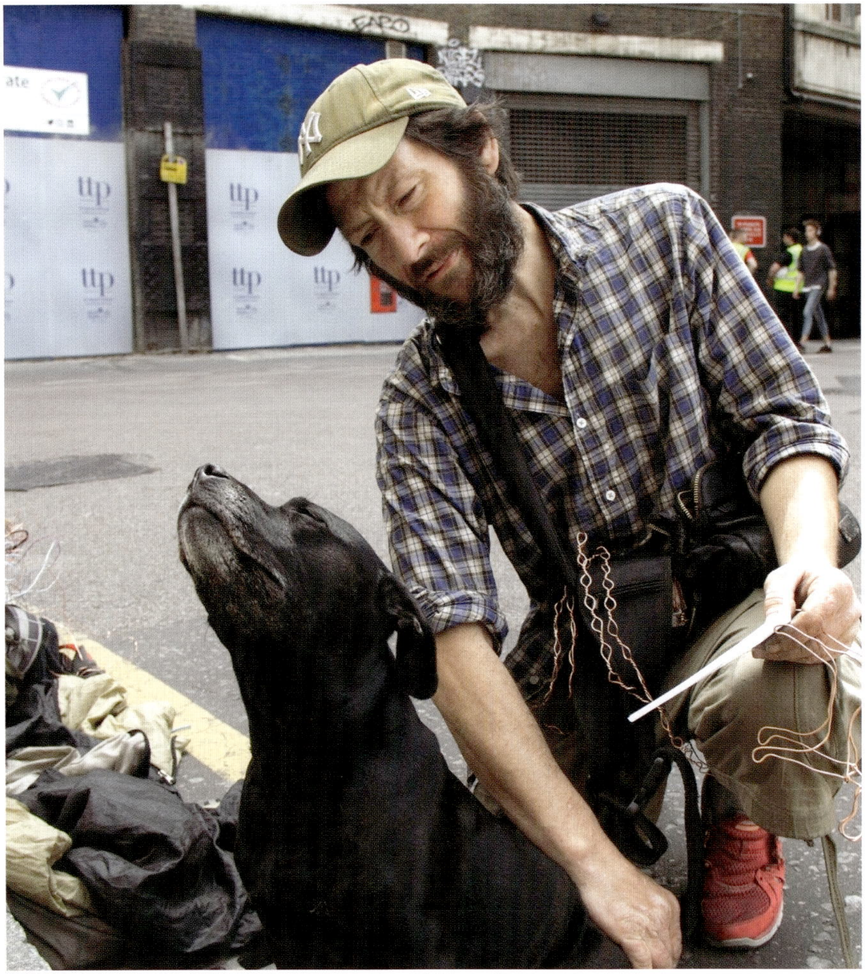

LUNA Cobham, Surrey, UK

Luna is a rescue from Cyprus, who now alternates between sitting with Jim in his office and having the run of the yard, where most of the action takes place: Jim and a team of fifteen work on vehicle conversions, creating spaces in American school buses for mobile spas or camper vans. He has worked with the celebrity architect, George Clarke, and the comedian, Johnny Vegas. Luna is Jim's shadow at work and at home. 'I don't know what I'd do without them,' says Jim, of Luna and his other dog, Harley. 'They are my best mates and my house mates.'

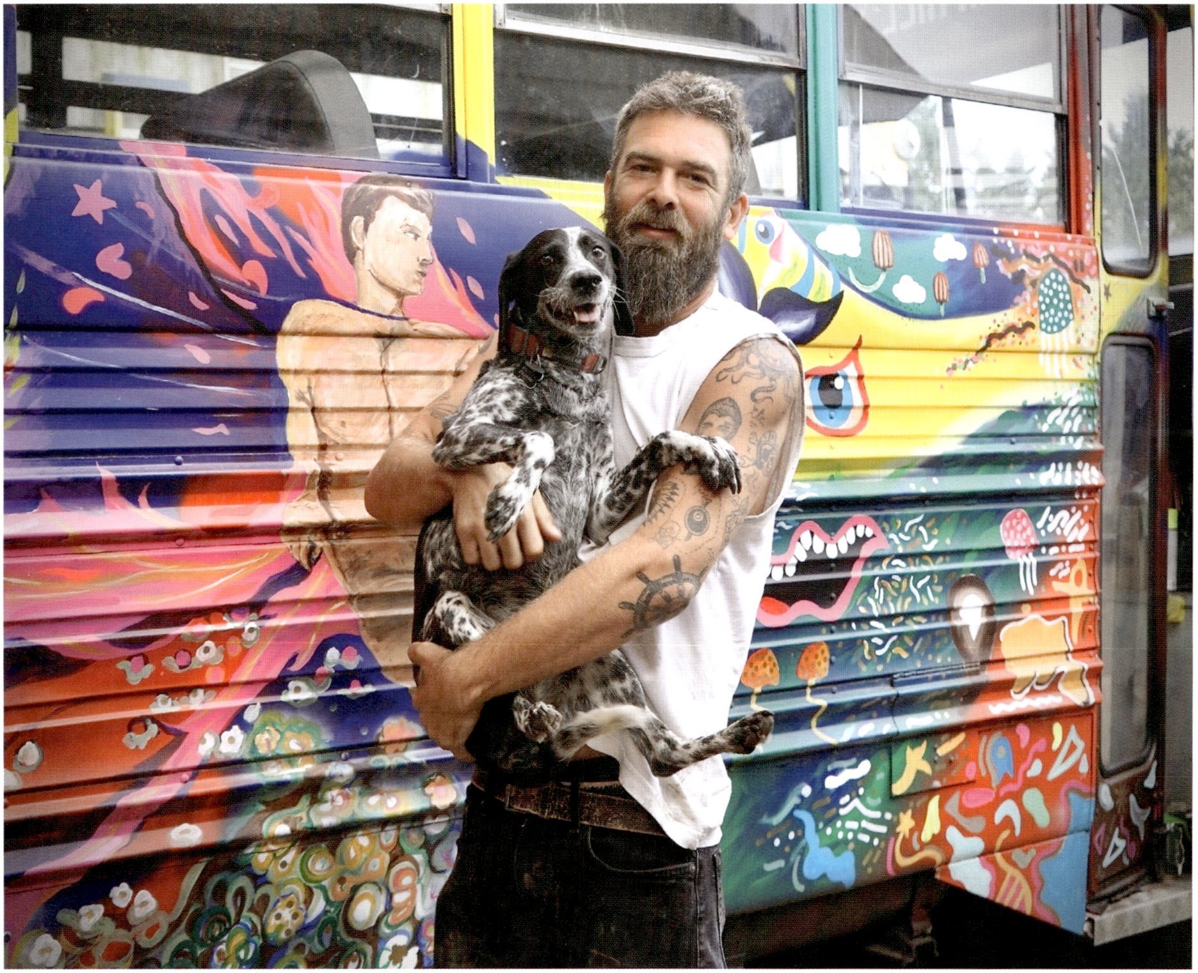

CASPAR Putney. London, UK

Part-Rottweiler, part-German Shepherd, Caspar is named after the cartoon character *Caspar the Friendly Ghost*, created in the 1930s. Hardly invisible, this gorgeous dog accompanies his owner, Tom, a tree surgeon, to work. Tom tried to teach him to drag logs, but Caspar generally prefers a supervisory role.

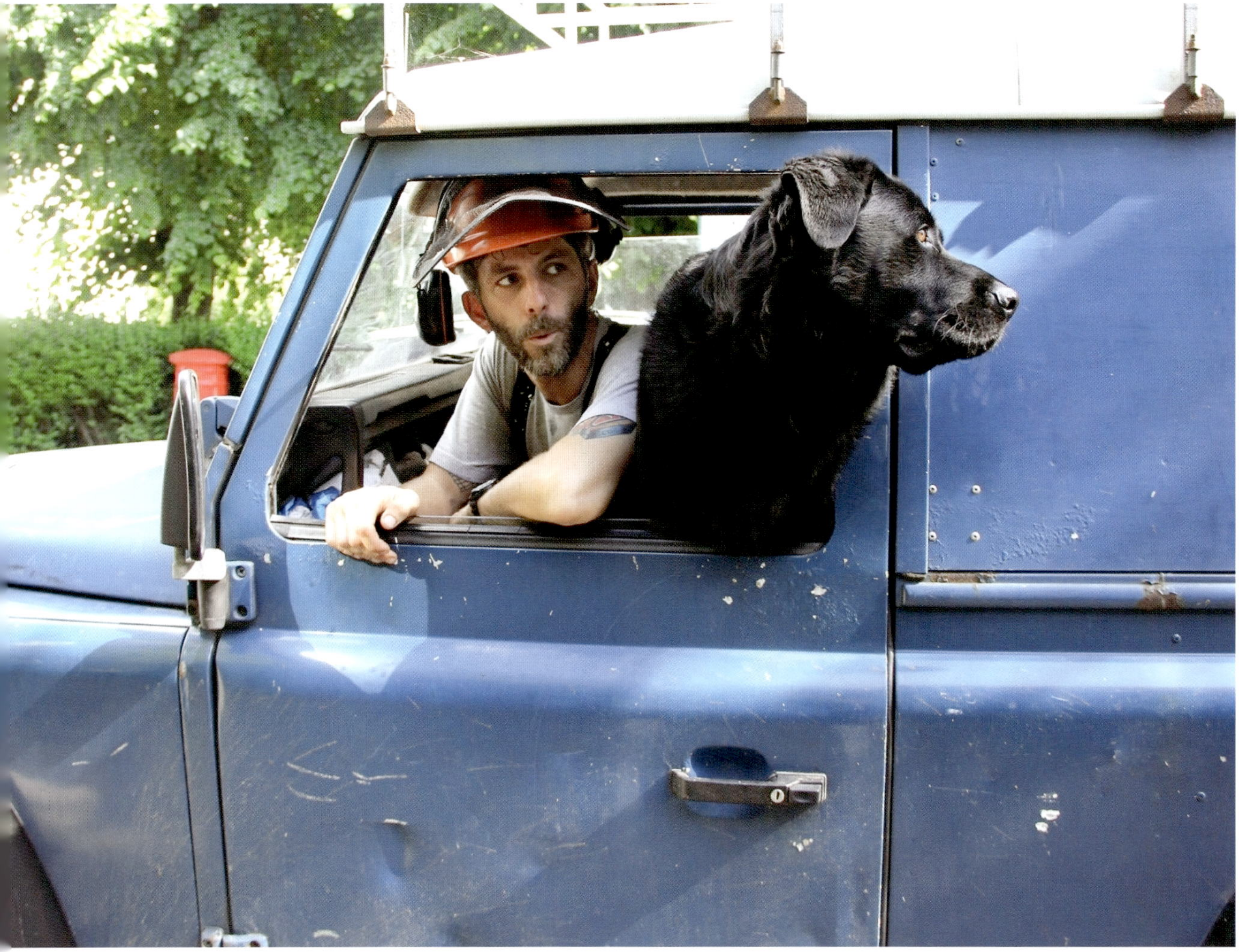

ONYX

Regent's Canal, London, UK

Emanuel, who runs a pleasure boat company on the Regent's Canal, is charming and clever at persuading clients to board, promising them a wonderful glide up the canal with the added bonus of Thomas James Smith, singer and guitarist.

Undoubtedly, though, one of the main attractions is Onyx, Emanuel's four-year-old black Labrador, who always comes along for the ride. From time to time, Onyx is allowed off to wander along the towpath. He is a local celebrity and regularly recognised.

In the summer, both Emanuel and Onyx sleep on board the punt.

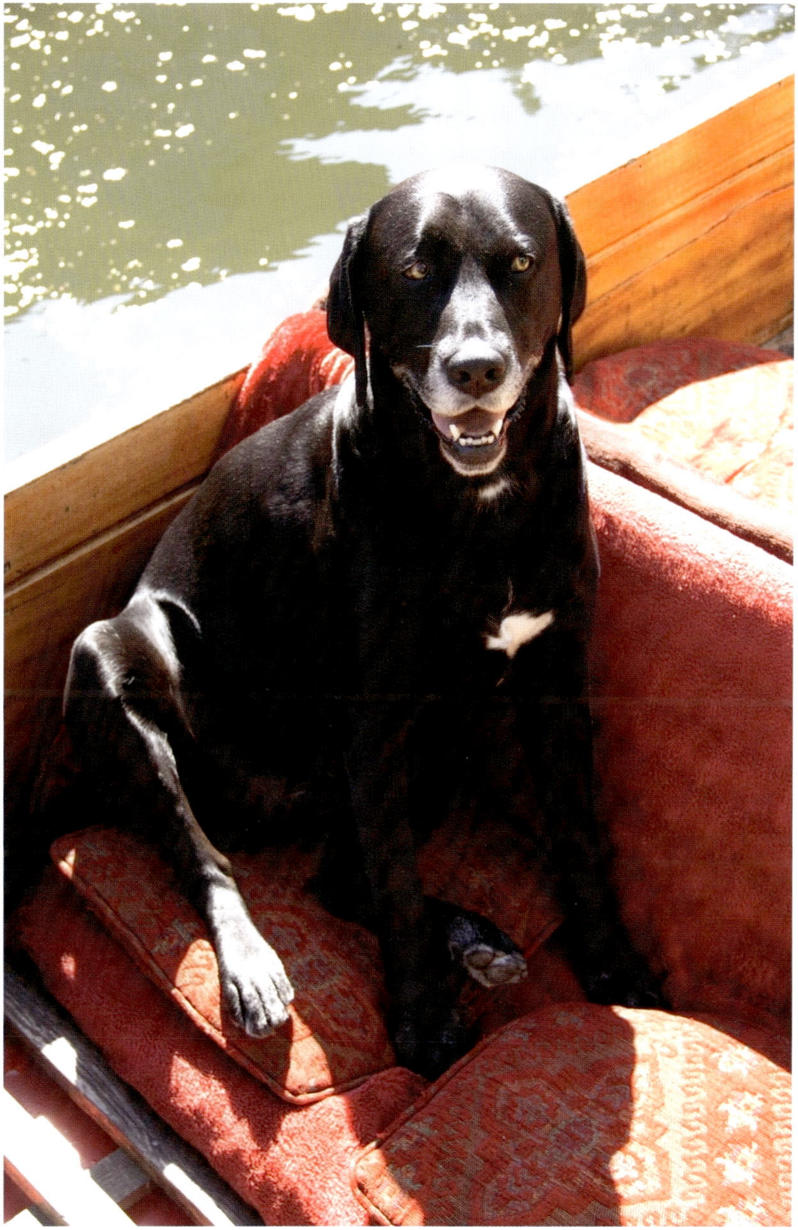

PERSEPHONE & JUNO High Clandon, Surrey, UK

Persephone, Goddess of Spring, and Juno, Queen of all gods, are the undisputed rulers of the English vineyard set up by Sybilla (the Pinot Queen) and Bruce (the Chardonnay King). Never far from Sybilla, they only break away to chase rabbits in the rewilded fields, and mallards off the pond.

In the autumn, they truffle hunt in a nearby orchard. At winter pruning time, they accompany Sybilla, who places their beds at the end of the vines, moving them along as she progresses. When not chasing off intruders, they are all charm, and meet and greet customers who come to the vineyard or to view the sculptures dotted around the garden.

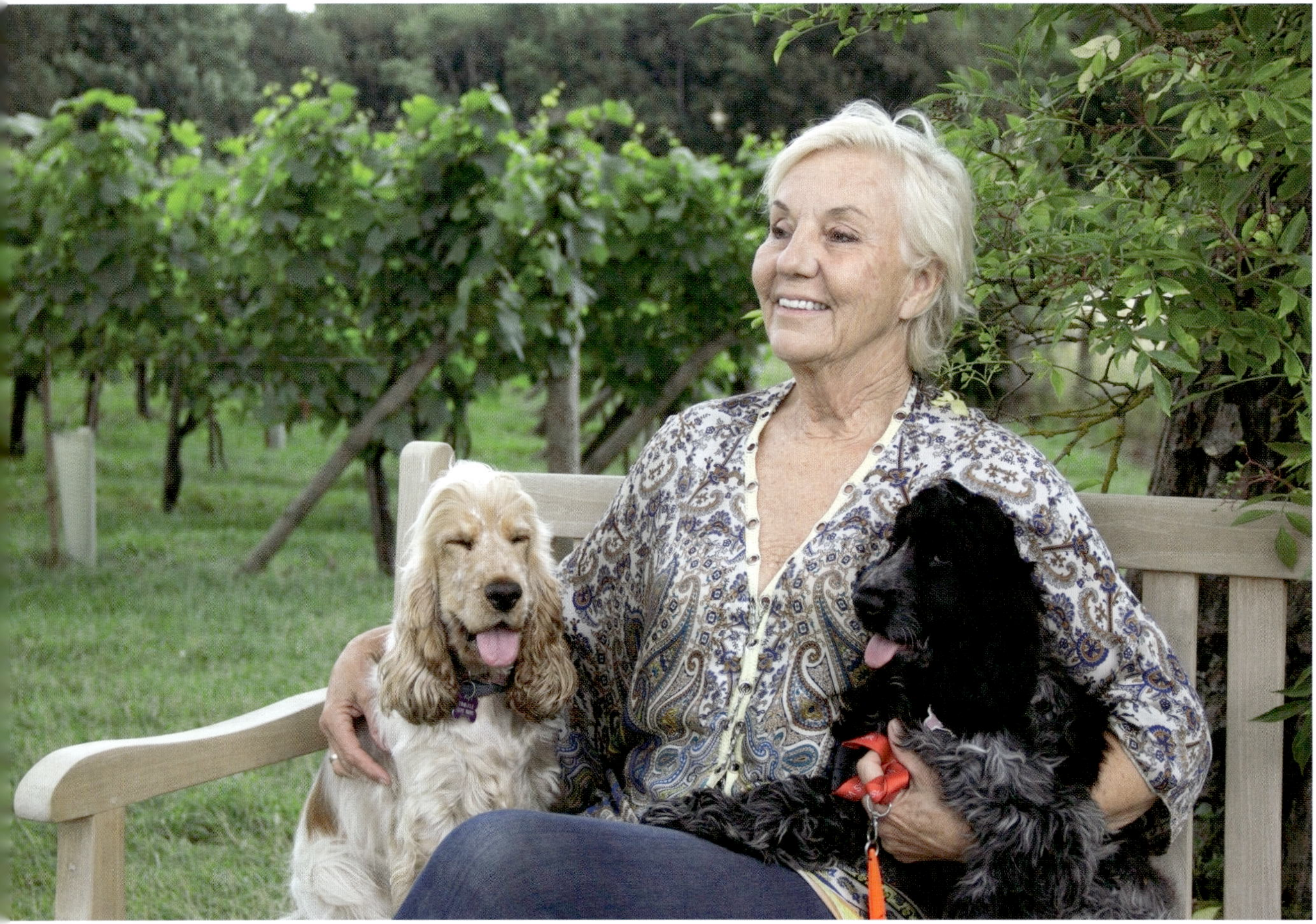

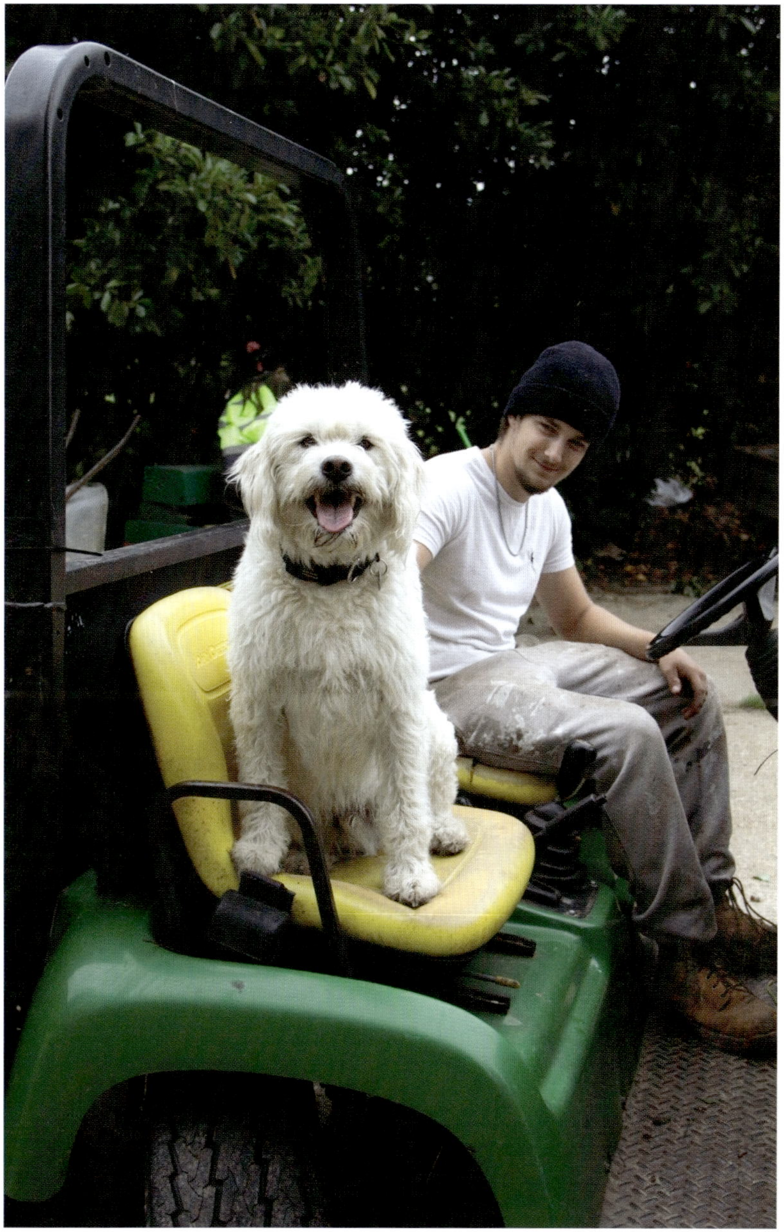

BONO

Chiswick, London, UK

Bono, a mini Labradoodle, was rescued as a puppy from an author who kept him in a cupboard under the stairs and rarely exercised him.

When head greenkeeper John first brought him home, Bono was unable to climb stairs as he had very little muscle mass, but he is now a valued member of the greenkeeping staff at Duke's Meadows golf course. His first job in the mornings is to chase off the heron that preys on the fish in the lake. Then he clears the geese off the fairways and finishes his morning chores with a pigeon- and crow-chasing session.

During the day, Bono flits from one greenkeeper to another, demanding attention, pats and the odd treat as he runs alongside the staff buggies.

He has been trained never to pick up a ball off the fairway, although he will run off with the greenkeepers' gloves if they are left lying around.

When the team gathers round a portacabin for elevenses, Bono joins them for a well-earned bowl of tea and his share of the biscuits.

PUPPY

Kochi, Kerala, India

Puppy the Dachshund looks up adoringly at his owner Appu, who is a mahout – an elephant trainer.

A mahout works with a single elephant for life, and forms a strong bond. Puppy can also look forward to a lifelong relationship with Appu.

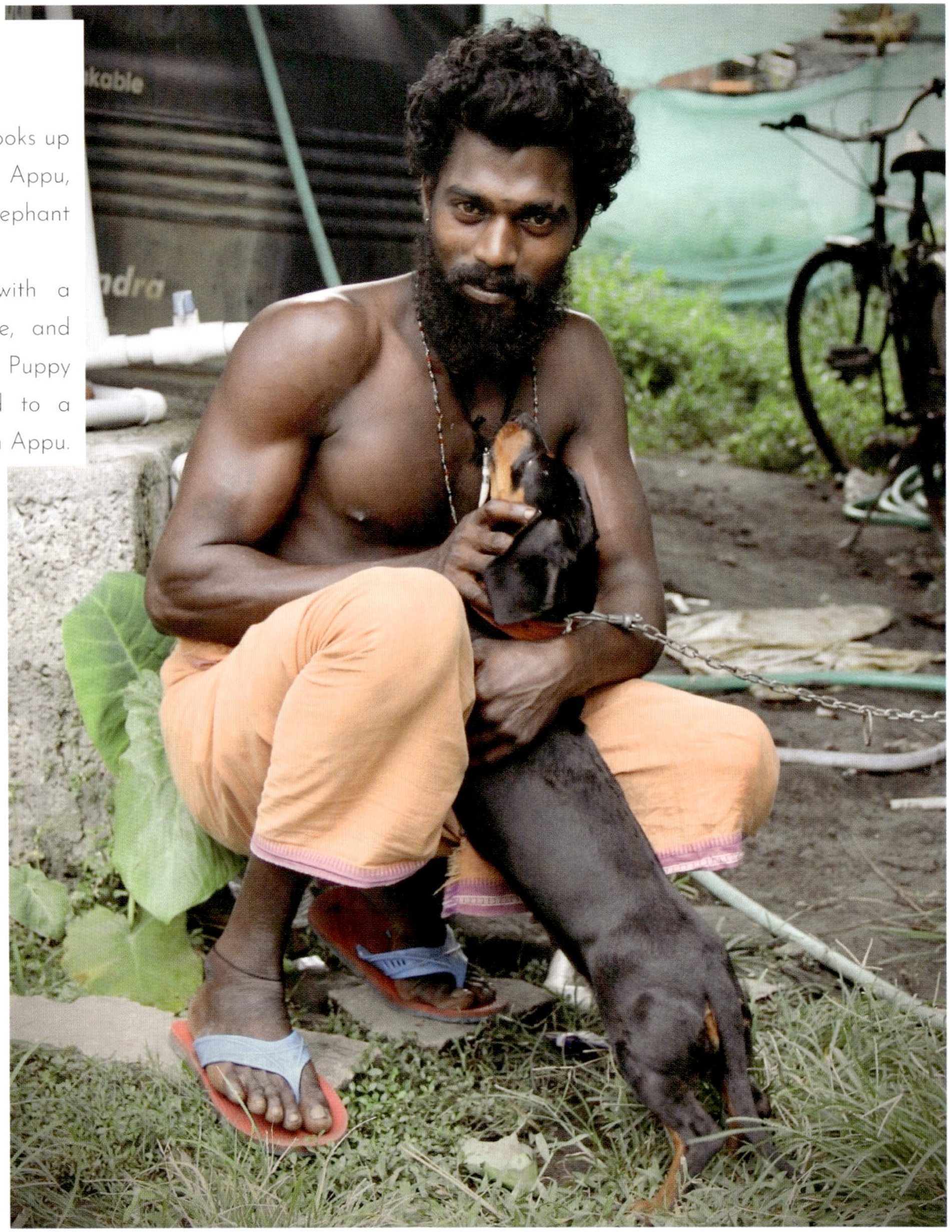

BRAMBLE & WILLOW Horsham, West Sussex, UK

'My world revolves round them and their world revolves round me,' says Ashley of Bramble and Willow, the two Teckels – Wire-haired Dachshunds – who accompany her everywhere at her Sussex campsite.

Ashley wanted dogs with more bounce than ounce and got more than she ever imagined with these two, as they love everything from travelling to Sunday lunch. They have been trained as sniffer dogs and are also gun-trained – for recall purposes only. When Ashley is busy, they enjoy spending time in the doggy 'pitch and putt' enclosure where they have dug their own holes.

Bramble and Willow act as a reminder to Ashley not to sit for too long at her desk. These cheeky – and occasionally stubborn – dogs are never far from Ashley's side. Here they pose, nosily but happily, in the Morris Minor pick-up truck converted into a camper van for Johnny Vegas.

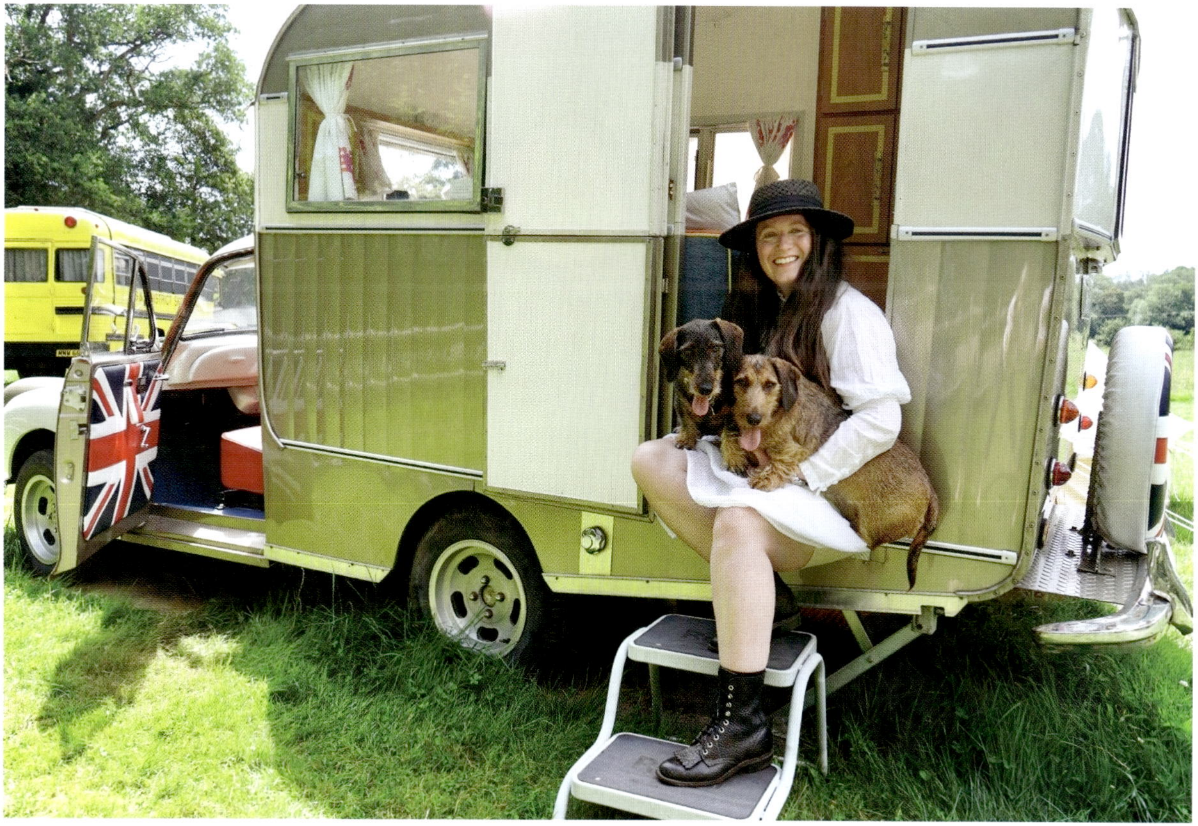

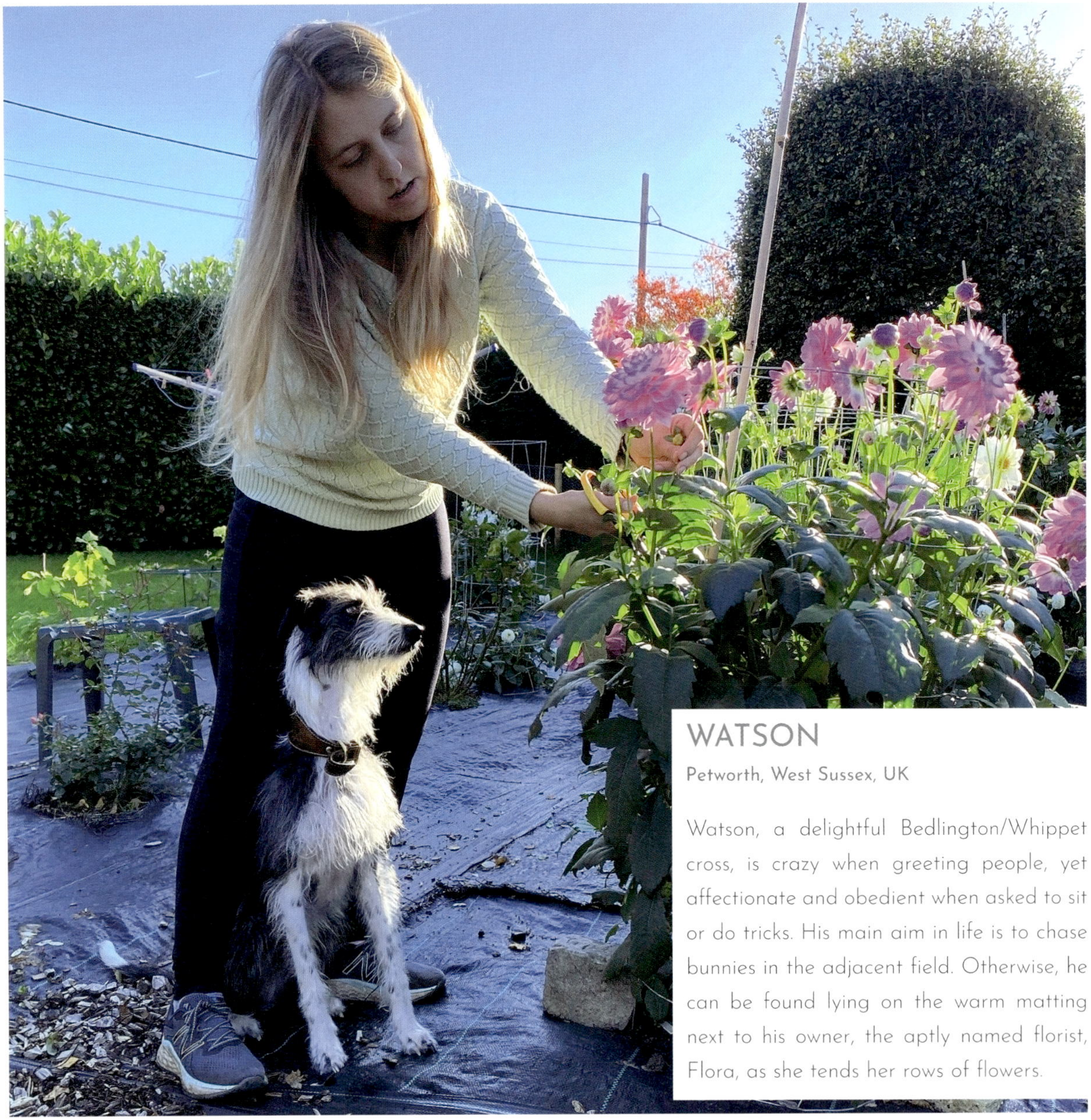

WATSON

Petworth, West Sussex, UK

Watson, a delightful Bedlington/Whippet cross, is crazy when greeting people, yet affectionate and obedient when asked to sit or do tricks. His main aim in life is to chase bunnies in the adjacent field. Otherwise, he can be found lying on the warm matting next to his owner, the aptly named florist, Flora, as she tends her rows of flowers.

CHOC & NING Pingelly, Western Australia

These Border Collie/Kelpie crosses are working farm dogs, who make sure no sheep is left behind. Ning's father was an Australian champion Border Collie. Choc adores riding on the back of the ute and he and the other farm dogs love rolling in dead sheep.

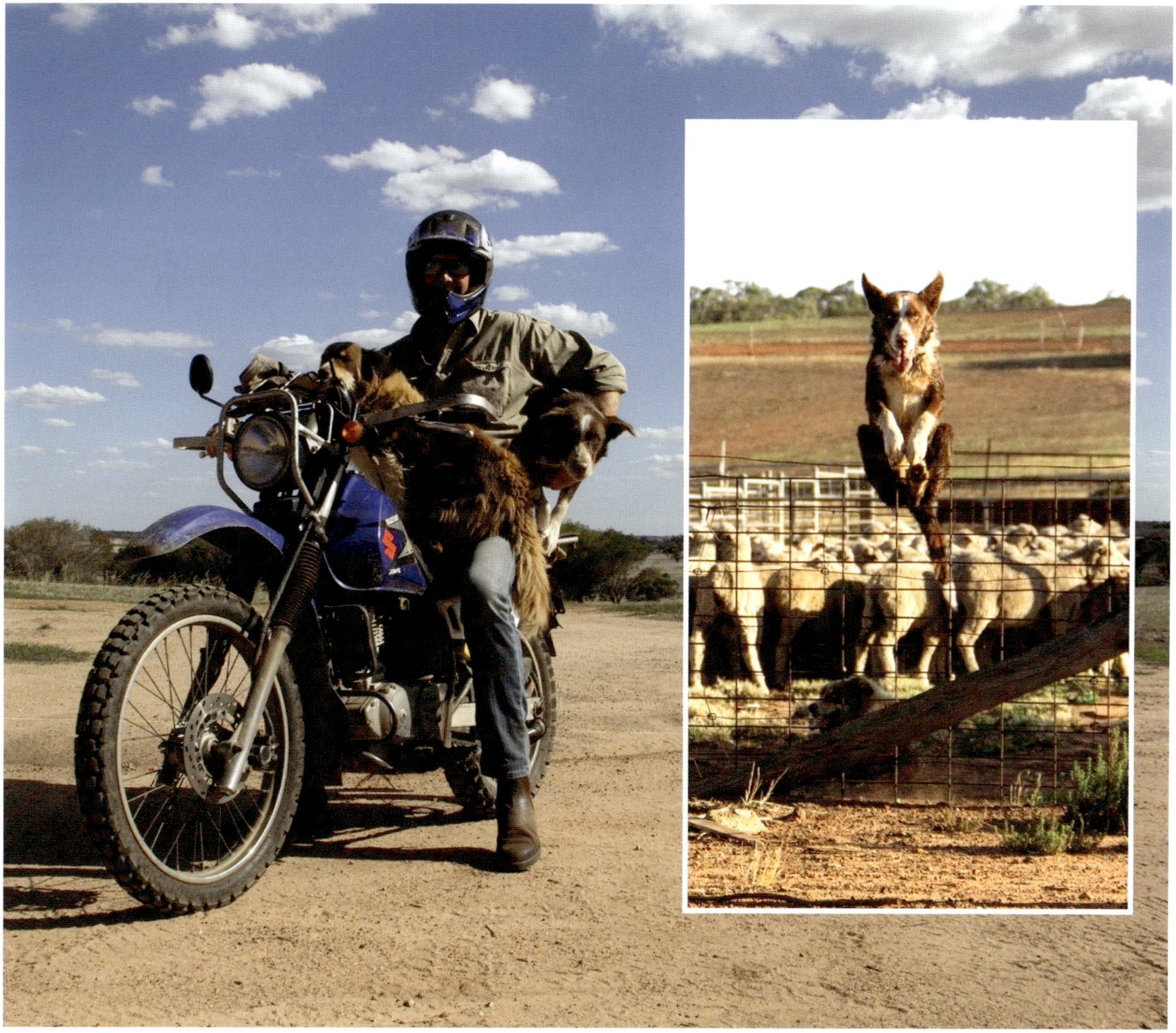

OTIS Richmond, Surrey, UK

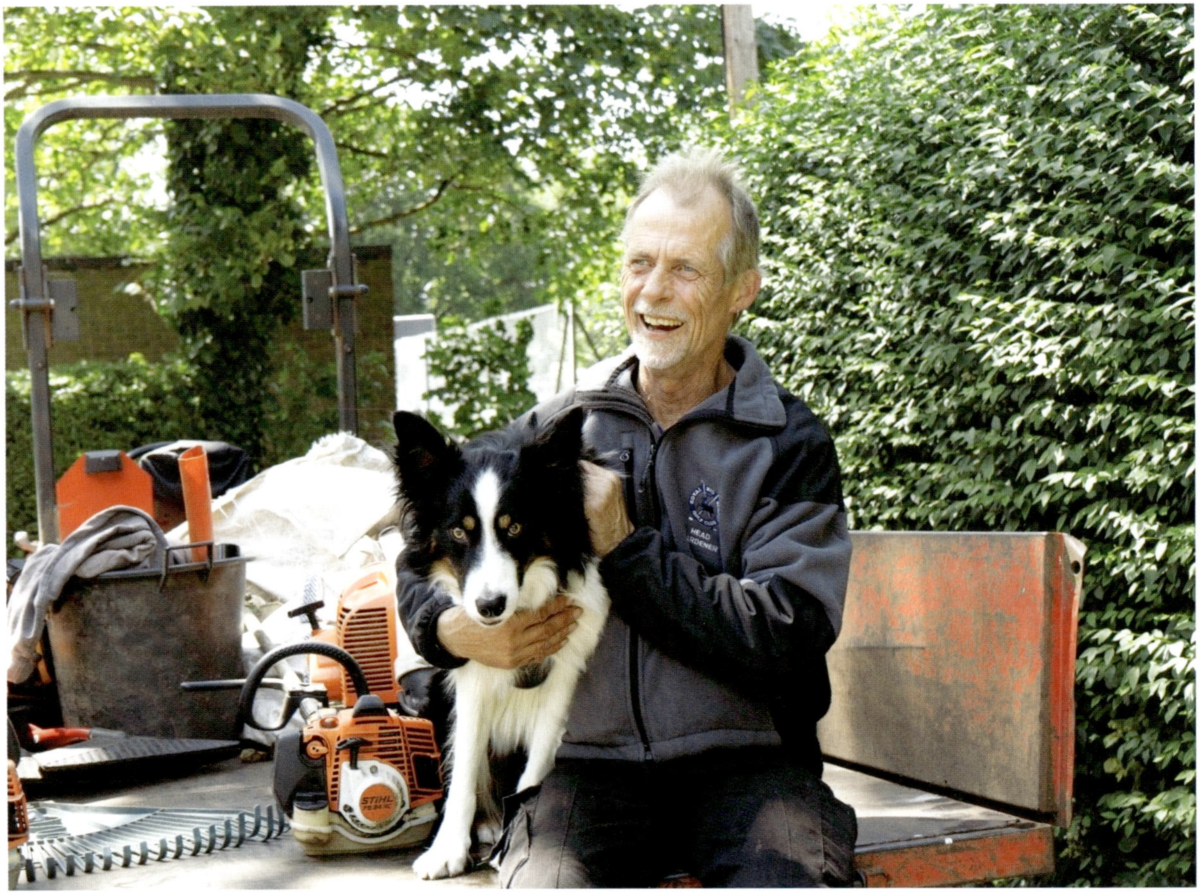

Otis was named after Otis Redding, because, according to his owner, Darren, he had soul. Otis is employed to keep the Canadian geese off the fairways of the golf course where Darren is head gardener. Otis is a rescue Border Collie and after an early life cooped up in a cramped caravan, now has the run of the golf course first thing in the morning and last thing at night.

Otis is a good badger spotter, which delights Darren as he is keen to photograph them. There are no paw marks in the bunkers and no missing golf balls as Otis has been trained to leave both well alone. His off-duty activities include chasing shadows.

TALIA & MURPHY Saffron Walden, Essex, UK

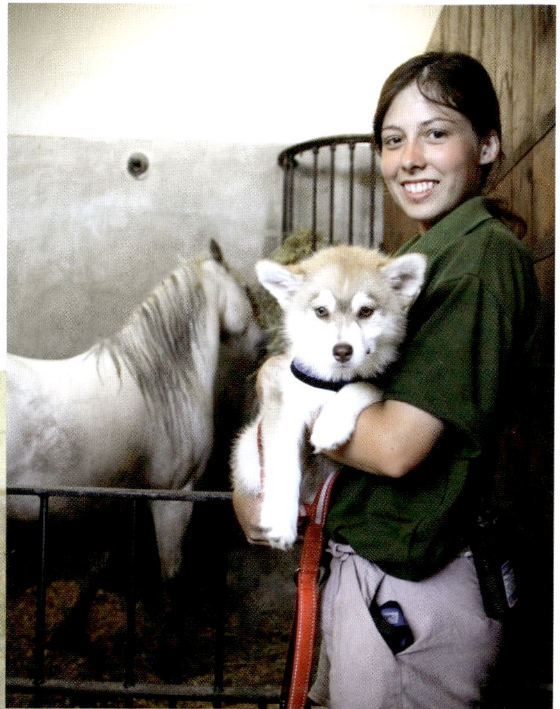

Sinead (right) and Fiona (below) are stable lasses, who take their dogs, Talia and Murphy, to work with them at Audley End House.

The day I visited, Talia the Pomsky pup was being trained to keep out of the way of horses' hooves, while Murphy the Labrador/Springer Spaniel was busy eating apples from the orchard and mapping out the different houses on the estate where he could source a treat.

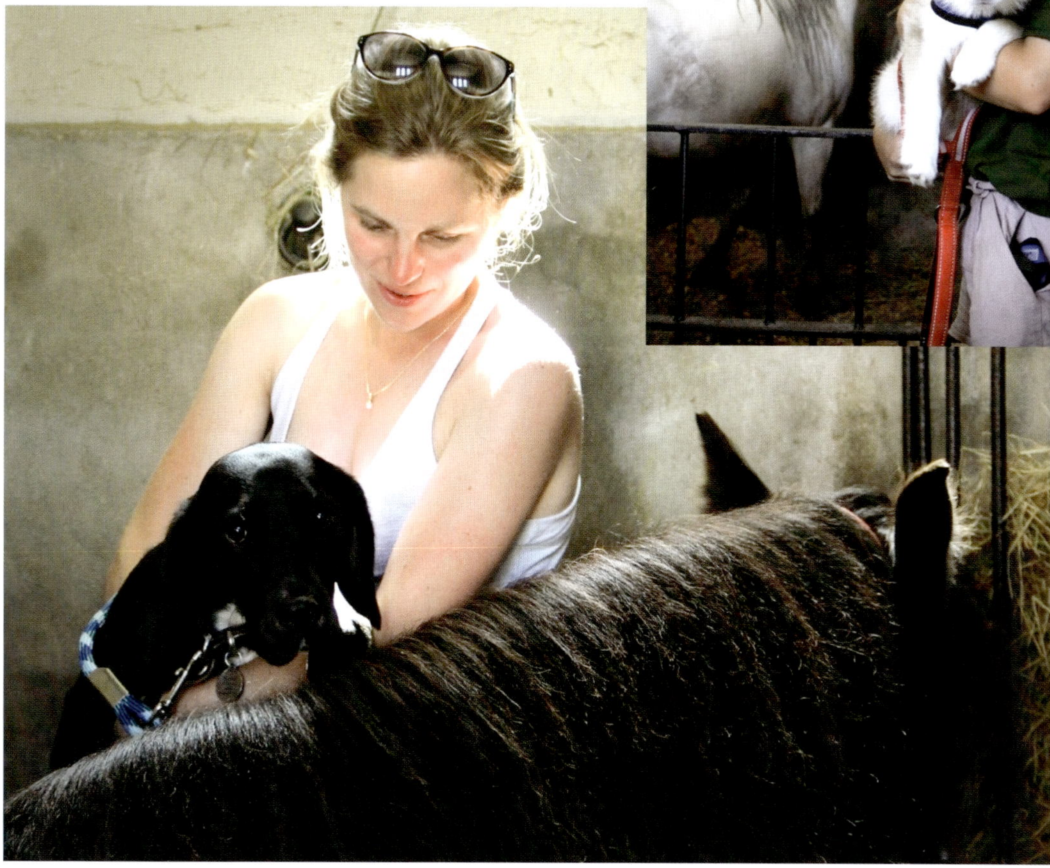

OFFICE DOGS

Some of my most rewarding visits have been to office spaces, especially those with multiple dogs, where the human/canine balance is perfect. Often, I can't say who has the biggest smile: the employees or the dogs. The atmosphere is one of ordered chaos, with dog treats, dog bowls and beds next to desks.

In private companies or co-working spaces, the canine presence is not only a bonus for the owner but also for other colleagues, who invariably have a stash of treats for any dogs that happen to pop their heads round the corner. And for solo office workers, the company of a beloved pet is invaluable.

MISSY & NELLY Wisborough Green, West Sussex, UK

Missy is a gun dog, who has adapted well to office life. She had never been in a car or a house until she met her owner, head auctioneer Will, but she is so well-trained – responding entirely to commands – that she does not need to wear a collar or lead. Nelly, Will's other dog, is also a Labrador but younger and more of a greeter.

After a long walk, when they arrive at the office, Missy goes straight to her bed while Nelly minesweeps the floor for crumbs.

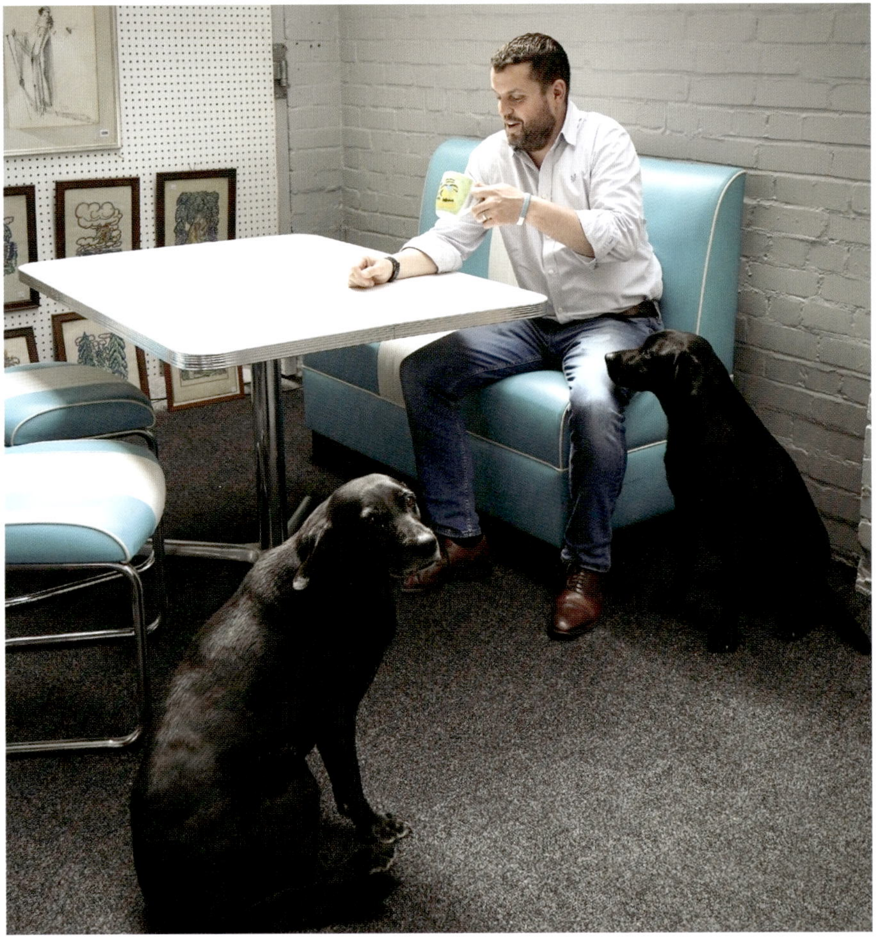

AGGIE Hastings, East Sussex, UK

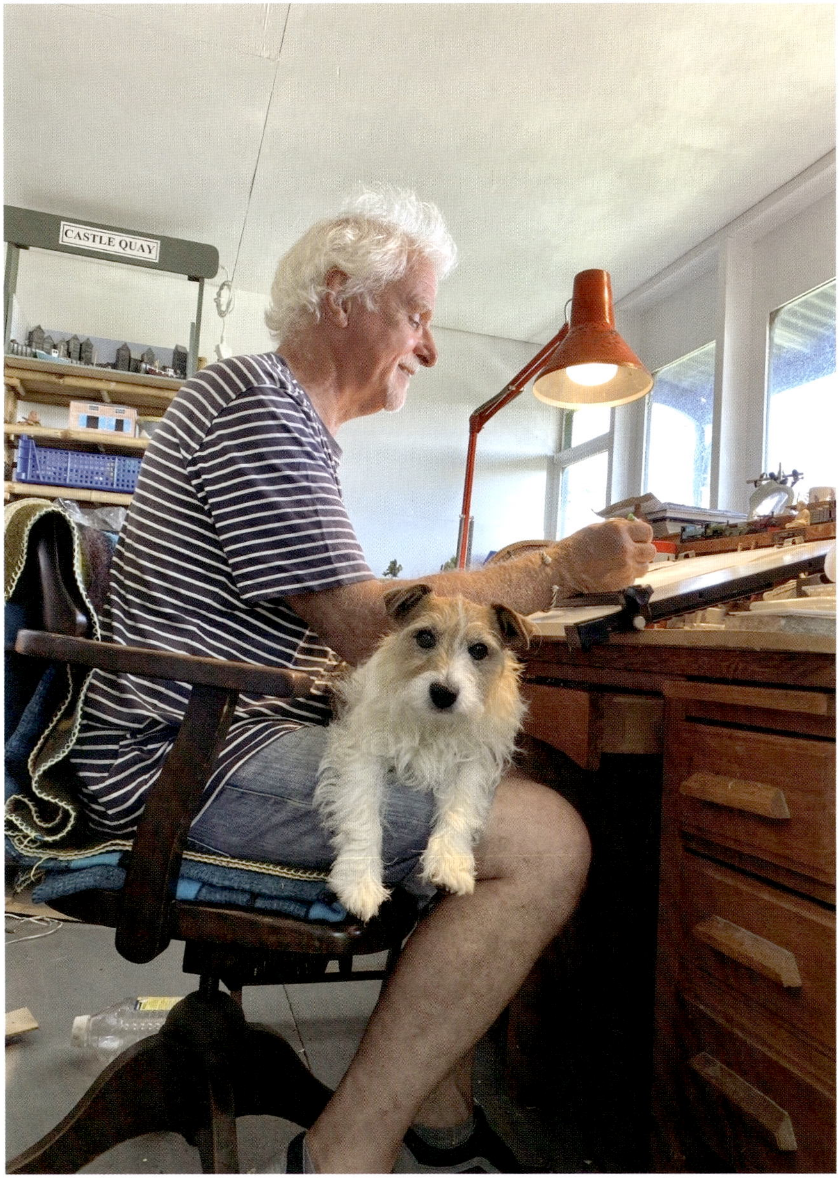

Aggie, a Jack Russell Terrier, was born in a rescue centre. Chris – a crime novelist, potter, sculptor, garden designer, and model train enthusiast – took her home as a puppy eight years ago. Aggie is Chris's inspiration and constant companion, and is instrumental to his detective novels where she features as DI Sonny Russell's sidekick.

Chris writes in a converted train compartment with views of the English Channel. There is no set routine; Aggie is flexible and goes with the flow and ebb of the tide. She loves to run along the beach, sometimes in circles, like a mad dervish.

Above Aggie's bed in the studio is a string of rosettes. She has won several dog competitions at local fairs, including waggiest tail and second best in show.

She accompanies Chris on his book promotion appearances and gets more likes on Instagram than her owner's novels.

MONTY, ELLA, CHARLIE & SCUBA City of London, UK

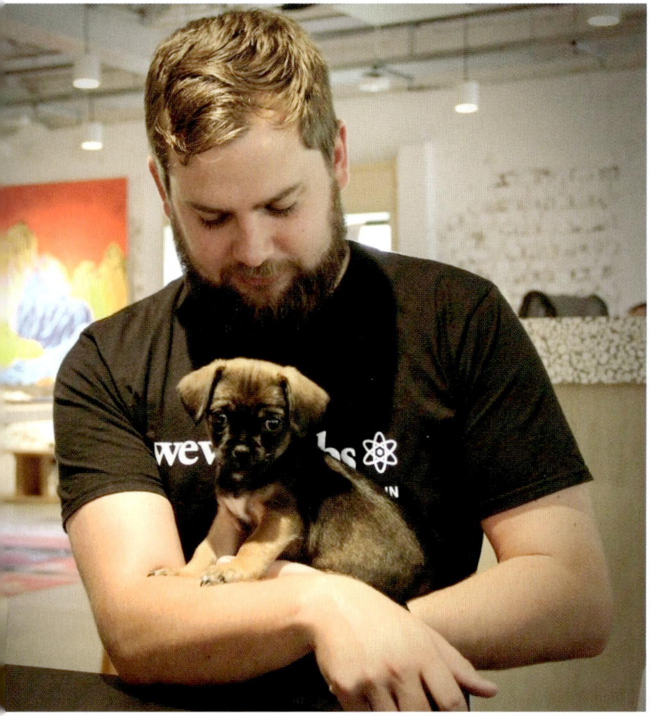

There are several dogs at this large co-working space, which makes it a very sociable venue for the pets.

Monty, left, is a Chug or Pughuahua – a Chihuahua/Pug mix. Only eleven weeks old, he is new to the world and to the office, where he comes with his owner, Florie, who decided it would be less stressful to get a dog than a boyfriend. Florie co-parents Monty with her office colleague, James, who takes his duties very seriously. When Monty is not playing with his collar, he loves to chew on James's beard.

Florie claims that 'everyone in the team is happier and more productive' since Monty has been there.

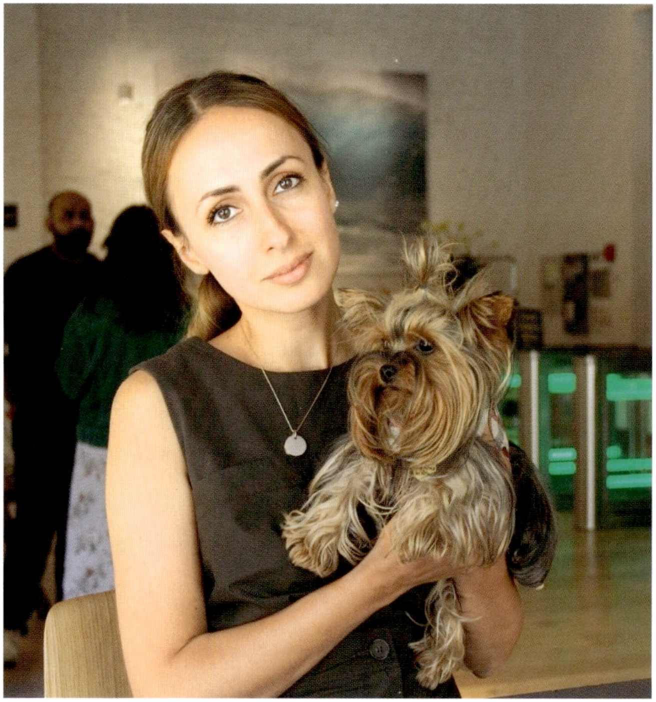

Yorkshire Terrier Ella, right, belongs to Yana who finds it much nicer working with a dog at her side. 'Home is where your dog is,' Yana says, and just looking at Ella helps lower Yana's stress levels.

Ella is the co-working office's diva. She is not good with the other office dogs, except for Dylan who is very patient with her.

Mondays are Ella's favourite days and she can't wait to get to the office, though she barks when Yana works overtime.

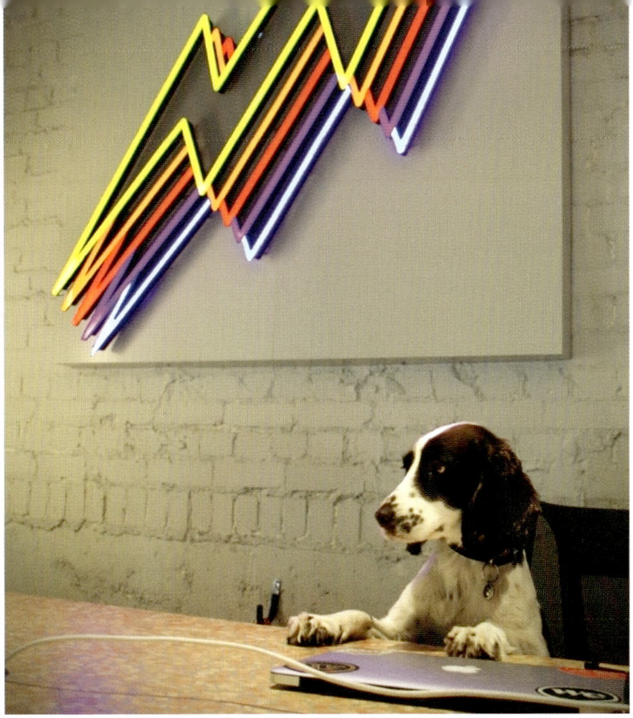

Charlie, three, left, is a rescue Sprocker (Spaniel/Cocker). He comes to this co-working office with his owner, Darren, who was impressed to find there was a dog present during his job interview.

Charlie has free run of the office and wanders off to the desks where he can guarantee he will get a treat. He is scared of the office alarm and the noise of the coffee machine, and refuses to walk along the polished floor of the coffee bar area.

In his spare time Charlie is a PET (Pets as Therapy) dog, and regularly visits a local care home where many of the residents have dementia.

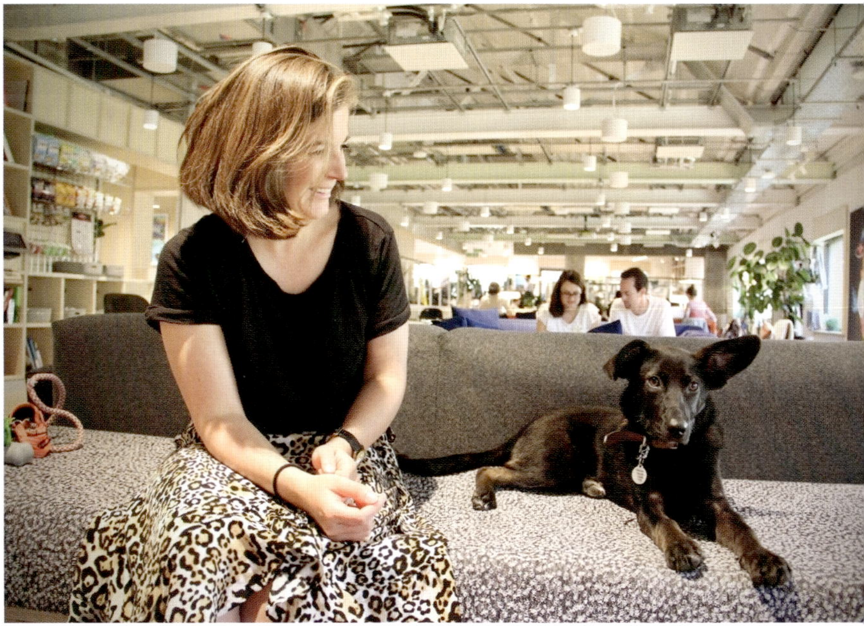

Scuba, right, is a young rescue dog whose name was chosen because her 'dad' loves deep sea diving. She is quite new to the co-working office where she comes twice a week with her owner, Mary. Although a little nervous at first, Scuba now loves the attention she gets in equal measure from office workers and other office dogs.

Scuba comes to work by tube and needs plenty of rest during the day. She is as exhausted by the journey as she is by the attention she gets from work colleagues and other dogs.

OLIVE Putney, London, UK

Work? I'm just here for the ride. Olive sits back as her owner, Caroline, an estate agent, concentrates. Olive is hoping Caroline might be planning their next 'holibob' – clifftop walks in Cornwall are a favourite.

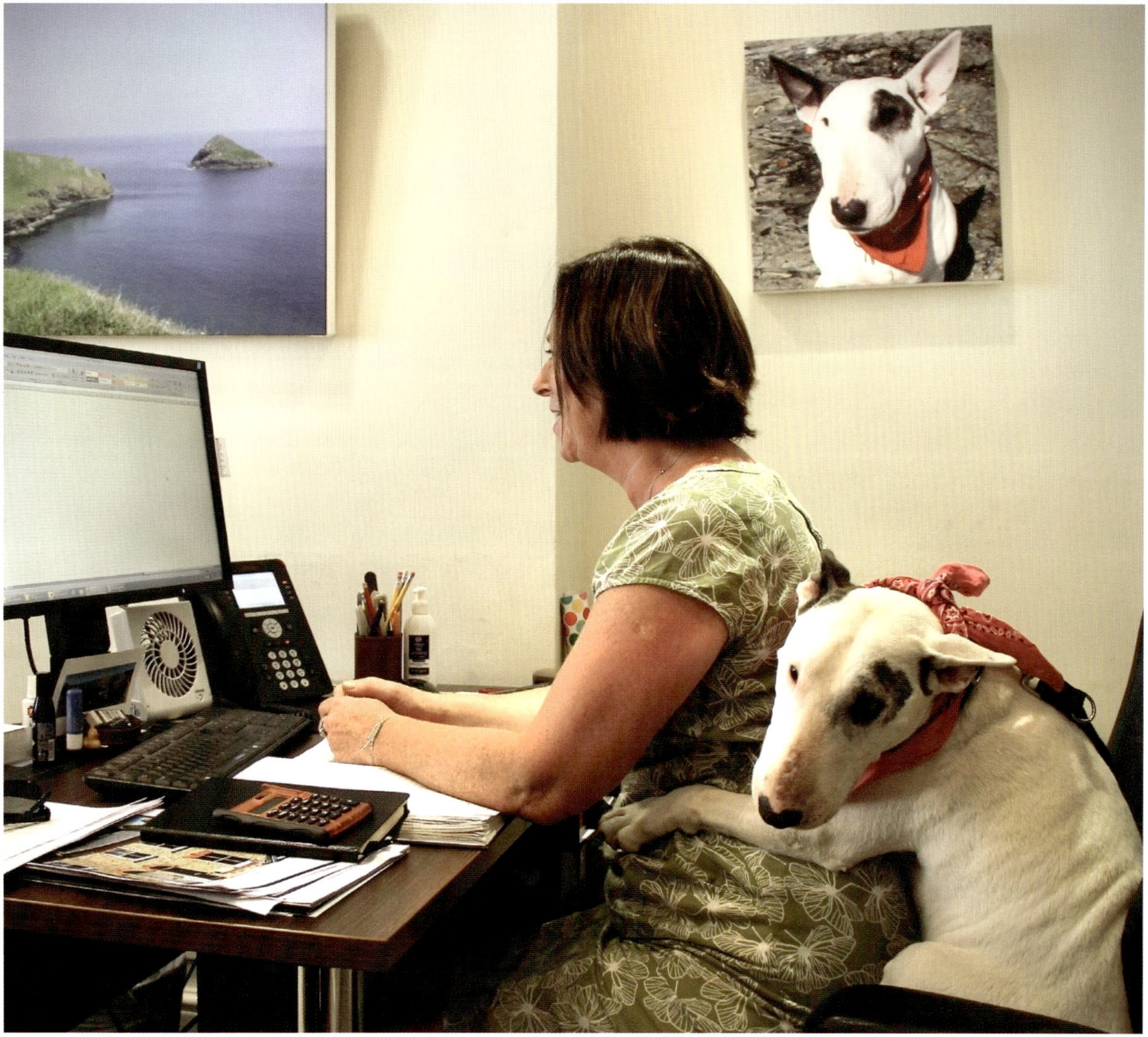

MAIA Phoenix, Arizona, USA

Dan chose this co-working space because it is dog-friendly and has good energy – he describes it as 'vibey'.

Maia, a Golden Retriever puppy, is still a little shy with other dogs. Dan nicknamed her Poker Face because she initially didn't smile much.

At home, Maia is always on the hunt for stray socks. She loves watching sport on TV and is a Phoenix Suns supporter.

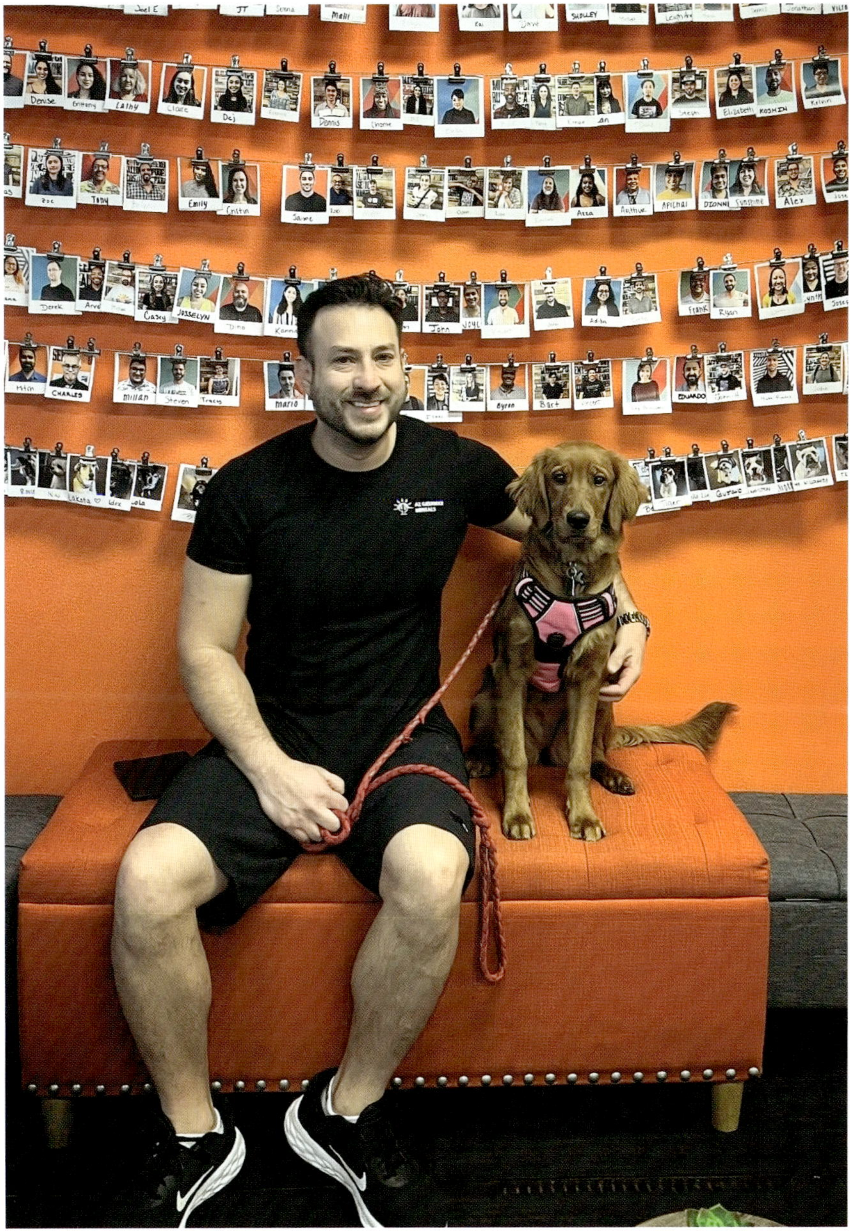

GEORGE Horsley, Surrey, UK

George is a beautifully behaved German Wirehaired Pointer, rescued by Richard from a Spanish pound, just two days before the dog was due to be euthanised. He now has a lovely bed, placed near Richard's desk at the railway station he manages. When Richard is in the back office, George alerts him with a little woof if someone needs service at the ticket desk.

George became a celebrity when news broke that Richard was handing in his resignation, having been told he could not continue to bring the dog to work. There was a local outcry, and nine thousand people signed a petition to encourage South Western Railway to reconsider. Fourteen national newspapers carried the story and even the then Transport Secretary, Grant Schapps, became involved. SWR carried out a risk assessment, and permission was granted for George to come in with Richard each day – setting a happy precedent across the SWR network.

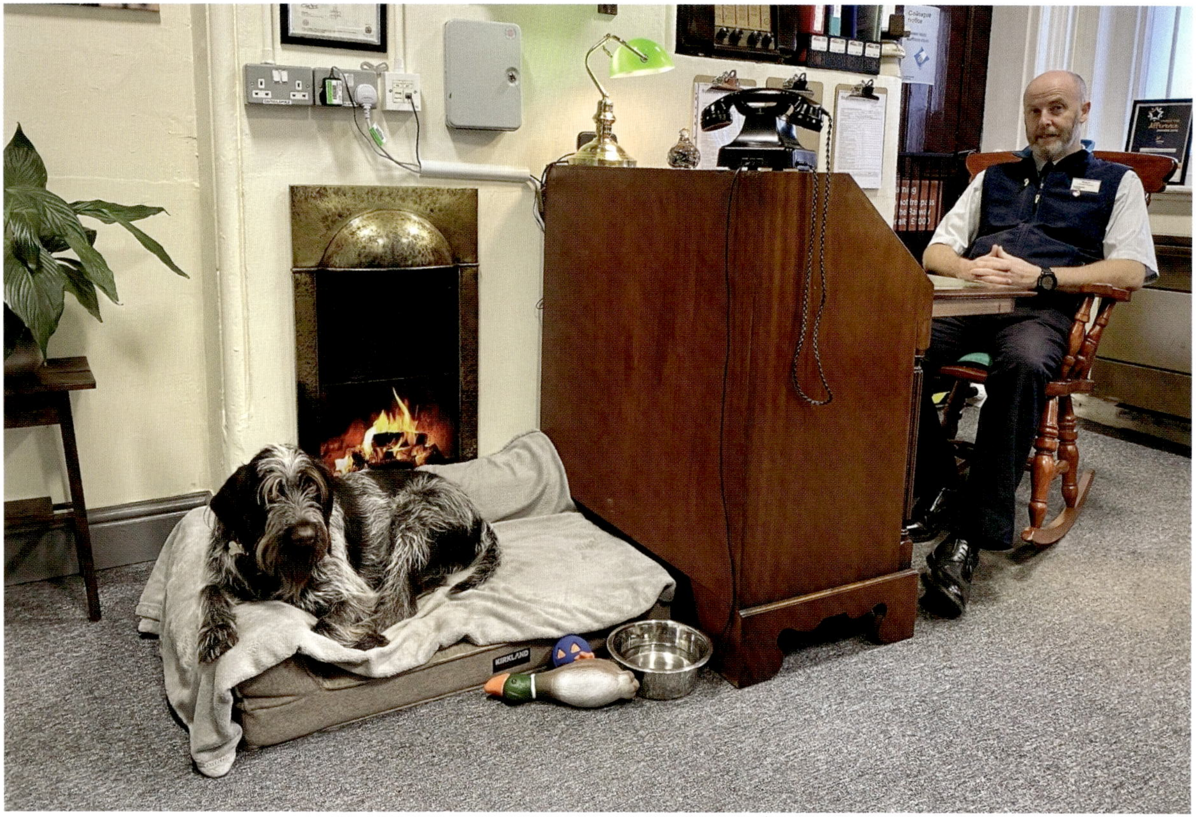

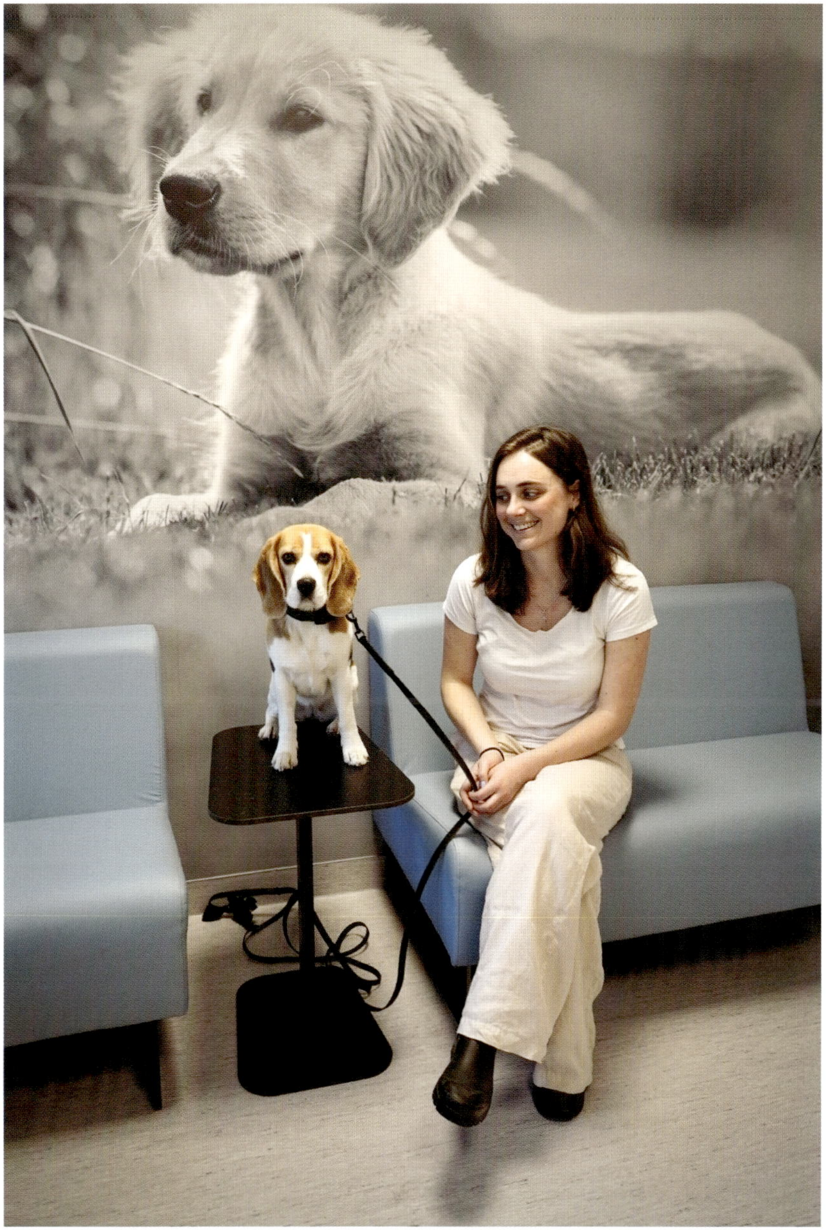

MOLLY

Gothenburg, Sweden

'She thinks she rules the world. Molly thinks everyone is here for her,' says Anna, a Swedish HR executive, who is the creator of the Dogenburg Instagram page.

Anna acquired Molly, a Beagle, during lockdown, and has been bringing her to the animal hospital where she works ever since. Molly was a tricky puppy, as she was 'high on life', but she now loves coming in and hanging out with her 'roomies' while Anna is at her desk. The dogs are taken out for walks at lunchtime.

Molly knows when it's time to go home and displays a different kind of happy at the end of the working day. Her full name is Miss Molly Malone, after the traditional Irish ditty. When choosing the name, Anna wanted one that reflected her Irish roots. She did not know at the time that Molly happens to be the most popular female dog name in Sweden.

PLONKY, AVA, MUFFIN, MAUD & MORGAN Frome, Somerset, UK

The owner of this computer solutions firm is so dog-friendly that at least a third of the staff bring their dogs into the office on a regular basis.

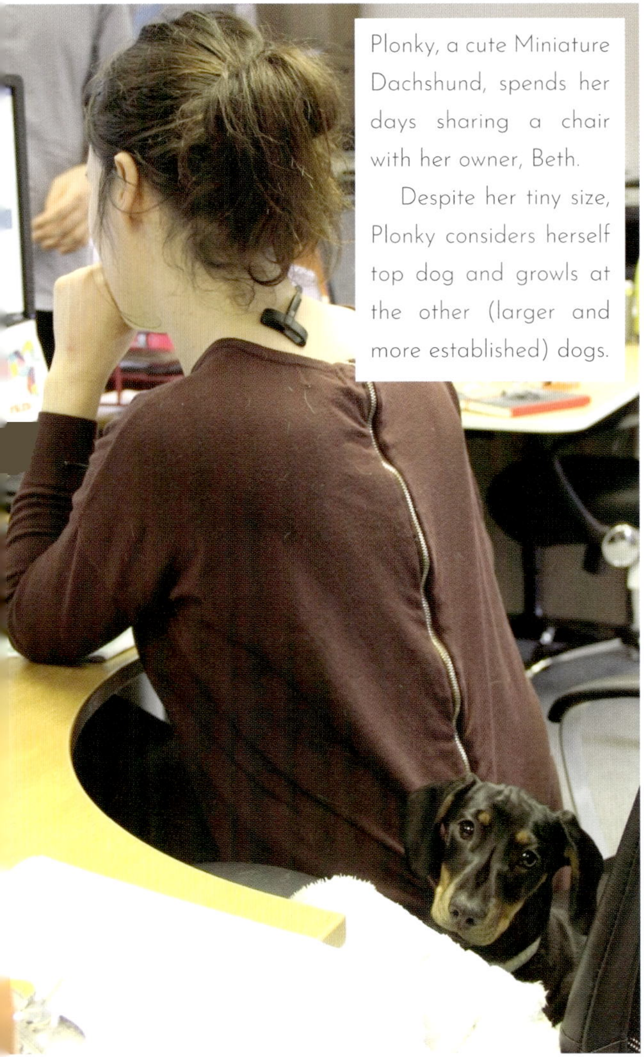

Plonky, a cute Miniature Dachshund, spends her days sharing a chair with her owner, Beth.

Despite her tiny size, Plonky considers herself top dog and growls at the other (larger and more established) dogs.

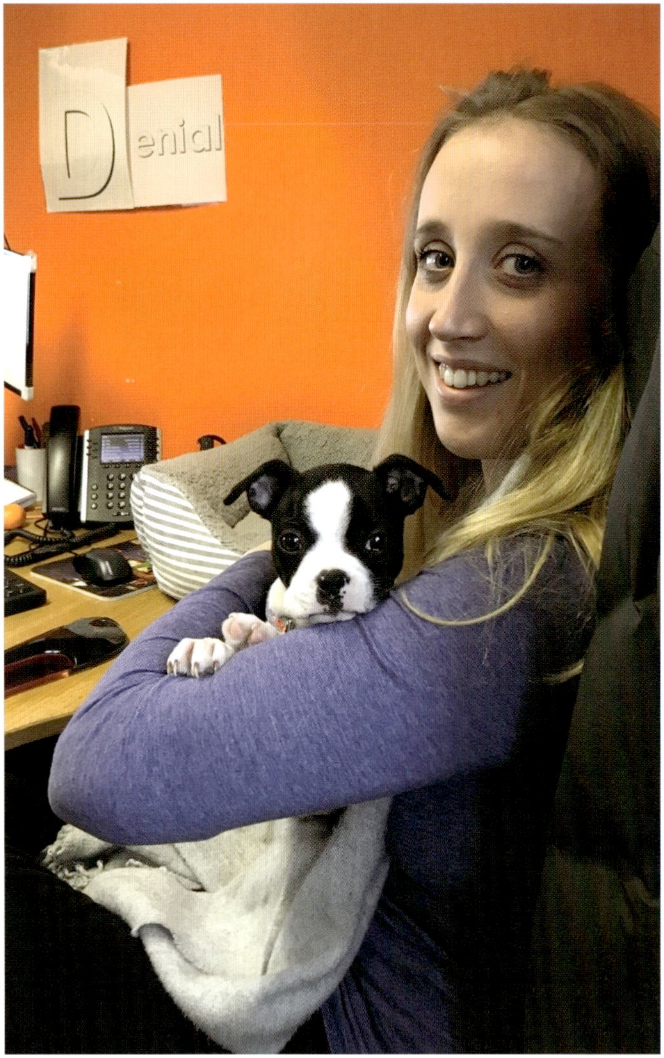

At just nine weeks old, Ava, a Boston Terrier, is too young to be allowed on the office floor. Like a baby, she sleeps most of the day in her bed, next to her owner, Lauren.

CLOCKWISE FROM RIGHT:

Muffin, half-Shar Pei and half-Cockapoo cross, is very sociable and runs around the office greeting everyone. As a pup, he was a bit nippy, but is now well-behaved and will sit on people's laps while they work. Not so much top dog as lap dog.

Maud is a shy, young Whippet/Bedlington Terrier, who timidly tries her luck at having a ball thrown for her by dropping it at people's feet. She will play with some but not all of the dogs, and likes to retreat to her own little spot under owner David's desk.

The senior dog at the office is five-year-old Morgan, an English Pointer rescue, who has his own chair in the conference room, where he sits during meetings. He has been known to help himself to food in employees' bags and has a penchant for croissants.

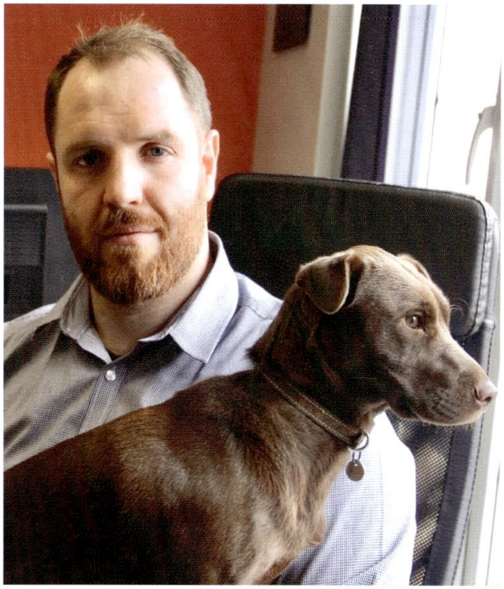

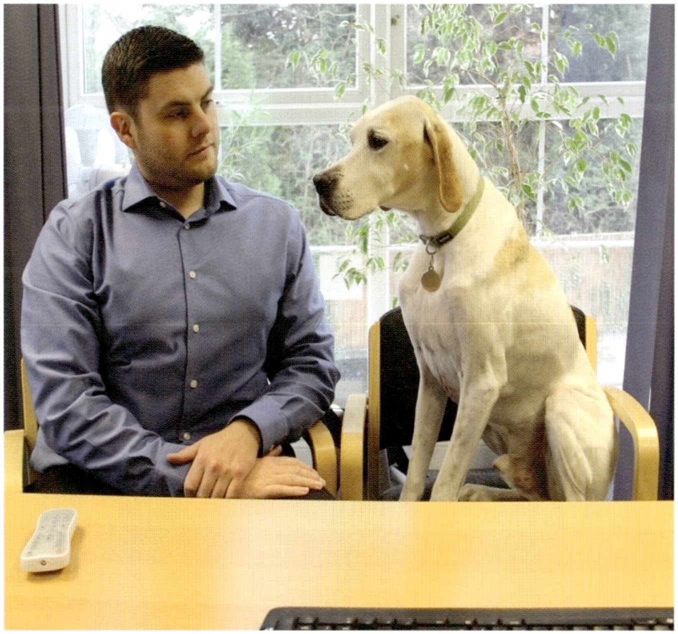

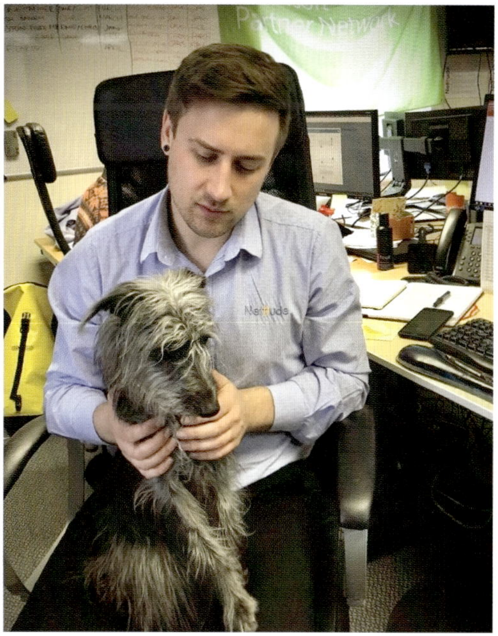

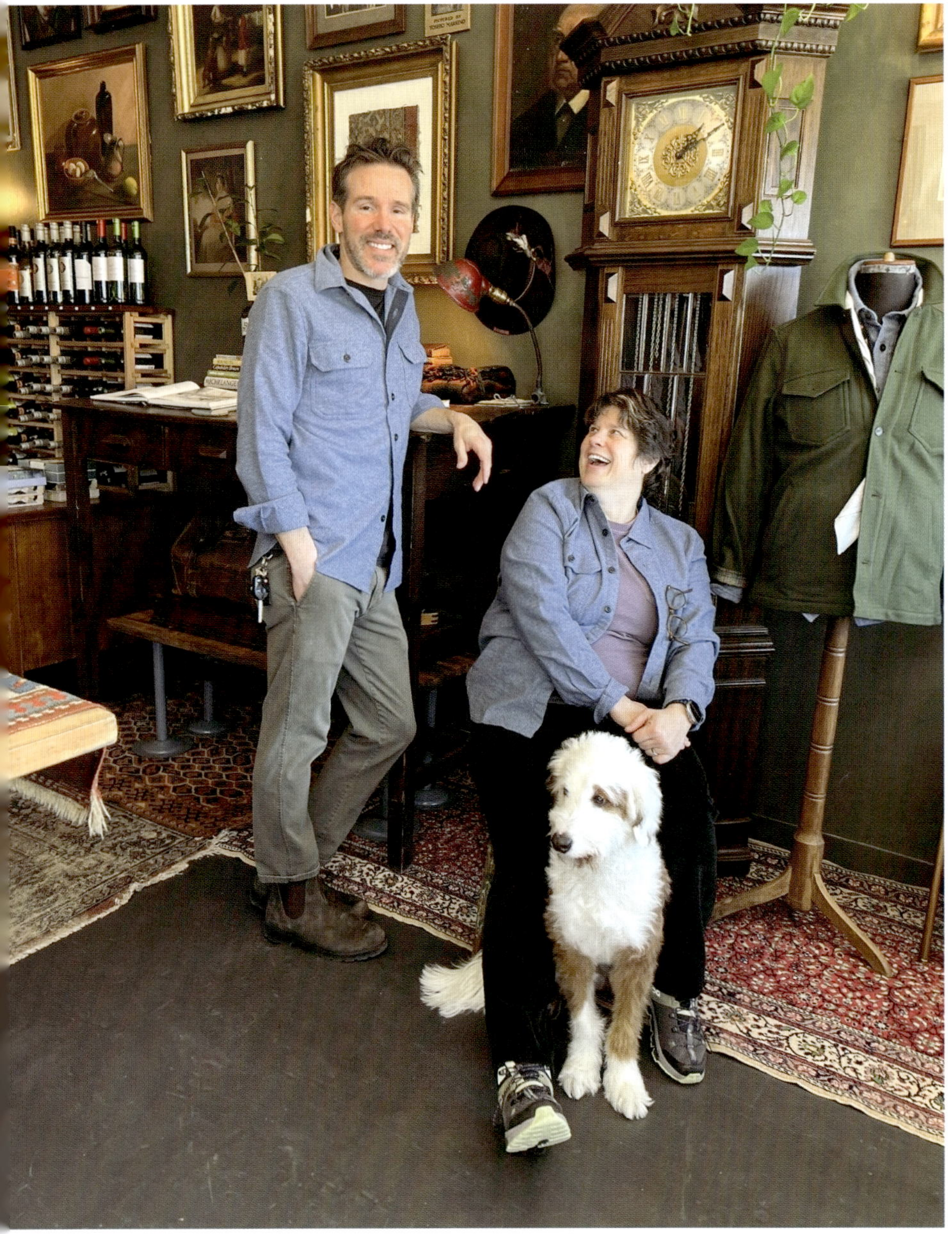

OAKLEY

Fayetteville, North Carolina, USA

Oakley, a mini Bernedoodle, is four years old. 'I'm his support human, because he's so skittish,' says his owner, Jennifer, a realtor. Oakley is a lockdown dog, whom Jennifer bought from an Amish community breeder. It's the Bernese side that is skittish, while the poodle side is smart.

On Saturday mornings, Jennifer brings Oakley – and breakfast – over to her friend, Patrick, who runs the antiques and coffee shop down the road. Based on his experience of Oakley, Patrick is now very keen to own a dog and bring it in with him to work. The dog will likely feature alongside Oakley in the photographic book he hopes to publish about his eclectic shop.

Back at the realty office, Oakley tends to go to his safe place under the conference table when clients visit. And, just as Jennifer calms Oakley down, the dog calms her down when she gets stressed at work. A mutual support team.

TINGO

Amsterdam, Netherlands

Tingo is a Congolese hunting dog, a breed that is traditionally associated with the Batéké people. He was rescued by human rights lawyer, Kelly, who, on one of her visits to the region, spotted him in the street. He was the smallest of a litter of five, and she made a sling out of banana leaves to carry him back in. From his emaciated state, he was brought back to health in seven weeks.

Now Tingo travels everywhere with Kelly and has more gear than she does. At home in Amsterdam, he waits for Kelly to finish work so that they can go biking or paddleboarding on the canal near her flat.

Apparently, Tingo understands English, French and Lingala, although – inconveniently – he has forgotten the word 'come' in all languages.

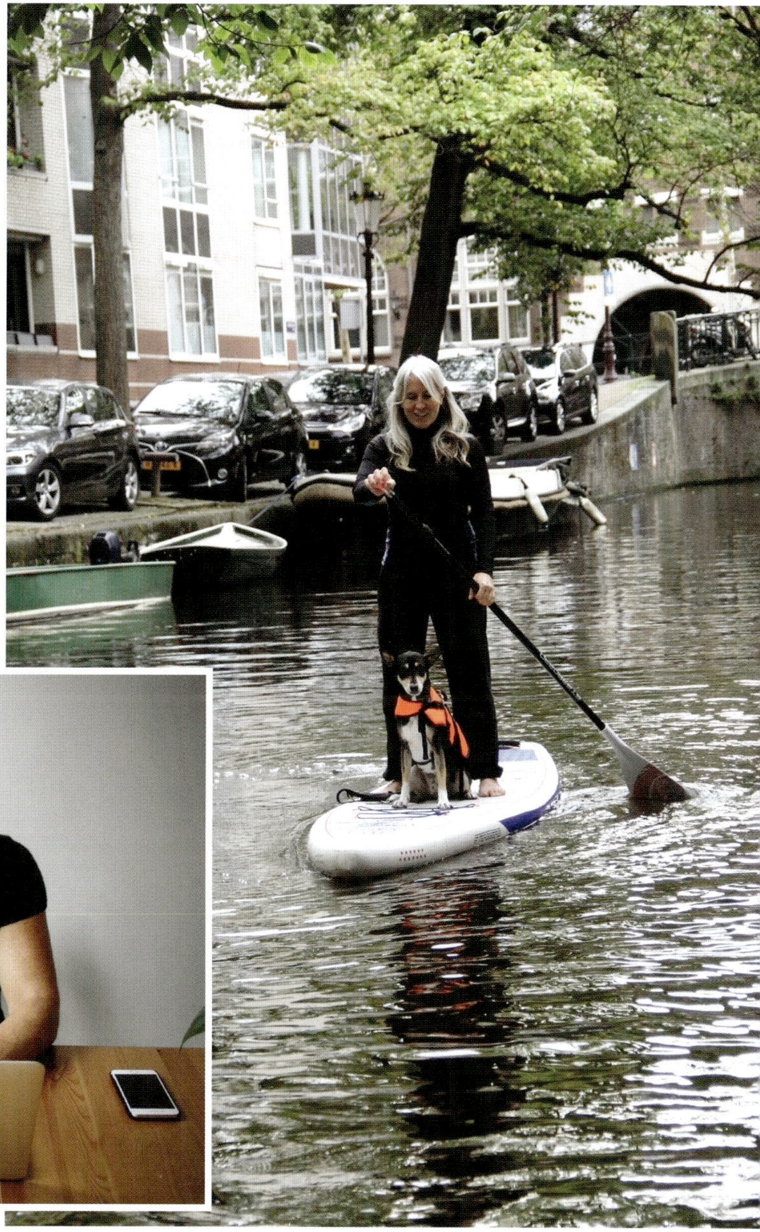

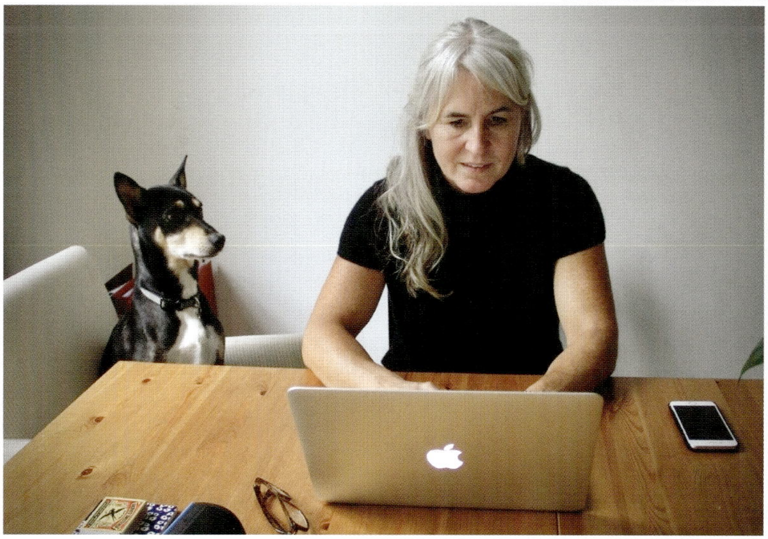

FLORENCE & CERYS Holt, Wiltshire, UK

Florence (below), aged nine weeks, newly jabbed, was behaving impeccably on her first day in the office. Samoyeds are quite placid and ideal for an office environment.

Cerys (right) is a short-haired Border Collie whose parents herded cattle and whose grandfather was a sheep trials champ. According to her owner, Andrew, Cerys has two modes – lying down doing nothing or full-on, going absolutely nuts in the field next to the office. Andrew and his wife acquired Cerys when they became empty nesters, and Andrew brings her to the office most days. She helps his sanity – she is loving and lively – and also keeps him fit, as she needs a lot of exercising.

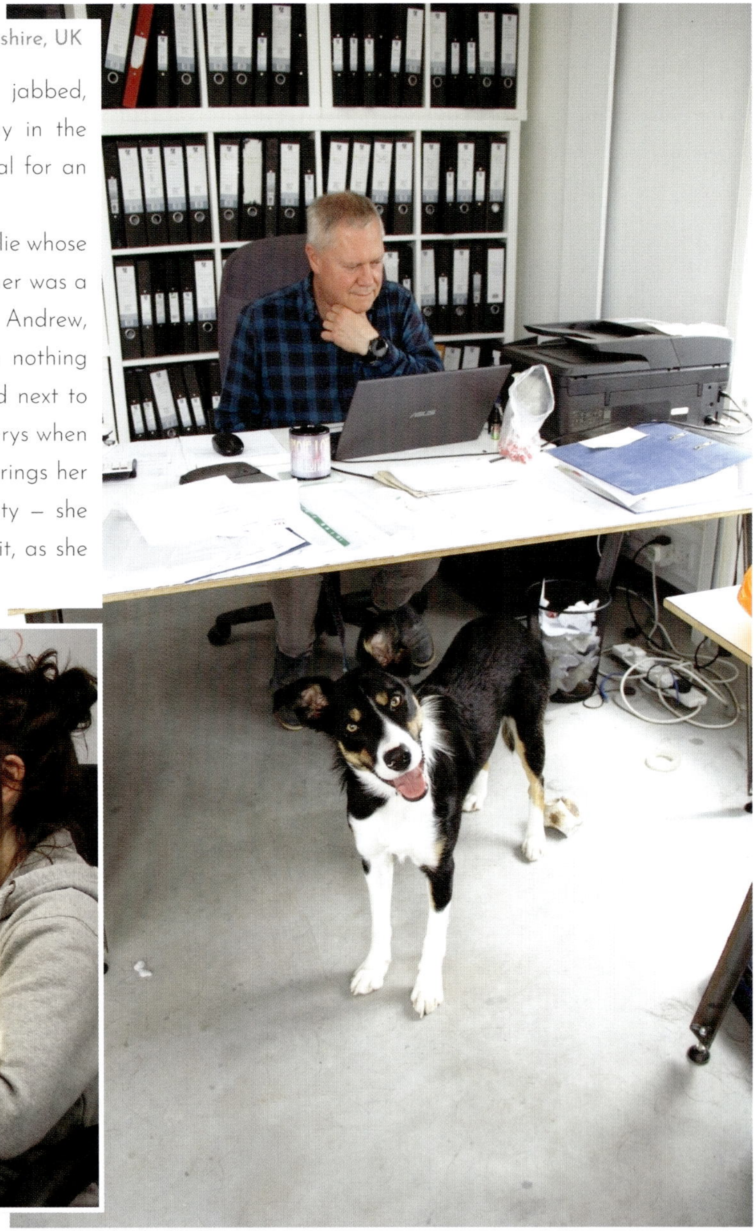

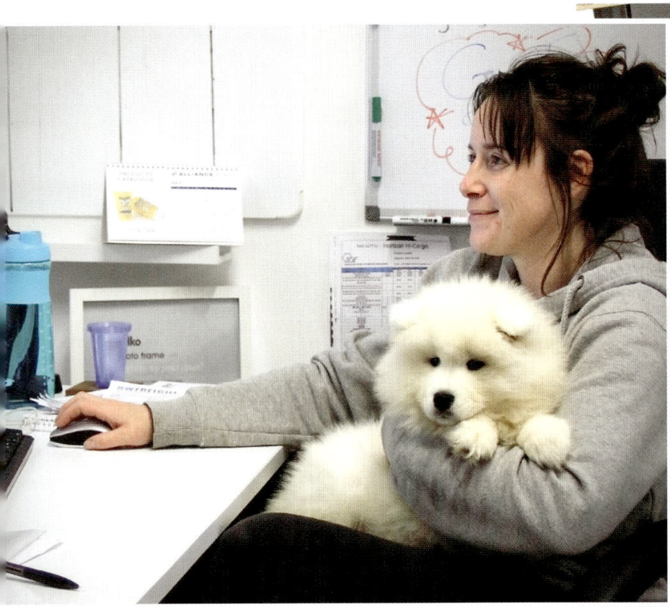

LEDLEY Hammersmith, London, UK

Laura's husband made a promise to her at the altar that she could get a dog, and named him Ledley after the former Tottenham Hotspur football player Ledley King. Ledley, a Cavapoochon, is an office nomad, as Laura has taken him to several different workplaces in London. Now that Laura works for herself, at a co-working office, Ledley comes to work with her every day. He starts his morning off by greeting everyone on the train, then continues at the co-workstations, where he says hello to each person there. He is very much an indispensable part of Laura's team and is a calming influence during meetings.

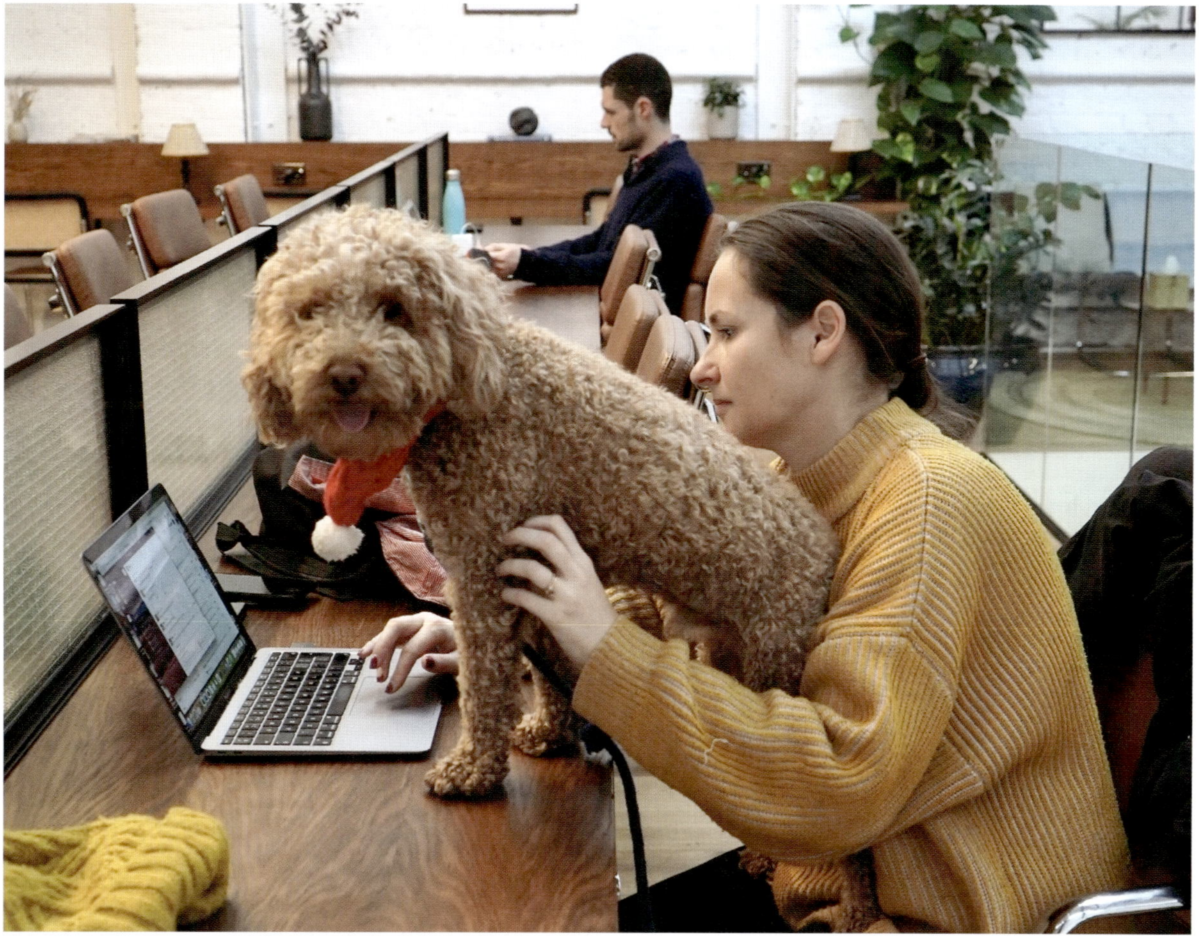

FORCES DOGS

Major Matthew Towl (opposite) was minding his wife's interiors store when I walked past. We got chatting and I discovered he worked at the nearby Royal Dragoon barracks, taking both his dogs in with him. When he mentioned that there were several dog owners who also took their dogs to the barracks, I asked if he and they would like, and be permitted, to take part in my project. His generosity and the results speak for themselves.

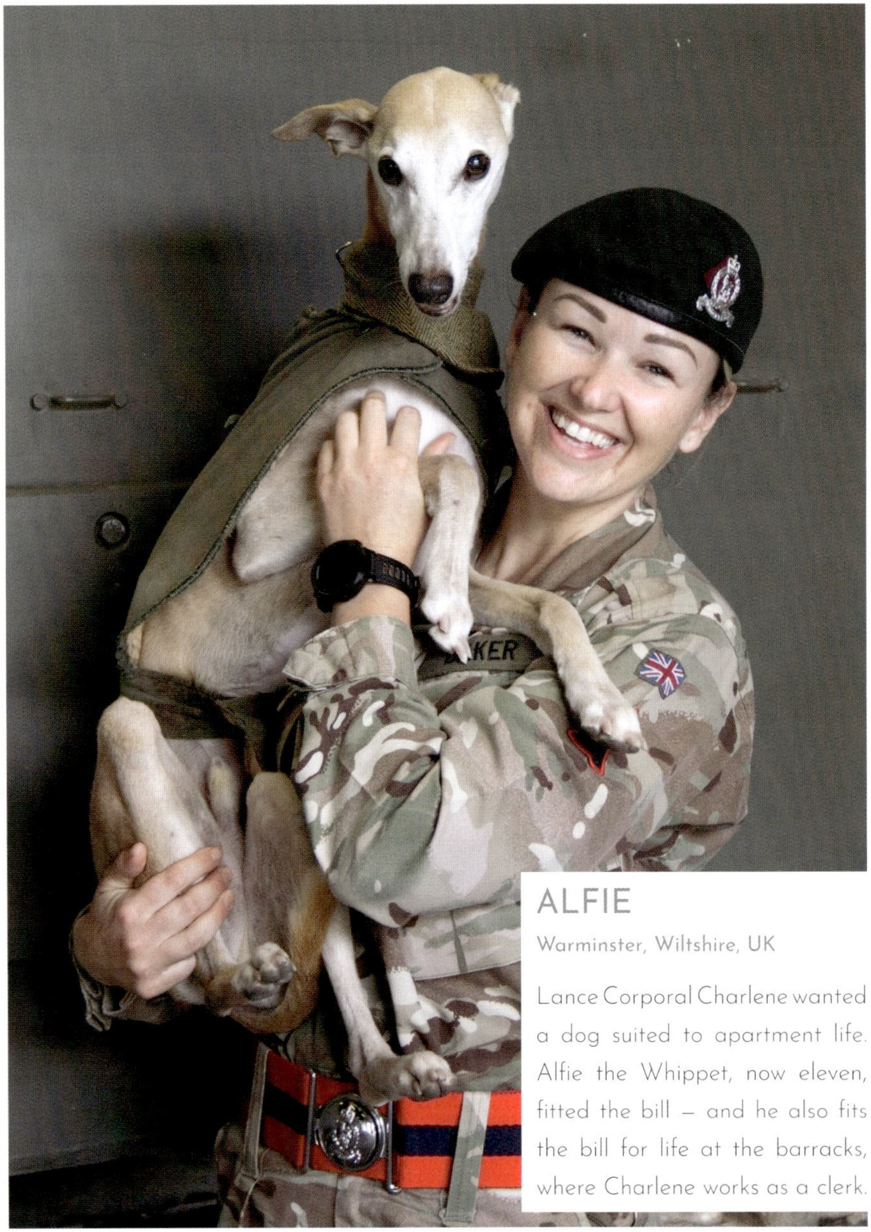

ALFIE

Warminster, Wiltshire, UK

Lance Corporal Charlene wanted a dog suited to apartment life. Alfie the Whippet, now eleven, fitted the bill – and he also fits the bill for life at the barracks, where Charlene works as a clerk.

MISSY & SASHA

Warminster, Wiltshire, UK

Missy, a five-year-old Vizsla, and Sasha, a six-year-old Labrador cross, make barracks life seem less regimented, according to Major Matthew Towl.

Missy was rescued from a house in Wales where she had been kept for breeding, and Sasha was saved by a soldier from being drowned on a French farm. Now they spend their days relaxing in the office or wandering the corridors in search of treats.

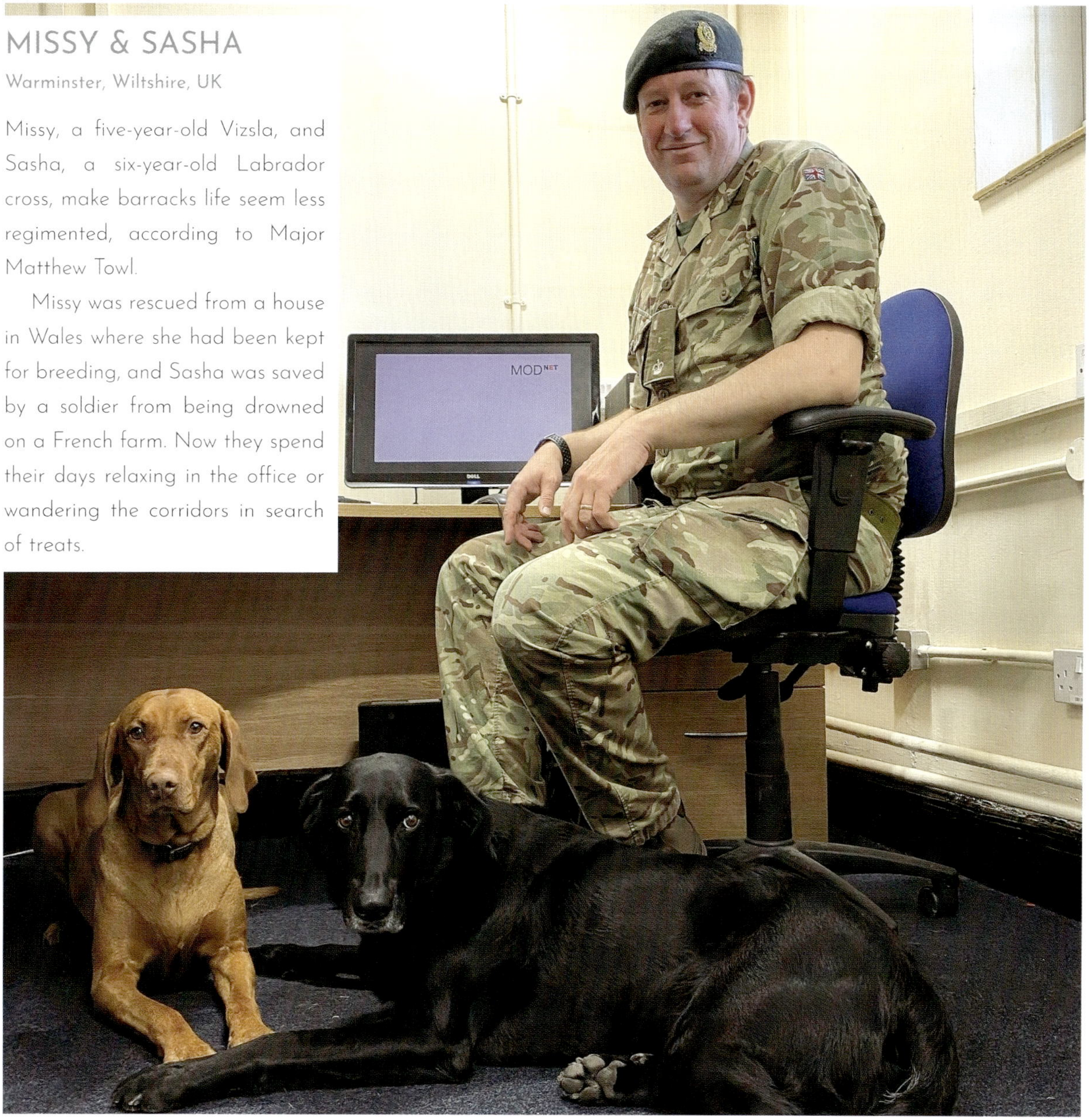

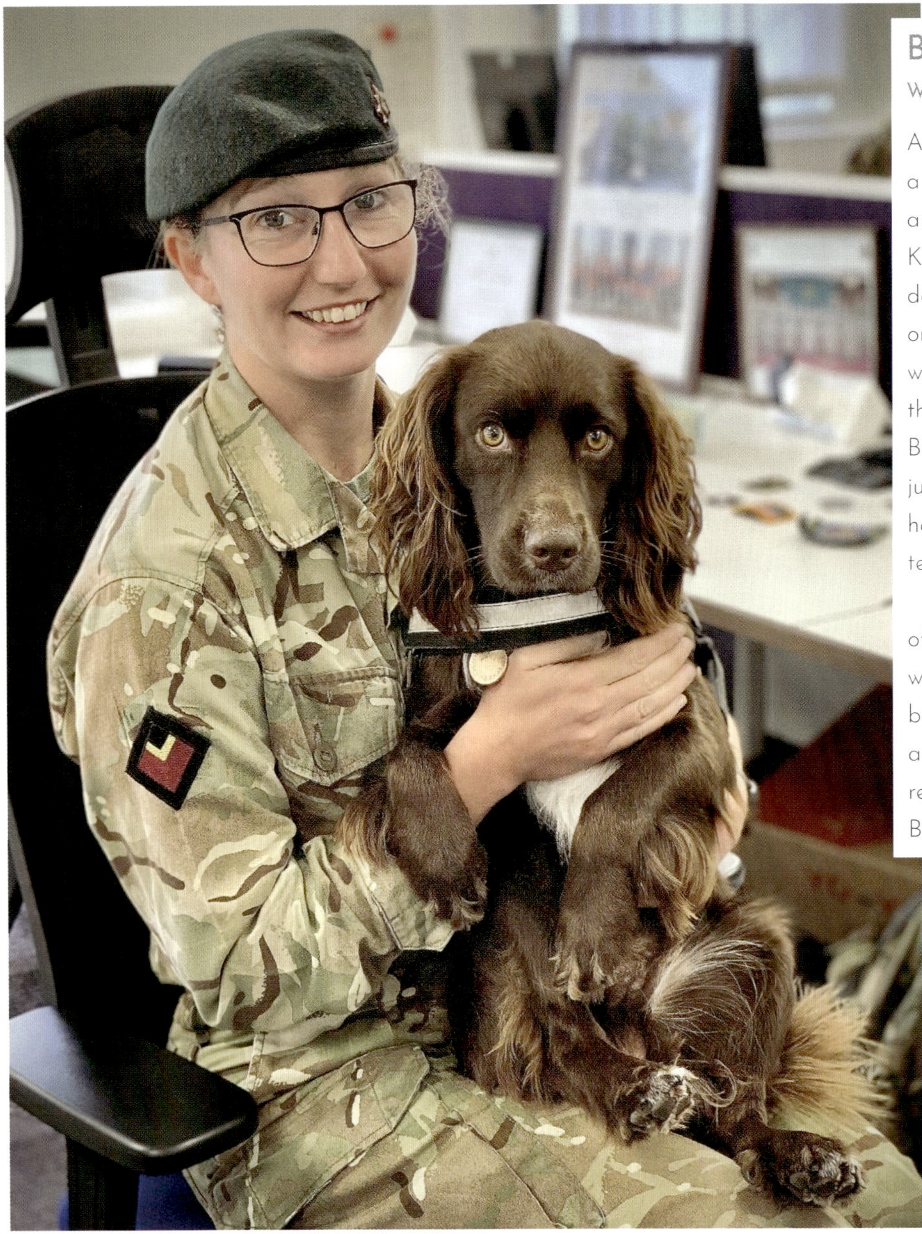

BLUE

Warminster, Wiltshire, UK

Active dogs such as Blue, a Working Cocker Spaniel, are popular here. Captain Kathy wanted an energetic dog to run alongside her on cross-country training, as well as to accompany her to the office. She makes sure Blue is well exercised – at just eighteen months old, he is currently a hormonal teenager.

After a long day in the office, with breaks for short walks, Blue starts to get a bit restless by about 4pm, and knows it's time for their regular big walk up nearby Battlesbury.

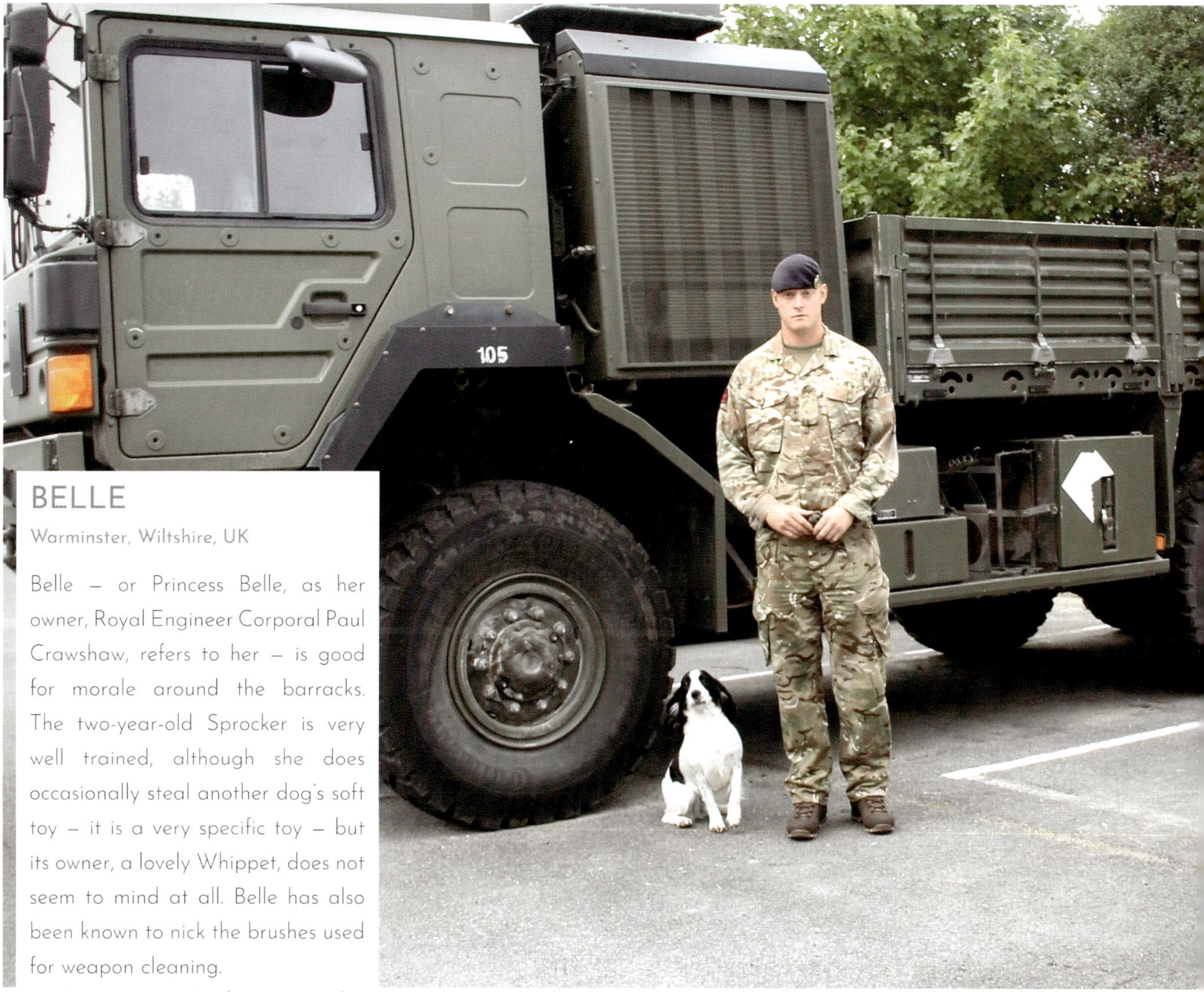

BELLE

Warminster, Wiltshire, UK

Belle – or Princess Belle, as her owner, Royal Engineer Corporal Paul Crawshaw, refers to her – is good for morale around the barracks. The two-year-old Sprocker is very well trained, although she does occasionally steal another dog's soft toy – it is a very specific toy – but its owner, a lovely Whippet, does not seem to mind at all. Belle has also been known to nick the brushes used for weapon cleaning.

As soon as Paul puts on his uniform in the mornings, Belle gets excited as she knows they are going to work and she will be fussed over.

THERAPY DOGS

These dogs have special powers. The value of their presence is immeasurable, and they bring an extra dimension to the workplace. Sometimes it's the owner that requires the dog's companionship to help them cope with the working day. Sometimes, the dog's role is to bring calm to communal situations. A dog can be the peacemaker for children or adults needing time out from an environment that is challenging them.

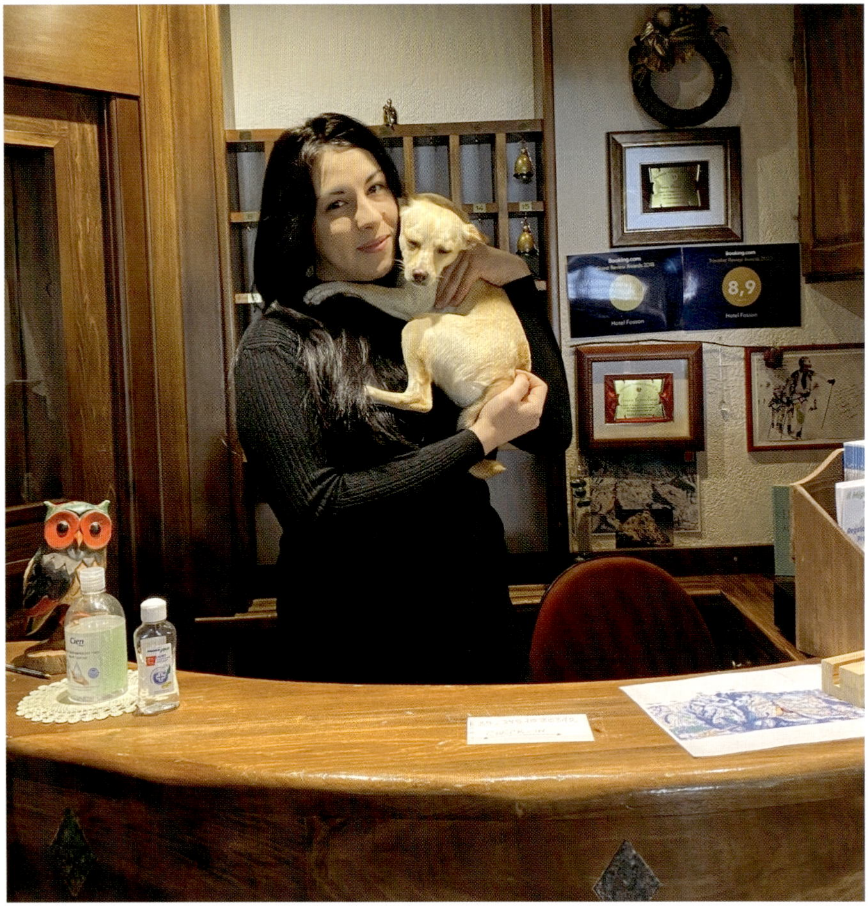

LUNA Breuil-Cervinia, Valle d'Aosta, Italy

When Antonella was younger, she had real anger issues. Her brother thought having a dog around might help her. Initially she was resistant, but gradually came round to accepting the Chihuahua that he brought home. She had a dream about a dog and the moon, so called her Luna.

The dog is now the main attraction in the hotel lobby where Antonella works at the reception desk. She says Luna is her therapy, helps calm her down and rarely leaves her side.

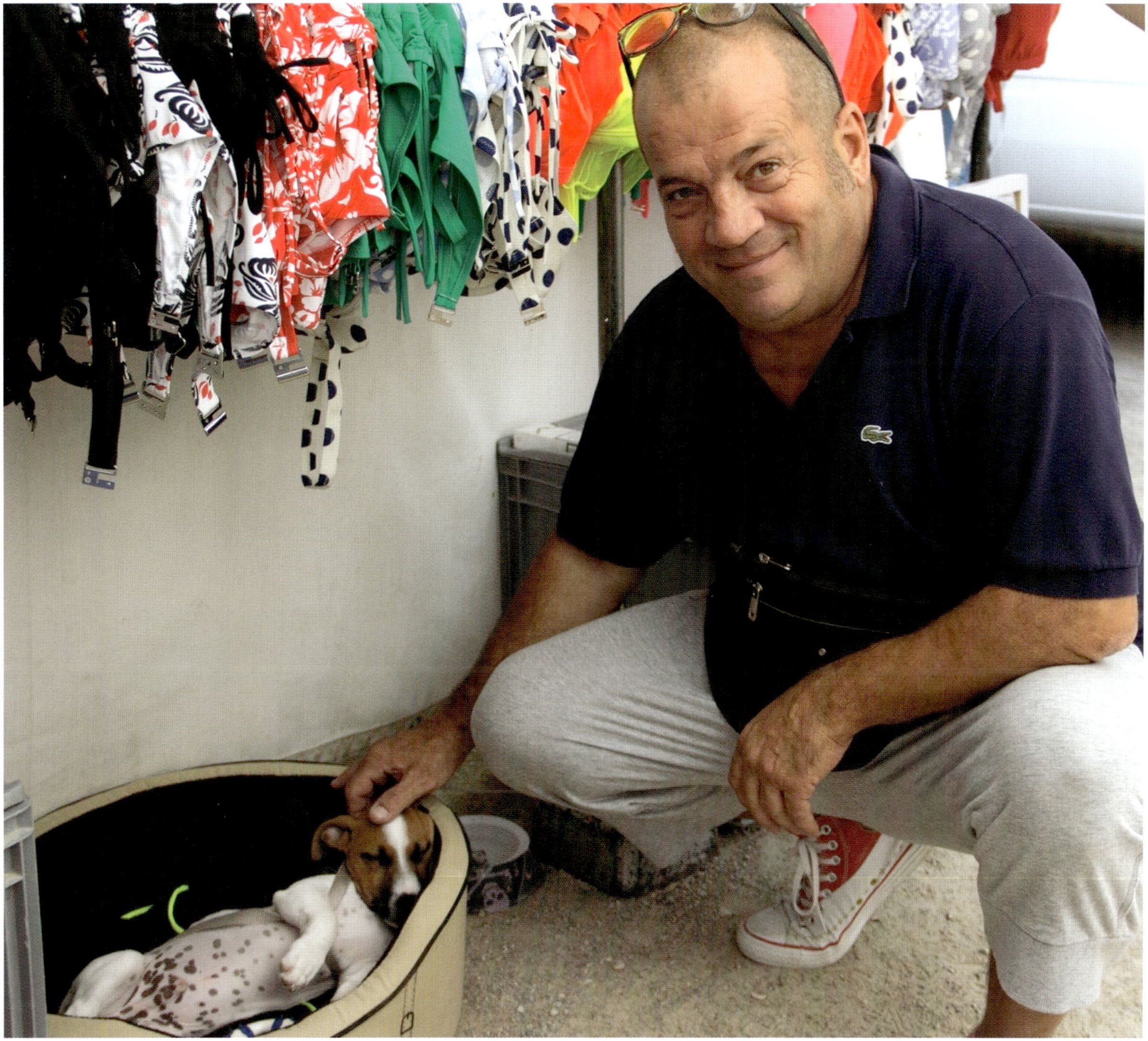

LEXO Saint-Tropez, Var, France

Lexo, a Jack Russell pup, is named after the anti-depressant drug Lexomil, which her owner, Gilles, used to take before she came into his life. The bikini stall holder says she is his anti-depressant now.

SAAR

Rotterdam, Netherlands

Saar, a Labradoodle, belongs to John, the head teacher of a school for children with learning difficulties. Saar's role is hugely beneficial as she is around to help the children if they are anxious or stressed. If kids become angry or frustrated in the classroom, they have an 'appointment' to see her and she helps calm them down. As Martine, one of John's colleagues, explains: 'She has no opinion on what is going on. People always talk – she doesn't.'

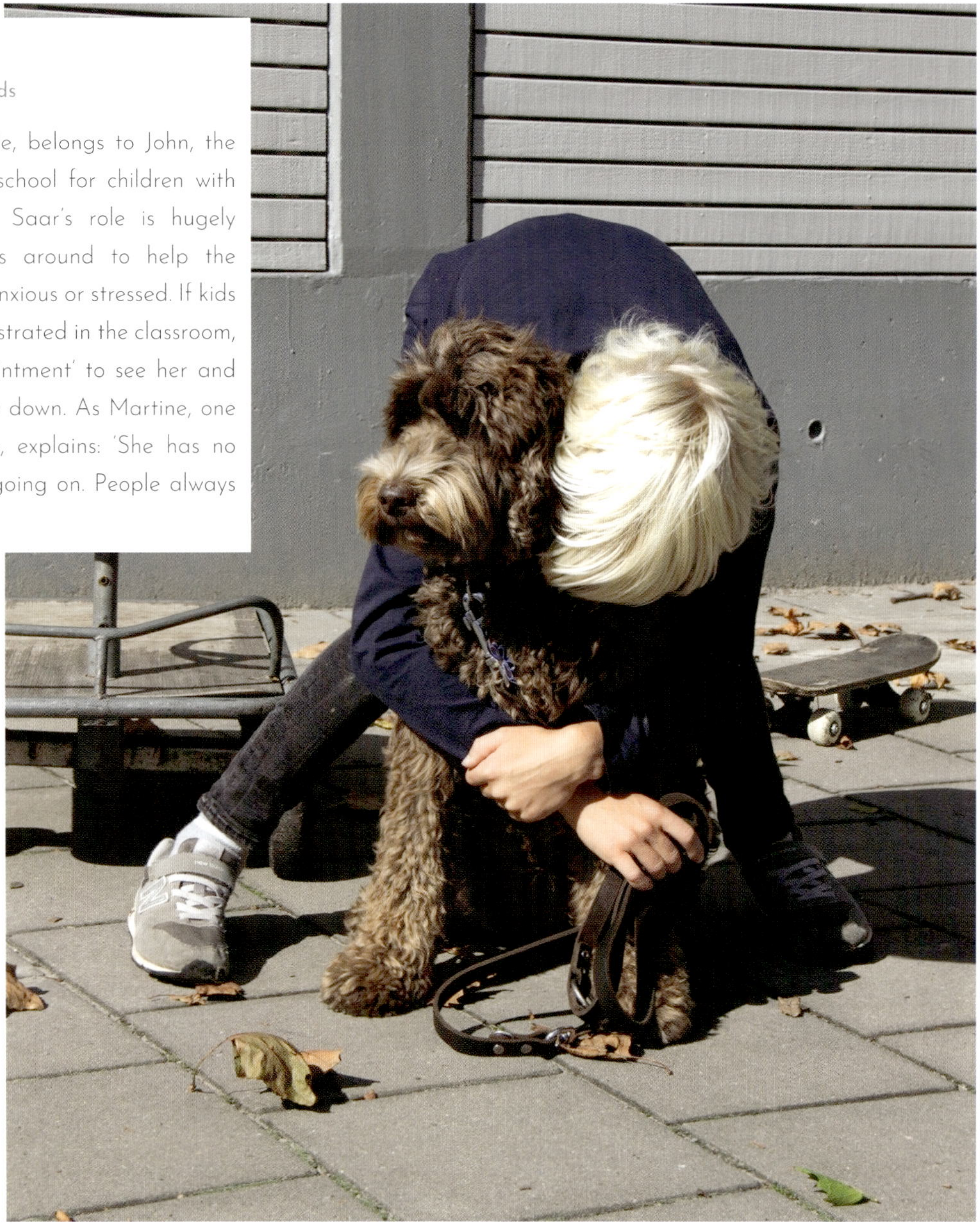

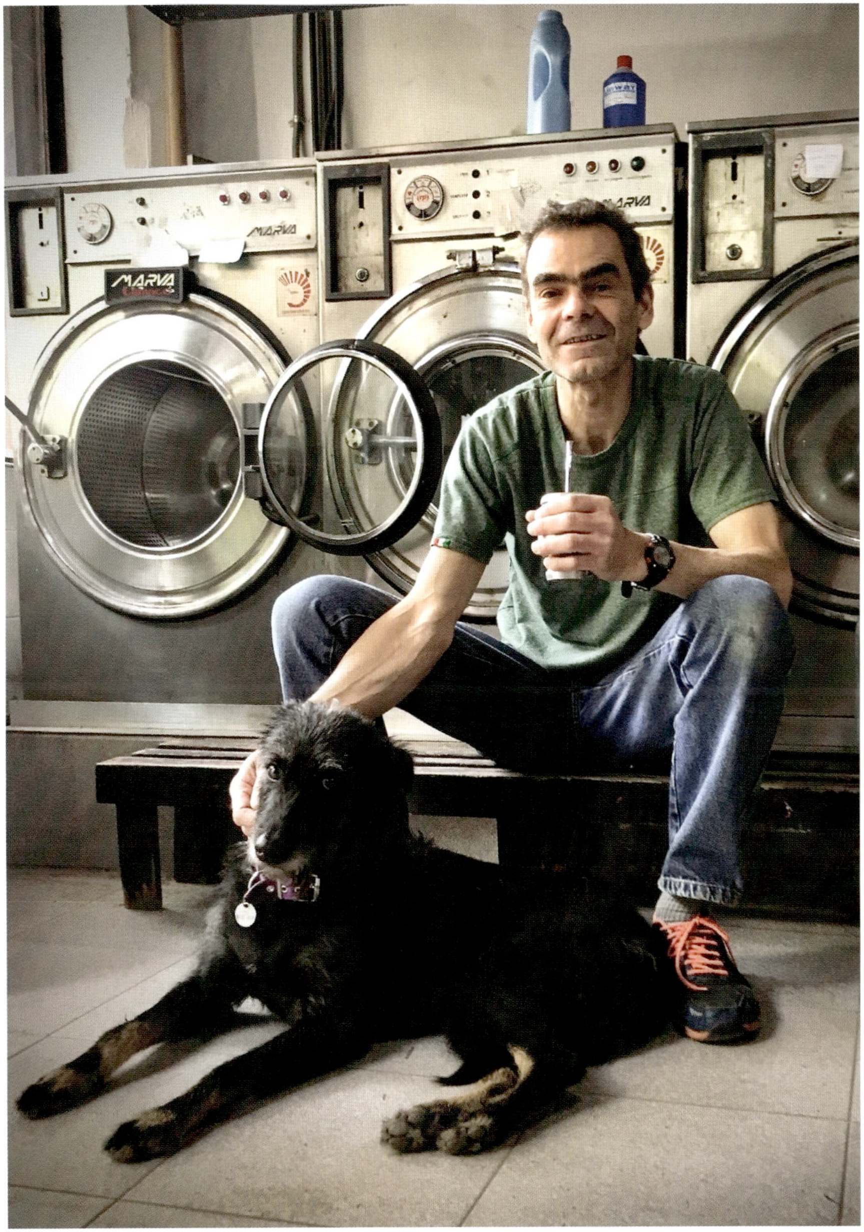

CABA

Buenos Aires, Argentina

Caba belongs to laundromat owners Fernando and Virginia, who were offered the dog along with Brillito (not pictured) by a lawyer who makes new owners sign a form promising to look after their rescue pets.

Both dogs love being at the laundromat and Caba is well known in the neighbourhood. She gets a daily pat from the local police officer and often returns with treats from shops nearby.

ARMANI, TYSON & SAKER

Orlando, Florida, USA

Armani, Tyson and Saker provide wonderful therapy to the autistic kids taught by their owner. The dogs are trained with crushed garlic and liver treats, and are beautifully behaved. Only problem – smelly breath!

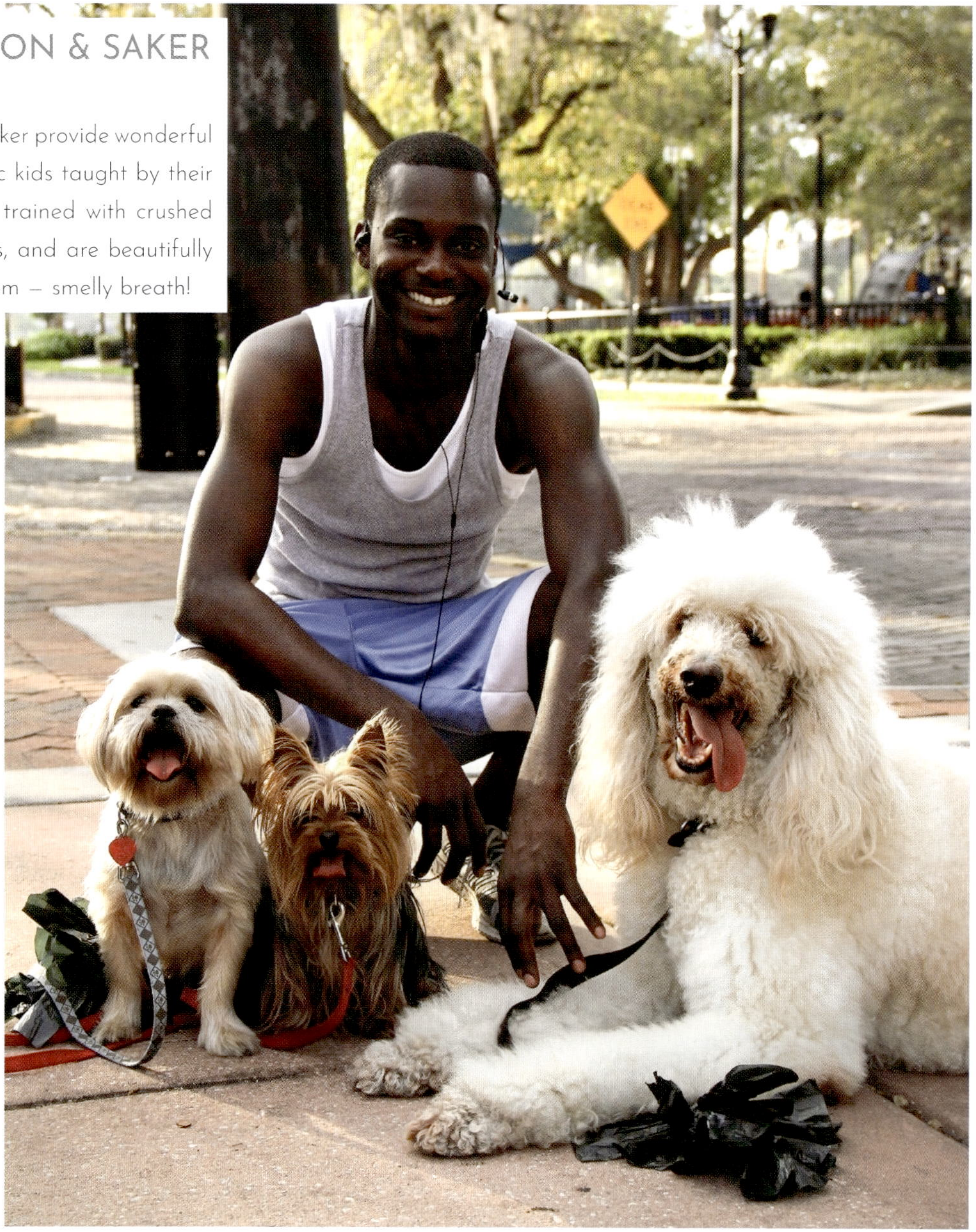

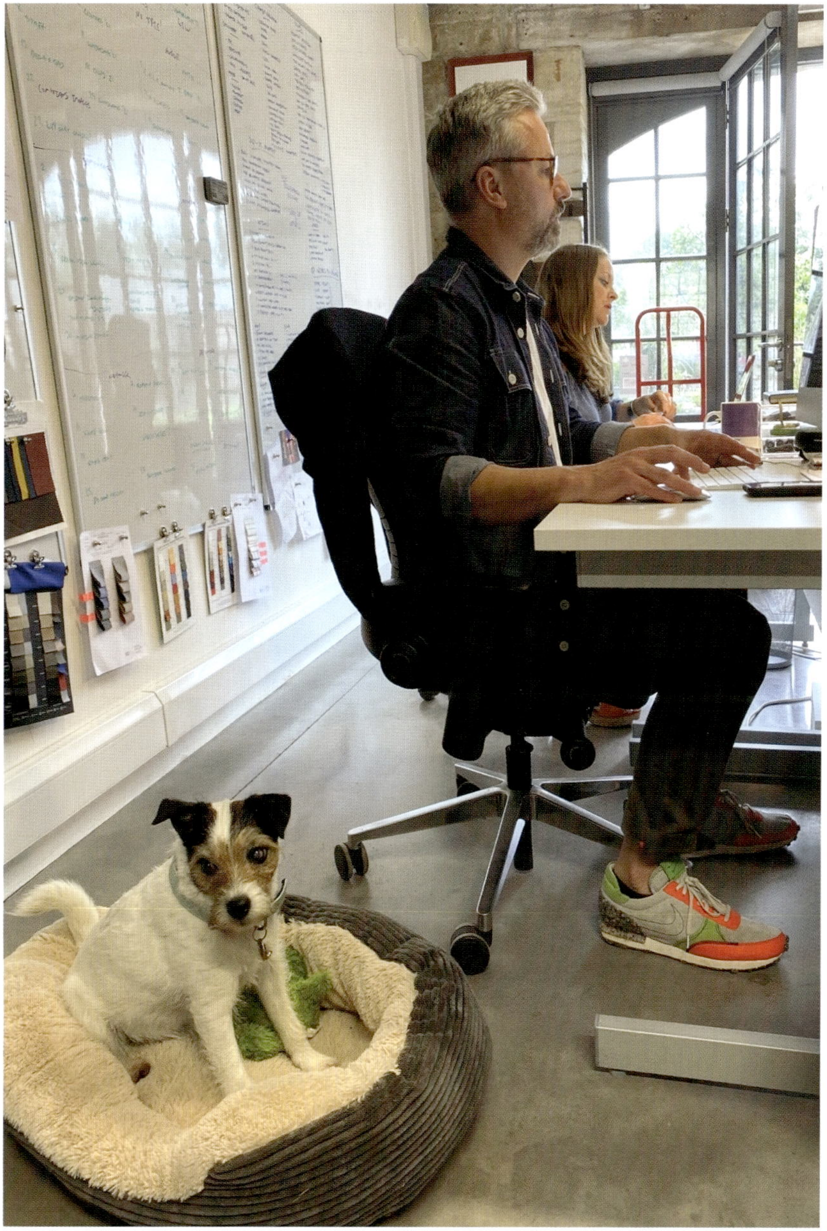

LILY

Holt, Wiltshire, UK

Nick suffered a mental breakdown in his previous job and managed to work his way through it with therapy. He designs and sells high-end men's outdoor jackets, and £10 of every sale is donated to the mental health charity MIND.

Nick and his wife, Emma Lou, acquired Lily, a Parson Russell Terrier, twelve years ago when Nick was working from home. Lily now accompanies them to the office where she provides the daily mental health support that Nick needs.

Lily has a saucy relationship with Whippets and, fortunately for her, there are two who regularly spend time at the converted tannery where Nick and Emma Lou are based. Lily will occasionally trot off and can be found pressing her nose up against a glass door of the office where Sonny the Whippet lies.

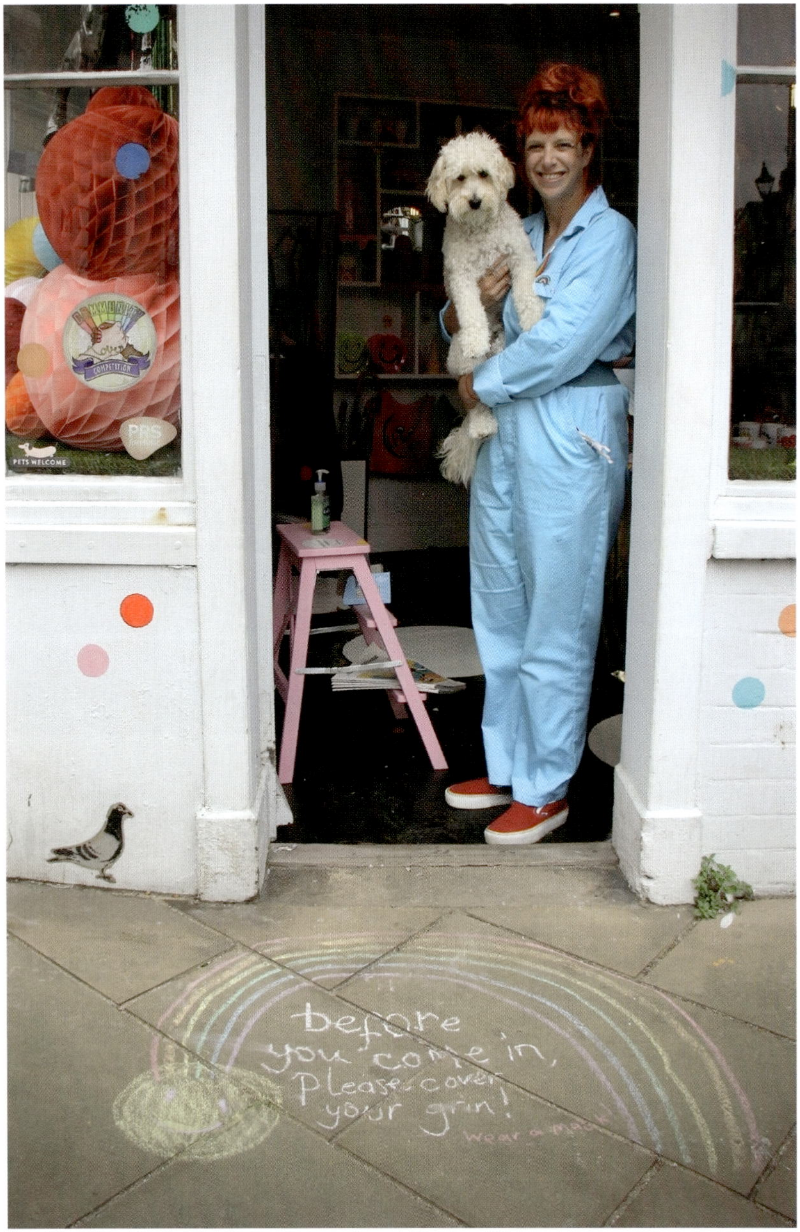

DUDE

Margate, Kent, UK

Dude gave his owner, Polly, the confidence to start a new life in Margate. Polly used to be an actress but, due to anxiety issues, decided to quit the stage and set up a gift shop in Margate Old Town. Dude is very much a feature there, and people come in just to see him.

He has turned out to be the best companion of courage when Polly most needed it.

Polly and her partner live above the shop. Dude, like a teenager, is not an early riser, although he will manage a walk on the beach before the shop opens.

He has only once absconded from the shop. He was caught by the local pub owner who called to say Dude was at the bar, having a swift half.

At the very end of each day, he goes back to the beach with Polly and sits on the paddle board as she negotiates the waves.

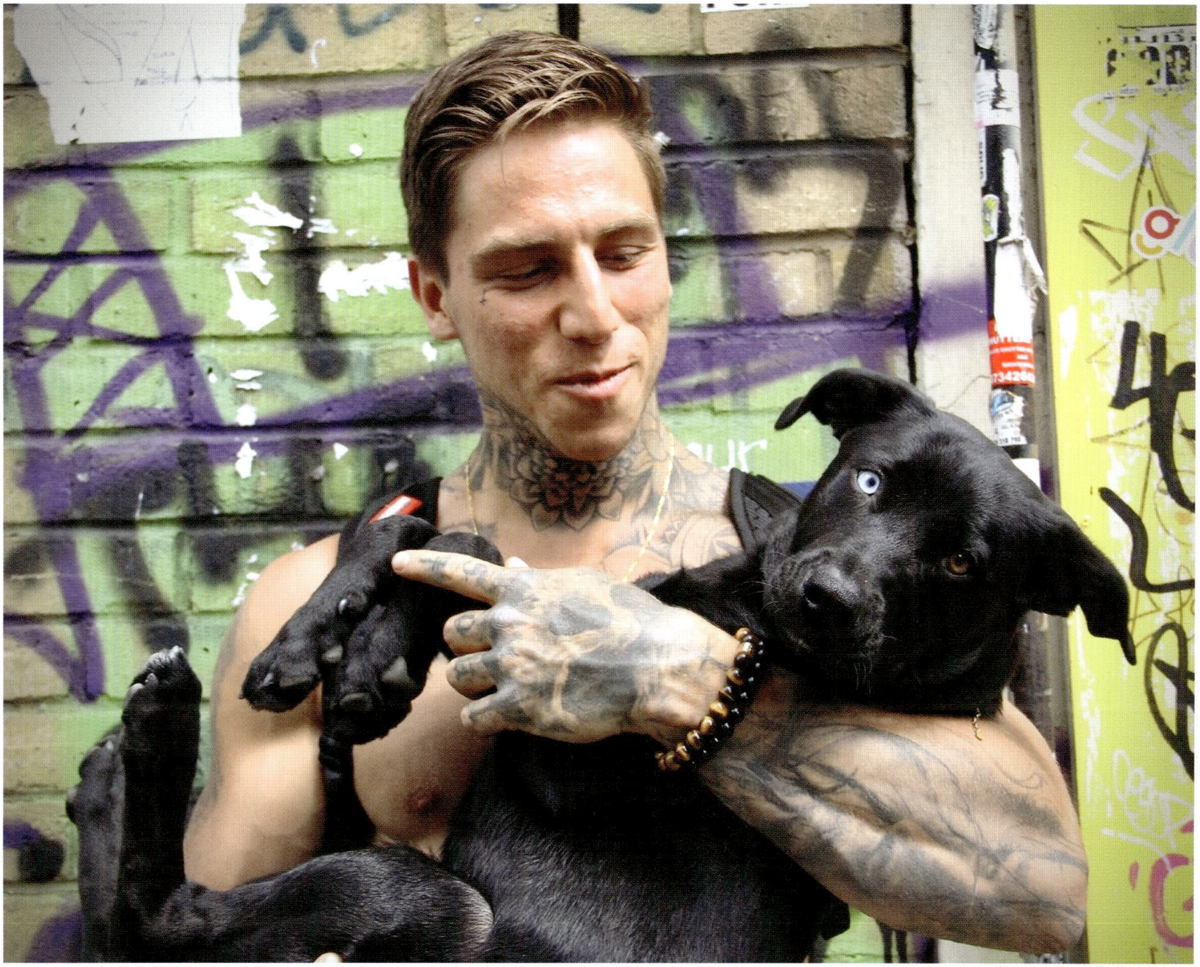

SHADOW Tower Hamlets, London, UK

Blue-and-brown-eyed Shadow, now five months old, was adopted by his owner, Janis, a model and currency trader, from a litter born to a dog in Janis's flat. Janis has had a troubled past; Shadow is his rock – officially, his ESA (Emotional Support Animal) – and goes everywhere with Janis: to the gym, photoshoots, work trips, etc. When he travels, Shadow sits on the plane seat next to him and has never left his side – hence the name. As young as he is, he never needs a lead when walking in London.

BRYN Islington, London, UK

Bryn is a silky-haired young Border Collie/Staffie rescue dog, whose owner, Caroline Fertleman, is an A&E doctor at the Whittington Hospital, London. Her colleague, Dr Heidi Edmundson, runs several initiatives to help boost staff wellness. One of her ideas was to have Bryn brought into the hospital once a week for an hour. Bryn tours the wards on a lead with Junior Doctor Rosie Sofair and invariably brings smiles to people's faces and receives plenty of stroking from staff and patients alike.

Both Heidi and Rosie are recording reactions to Bryn's presence – and Bryn recently stood between two arguing doctors who stopped to stroke him and ended their heated discussion.

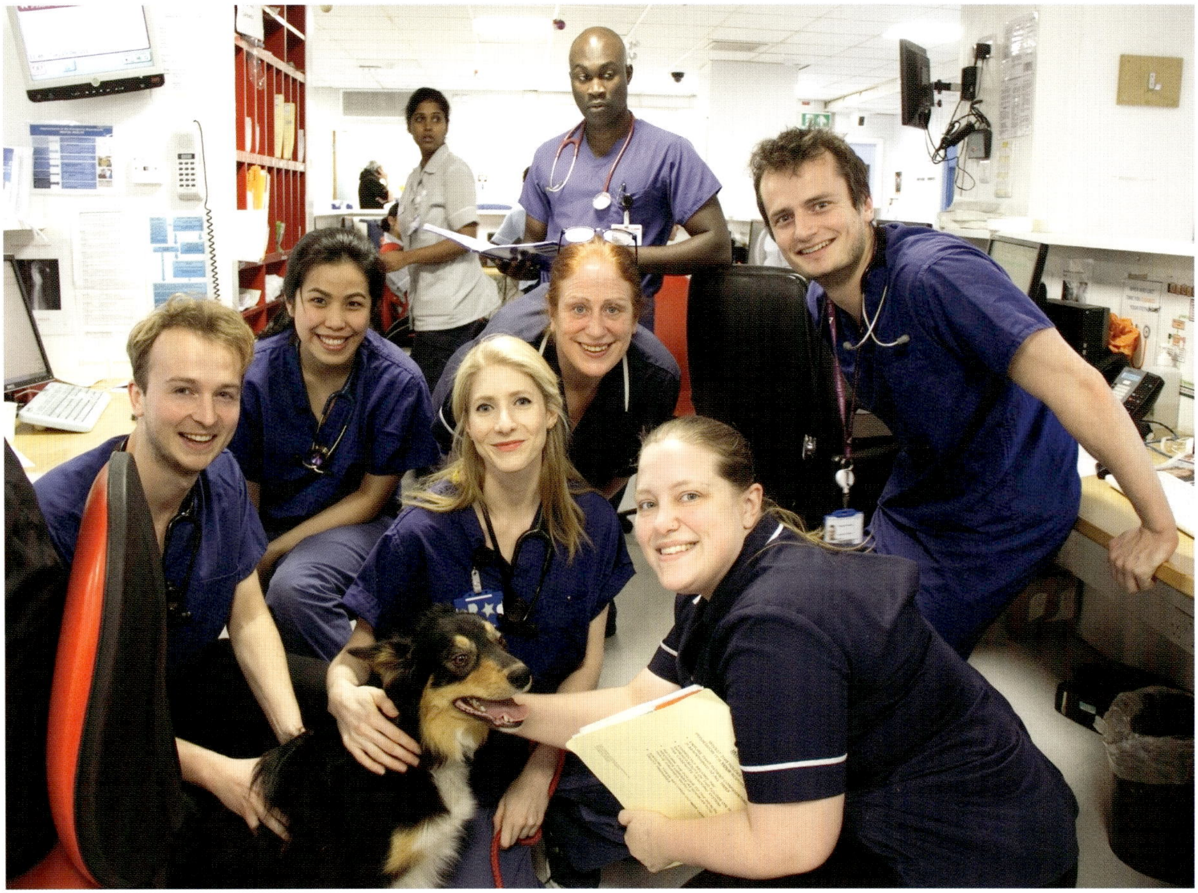

IZZY, POPPY & HUGO Enfield, London, UK

Izzy, Poppy and Hugo, seen outside Chase Farm Hospital, are affiliated to the Pets as Therapy charity. Pomeranian Izzy, left, with owner Amanda, loves people and helps calm patients before surgery. Sandra, centre, with her blue roan Cocker Spaniel, Poppy, divides her time between a supervisory role at Pets as Therapy and visits to hospitals, care homes and schools. Cockapoo Hugo, right, is a real character, who barks for attention but is quiet on the wards, where he seems to know who needs attention. Hugo's owner, Catrina, volunteers with him to give back the joy that therapy dogs gave her husband when he was seriously ill. Dog therapy visits to Chase Farm Hospital are managed by the Royal Free Charity, whose volunteers undertake a training programme to give them the necessary skills for this sensitive work.

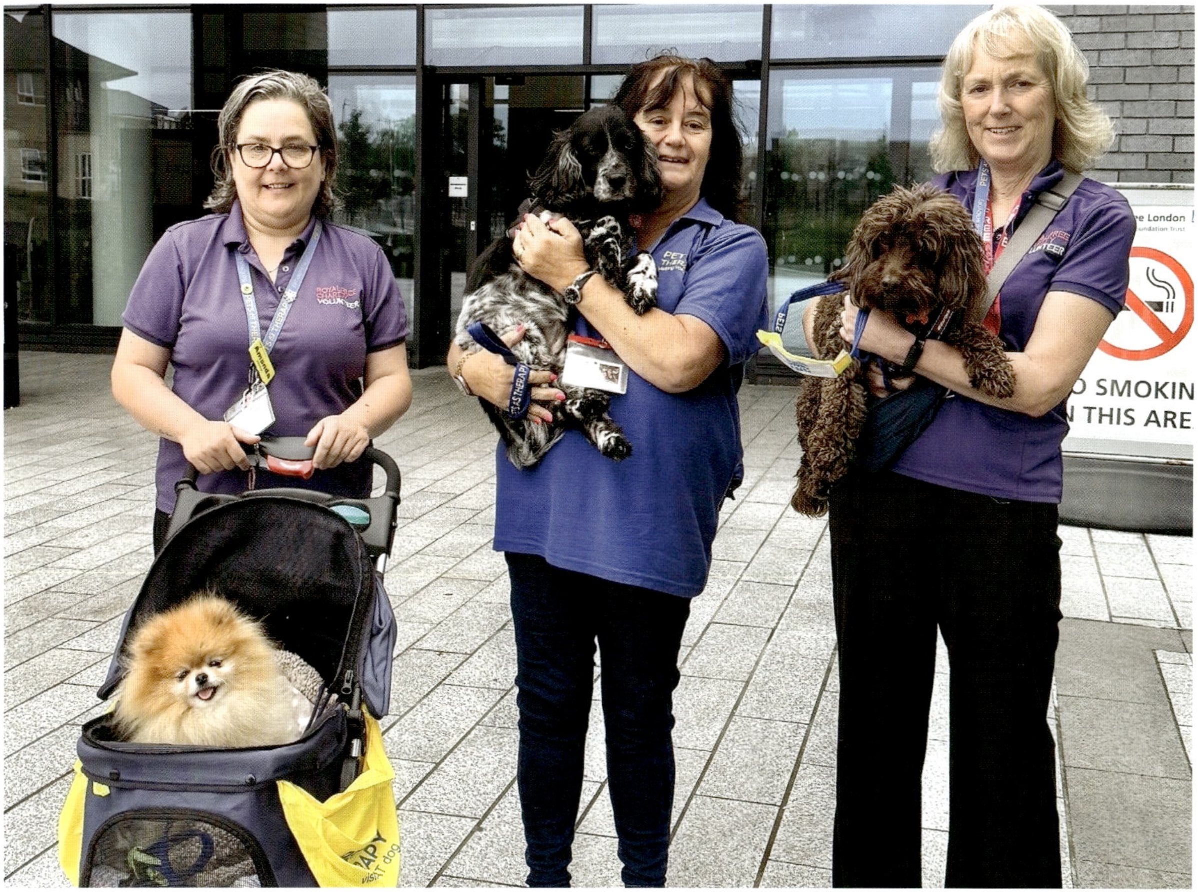

DOGS IN ENTERTAINMENT & HOSPITALITY

A dog will never complain if it must sit through rehearsals or be on duty at reception night and day.
It provides the added companionship that can help one get through a long public-facing day.
If you ask a dog 'What did you think of that, eh?', the response will always be the wag of a tail.
How encouraging is that?

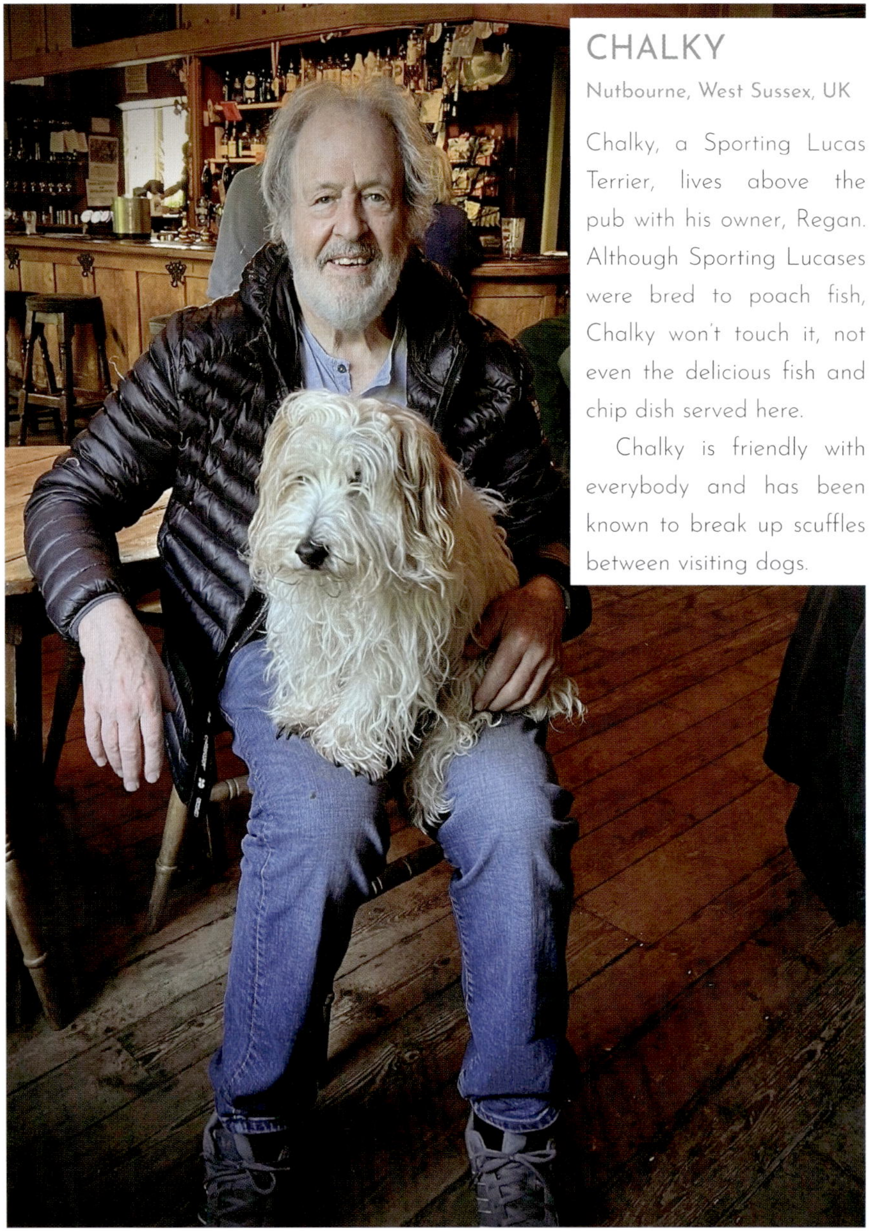

CHALKY

Nutbourne, West Sussex, UK

Chalky, a Sporting Lucas Terrier, lives above the pub with his owner, Regan. Although Sporting Lucases were bred to poach fish, Chalky won't touch it, not even the delicious fish and chip dish served here.

Chalky is friendly with everybody and has been known to break up scuffles between visiting dogs.

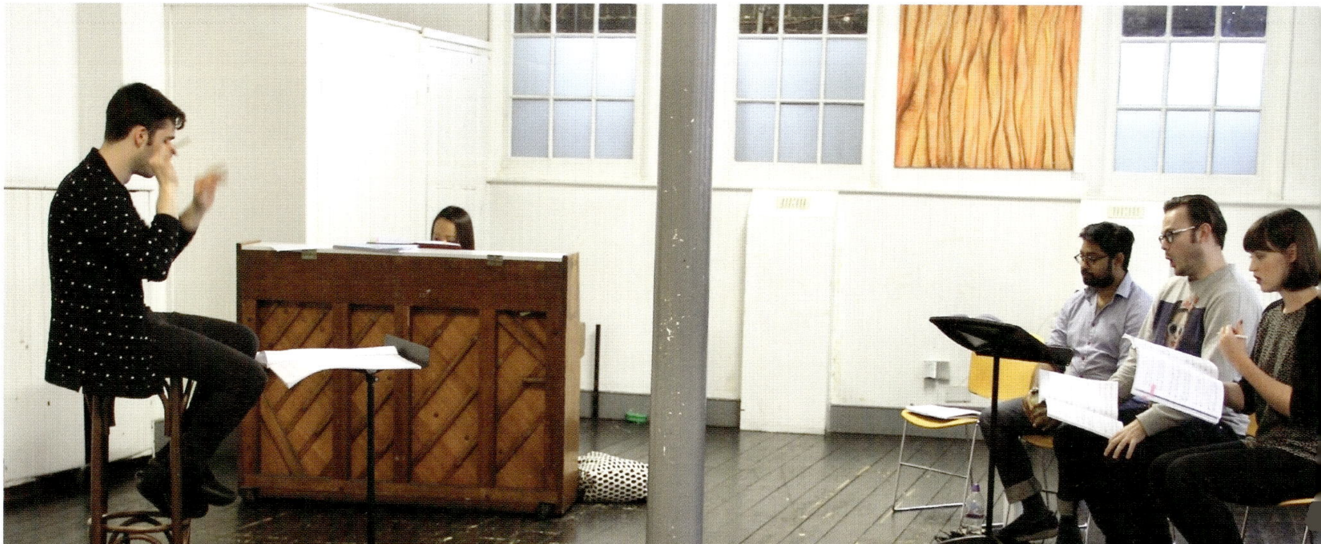

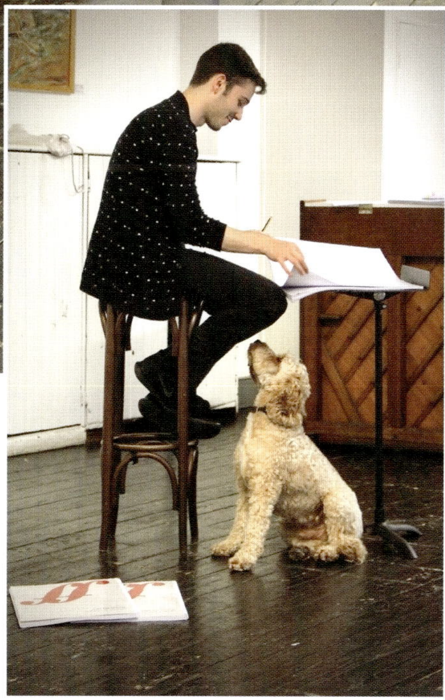

JARVIS Islington, London, UK

Named after the singer Jarvis Cocker, this Cockapoo comes with Oliver to his rehearsals as music conductor with the Melos Sinfonia. Jarvis sleeps through most rehearsals and does not move, even when singers hit the high notes.

RENÉE Downham Market, Norfolk, UK

Renée, an eight-month-old French Bulldog, is a family pet at this salon/café, where James and Ernie work at the hairdresser's salon at the back and Mum runs the trendy café at the front. Renée is normally very calm, but twice a day she goes mad and charges round the salon. She can spend hours staring at corners for no apparent reason.

Eric the Dachshund comes in every Wednesday and as soon as Renée spots him, she flips onto her back. She is normally very well-behaved and won't go beyond the threshold onto the road – although she will escape via the back fence to the building site next door for a treat or two. Although she is the youngest of the family's three dogs, Renée is very definitely top dog.

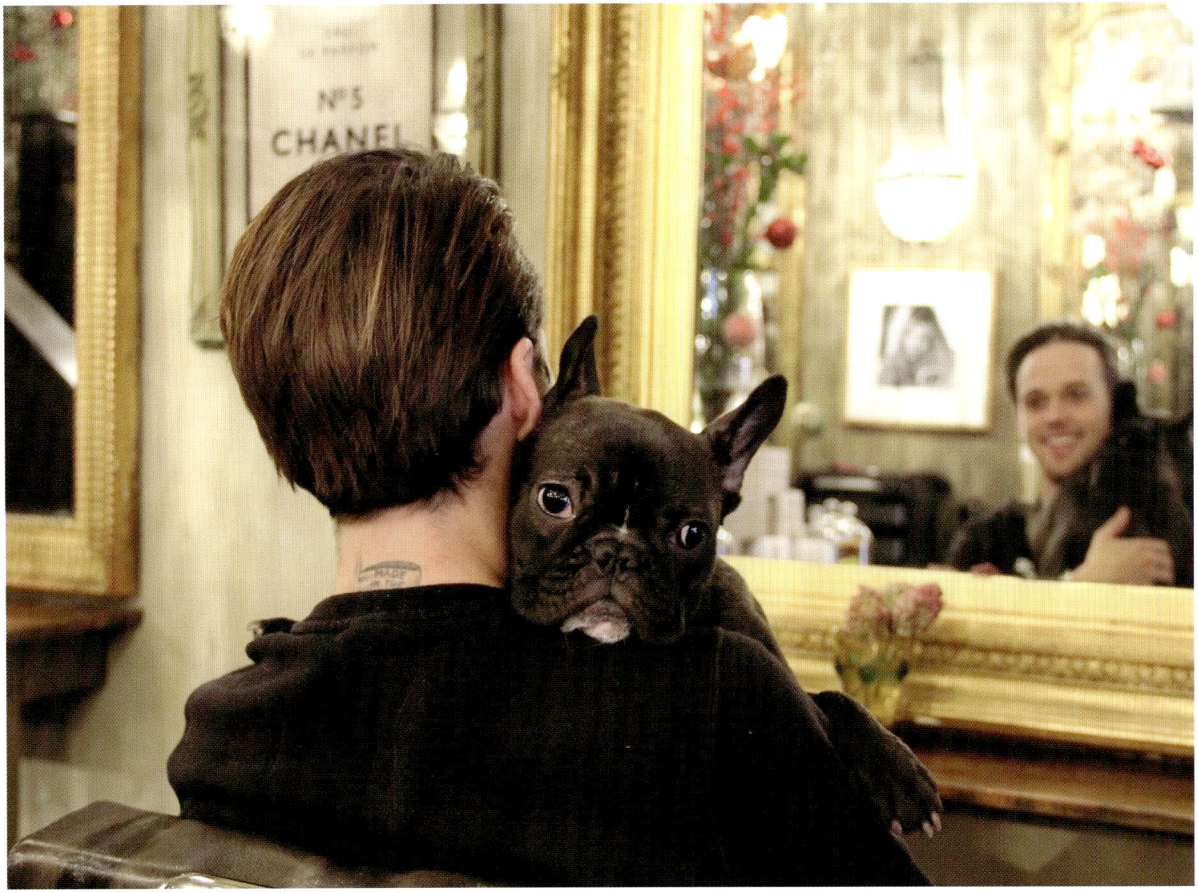

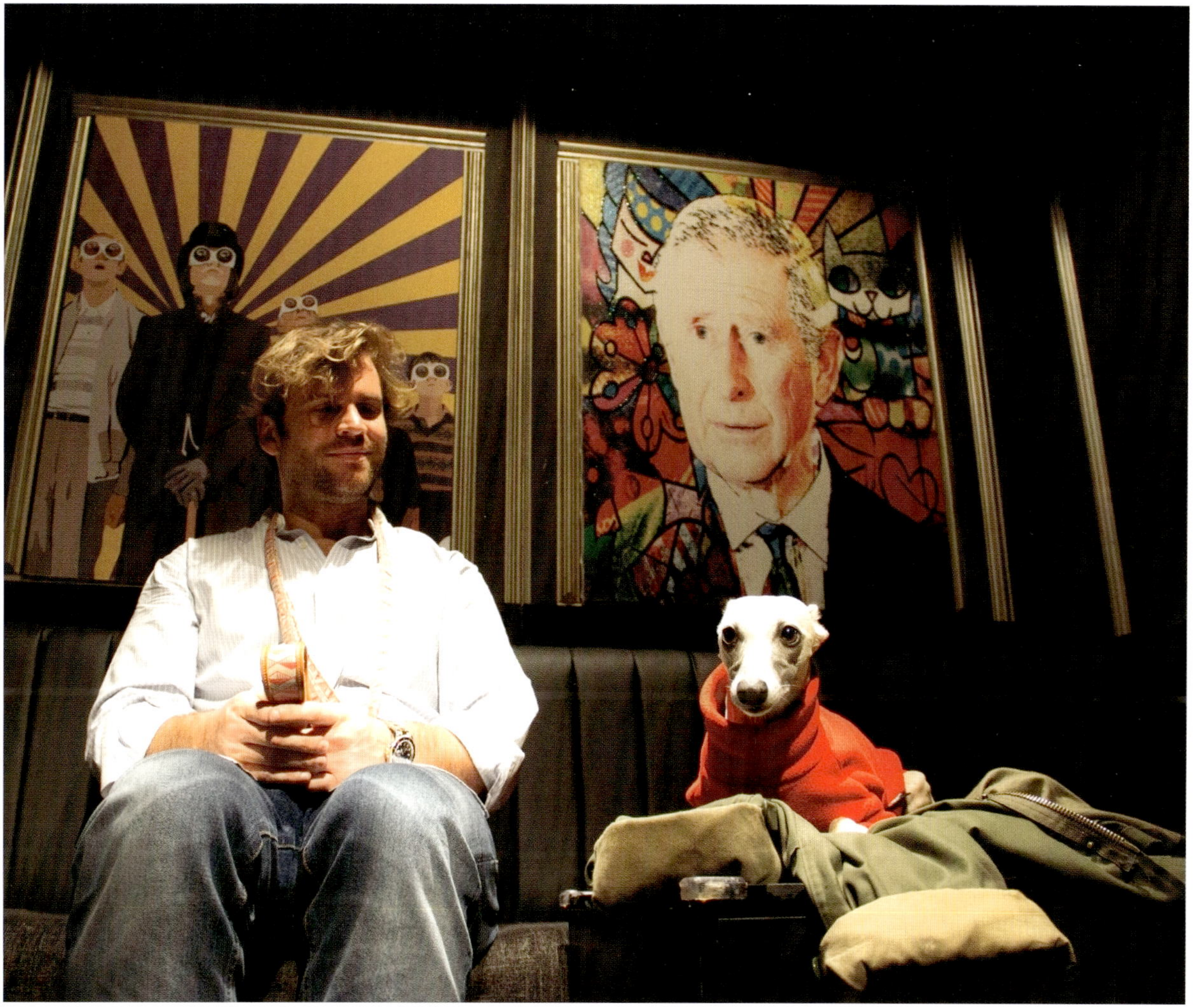

TWIGGY Mayfair, London, UK

Nightclub manager Alex describes Twiggy, a three-year-old Whippet, as his 'spirit'. She follows him everywhere round the streets of London, mainly off the lead, and goes for daily walks in Green Park. She has the run of the nightclub during the day, and when Alex is at work in the evenings, she keeps his side of the bed warm until he returns. She has her own Instagram page, where she is described as 'Comfort Seeker' and 'Croissant Stalker'.

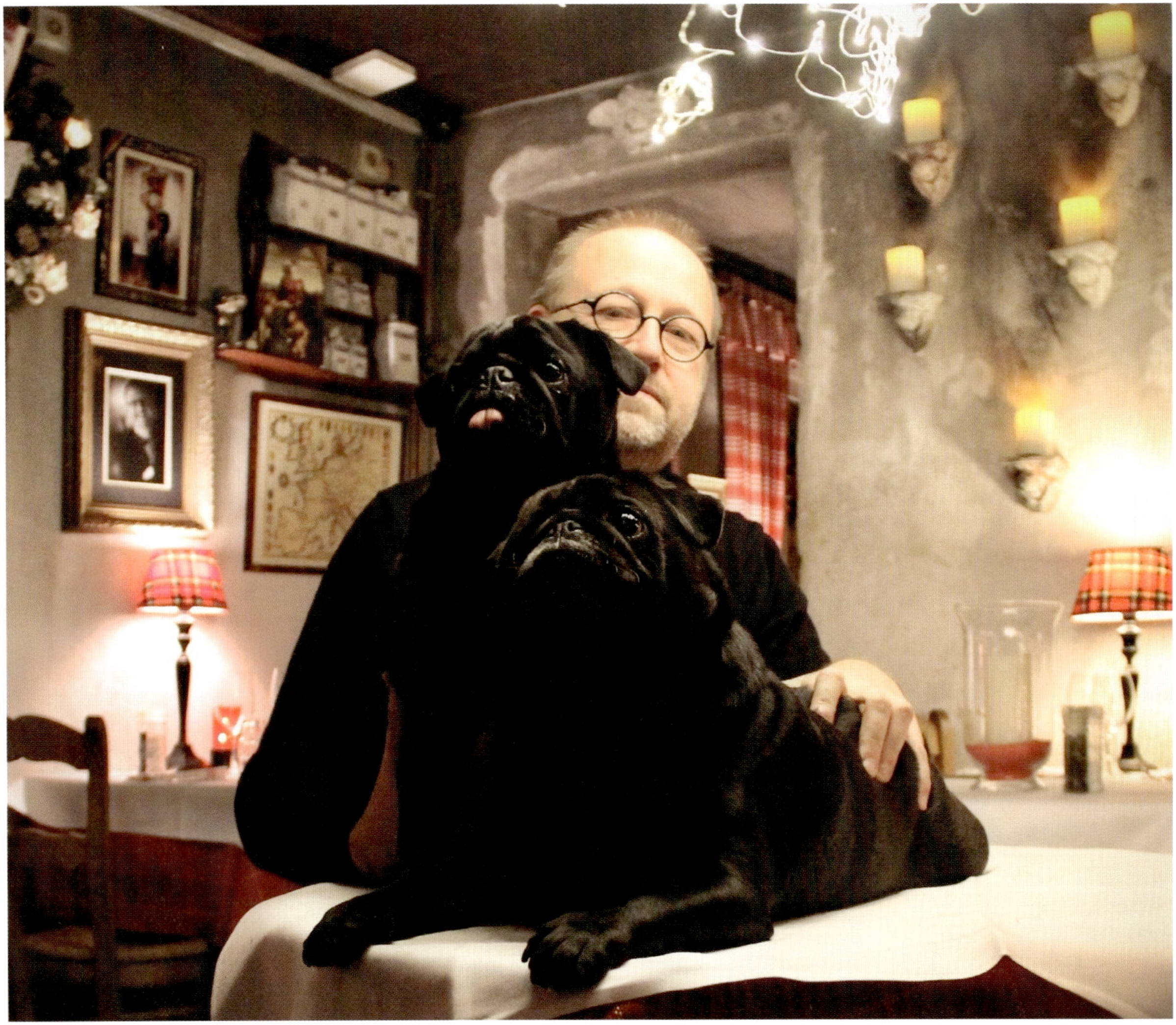

ROBERT & RENÉ Bruges, Belgium

Robert and René are Pugs, who were adopted from a divorced couple by the Belgian restaurateur and cookbook writer, Mario Cattoor. They are well-behaved enough to walk around the town without leads. Mario and his partner call them the shadow dogs – 'shadows of us and shadows of each other.'

ABBIE GIRL & OLLIE B2

Savannah, Georgia, USA

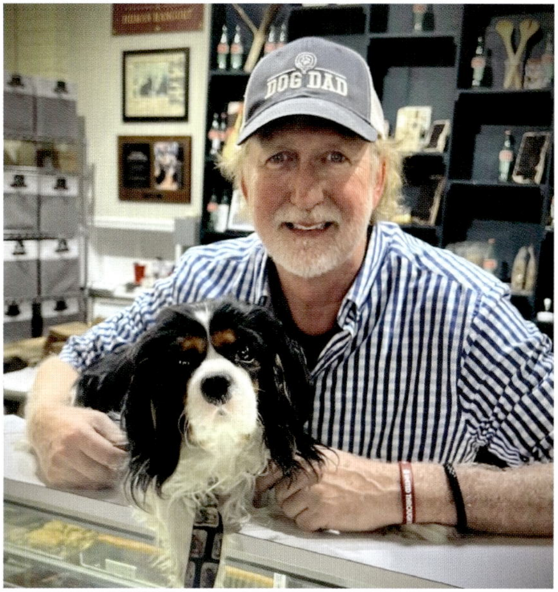

Abbie Girl, a rescue Labrador, is twelve, and Ollie B2, a King Charles Spaniel, is two. Together, they provide unconditional support and enthusiasm to Eric, even on the toughest days, in all his enterprises

His current venture is a dogs' deli, selling healthy pre-cooked dog food and doggy ice-cream. Humans are secondary here, although there is a nod to their needs, with a coffee station tucked away in a corner.

Eric placed everything in the large floorspace to fit around the position of the dogs' sofa, which he located directly opposite the large front opening onto the pavement. Abbie Girl and Ollie B2 lie in total comfort, snoozing or watching the world go by.

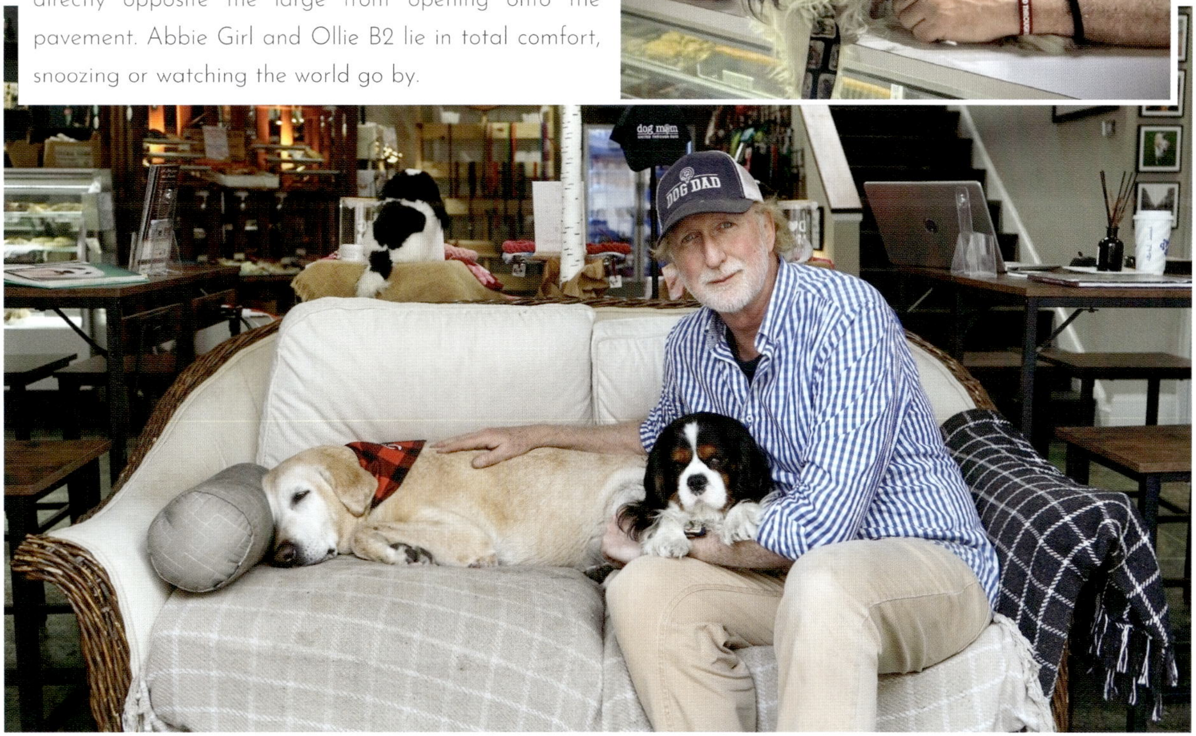

TIMÓN & PUMBA Buenos Aires, Argentina

Timón and Pumba were rescued by Guido, when he was running a five-star hostel in the Palermo area of Buenos Aires. Timón is very scared of people as he was badly treated before his rescue. They are very energetic pets and get plenty of walks but, like all good Argentine dogs, they lie down for their daily siesta. The dogs have brought Guido and his sister much joy, although Guido ruefully says, 'I am happier with Timón than he is with me!'

Guido is now an Instagram influencer and travels the length and breadth of Argentina in a campervan with his dogs, recording every single town and village he visits.

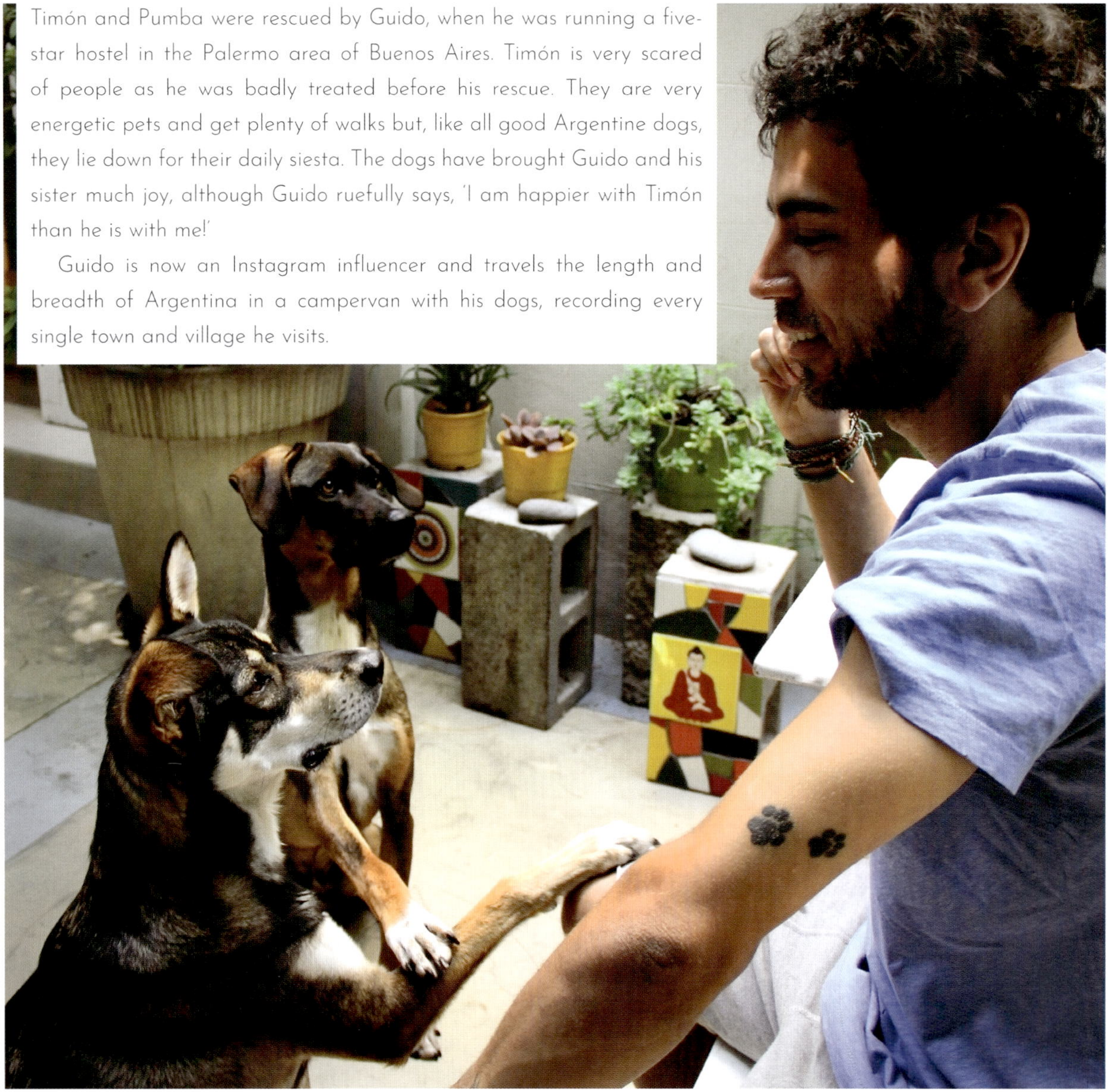

COPPER

Petworth, West Sussex, UK

Regulars who come for a coffee in the car park of this National Trust establishment frequently offer to take Hungarian Vizsla Copper for a walk while Paul and his colleague, David, man their silver trailer coffee shop – also referred to as a 'toaster on wheels'.

The dog now recognises some of the cars driven by his treat givers and regular dog walkers as they arrive. Paul says Copper really needs a booking sheet!

Copper gives a lot of love and, in return, receives plenty of attention. He is well-behaved, impeccably trained and knows not to chase the deer in the adjacent park.

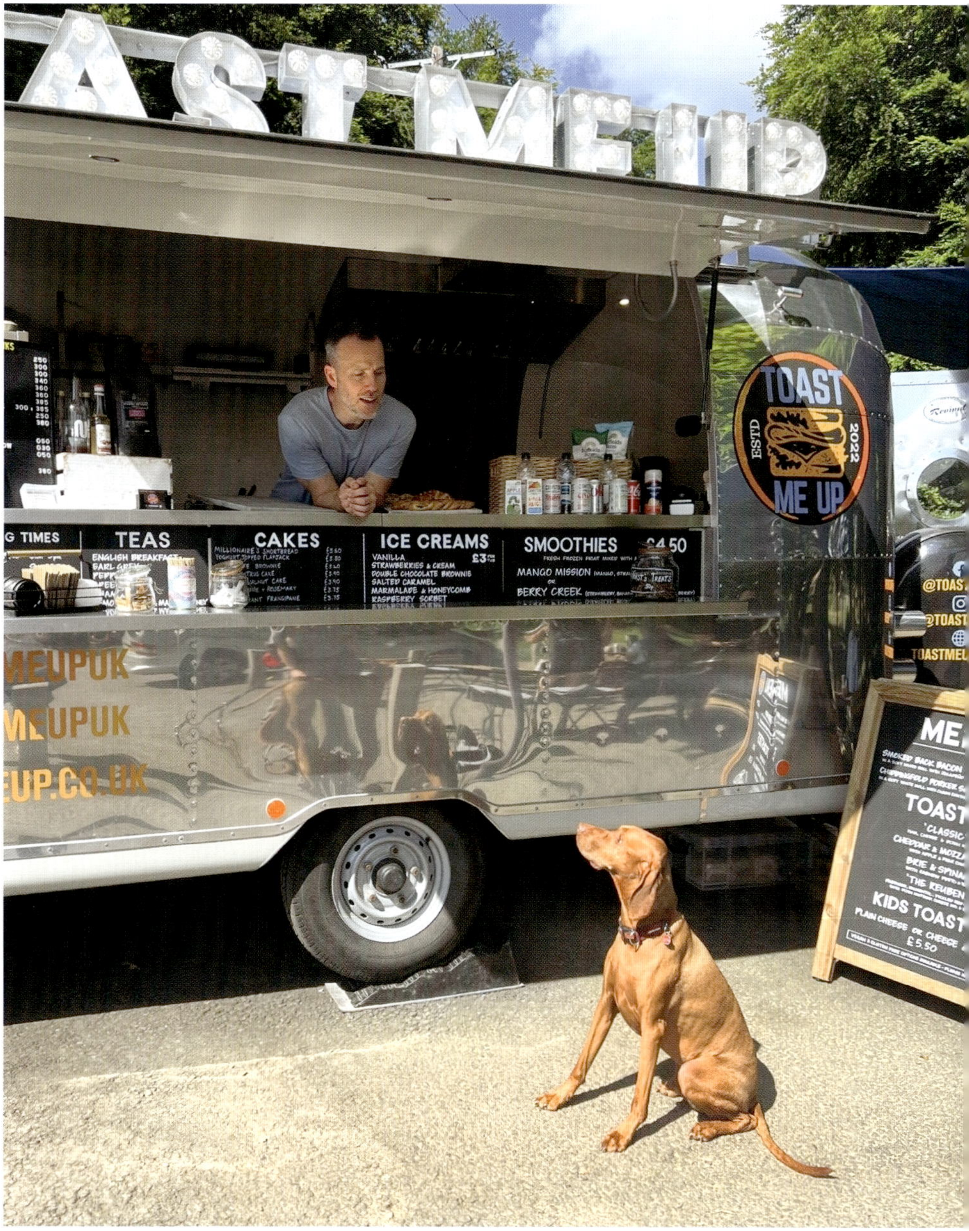

CHURCH DOGS

From vicars to vergers to volunteers, they all find their lives and their faith enriched by bringing their dogs into their daily spiritual space. No church and no cemetery is too large to accommodate the presence of dogs who greet, soothe or provide companionship to their dog owners and worshippers alike. And we all know that dog is God spelled backwards.

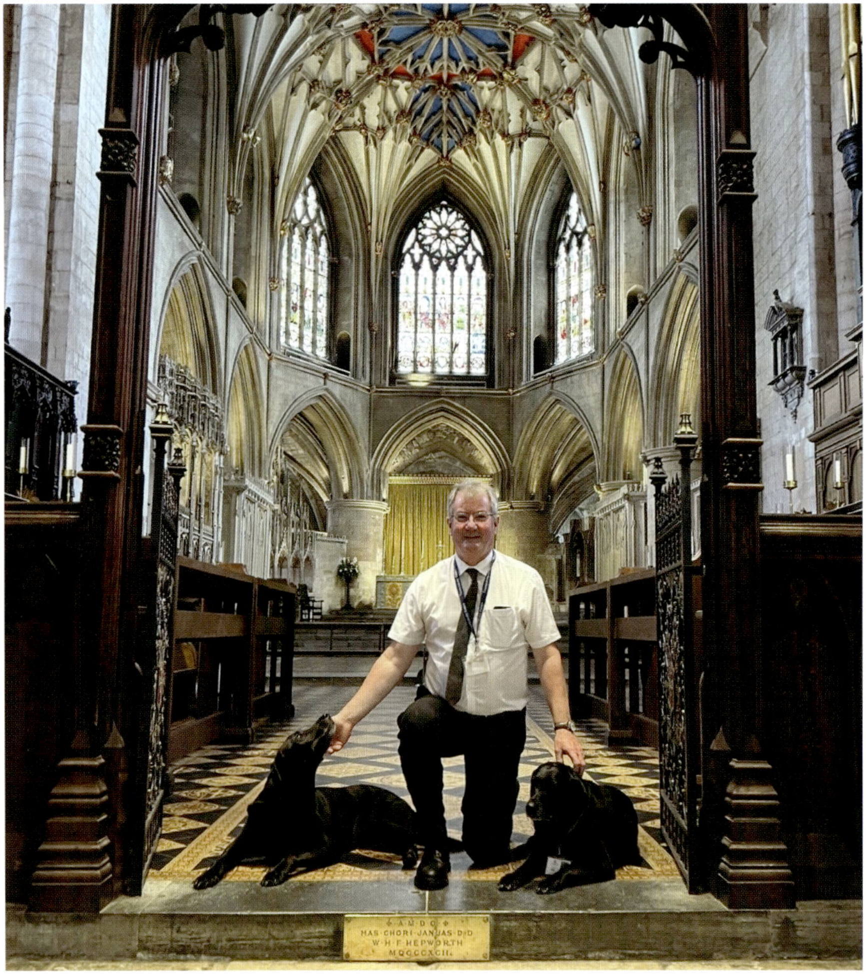

ERIC & FLORENCE Tewkesbury, Gloucestershire, UK

Chris is head verger of mediaeval Tewkesbury Abbey, and his Black Labs – Eric, ten, and Florence, nine – are his assistants. Chris prepares the church for services with the dogs in tow. They meet and greet visitors, and soothe anxious worshippers.

They are extremely well-behaved in the abbey and do not bark at other visiting dogs. They also visit care homes for the elderly, where they act as therapy dogs.

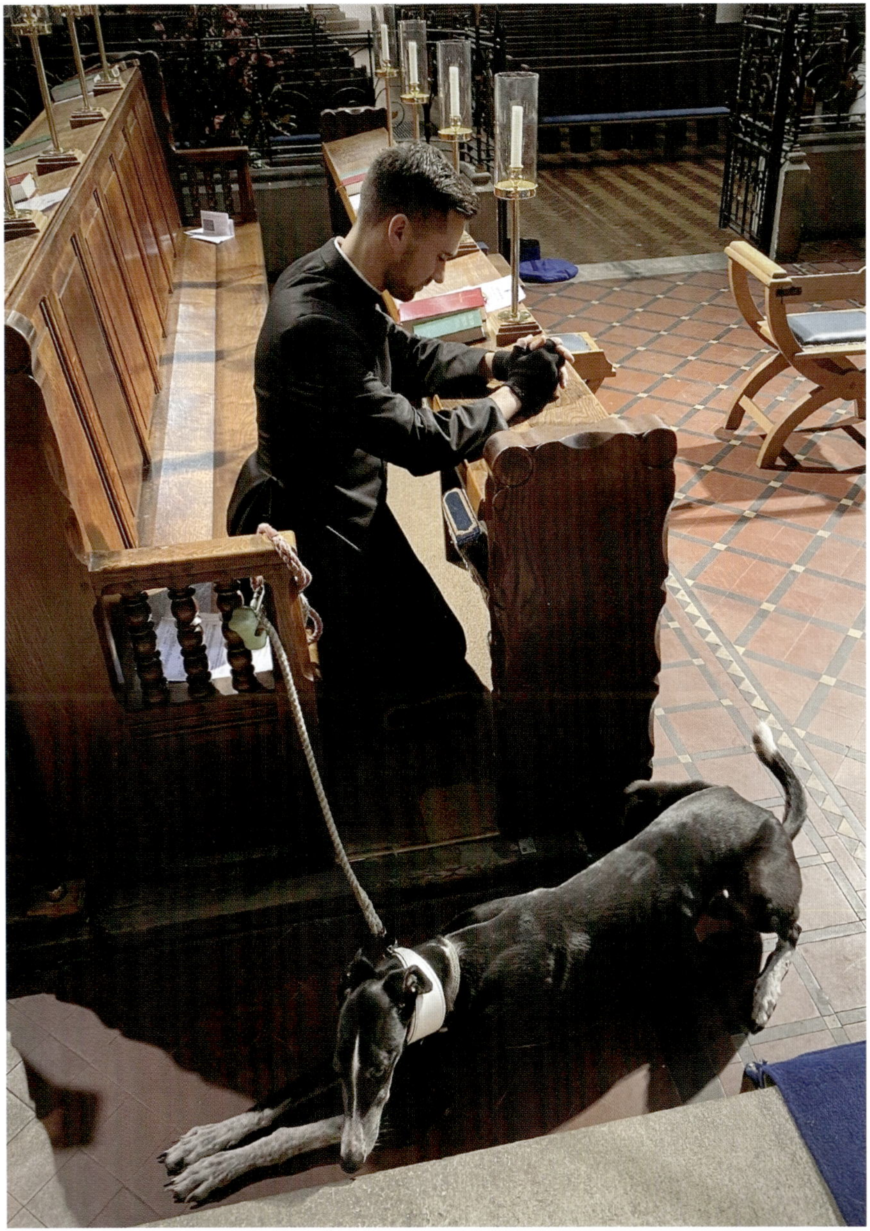

BEAU

Barnes, London, UK

This retired racing Greyhound had never been in a home or seen stairs until he arrived at the vicarage to live with Father Stephen.

Beau was a good racer in his day, but now needs little exercise and spends a lot of time sleeping. He is Stephen's companion both at home and at prayer time in the church.

DOGS ON THE MOVE

Like nomads, these dogs are happy to call home wherever their owners park their caravan, barge or coach – or wherever they set up work for the day. So long as their owner is there to provide stability, food and water, the dog will adapt to an ever-changing world. The dogs I come across in this ambulant way of life seem to know their owner's unwritten rule: when we are on the move, you don't move.

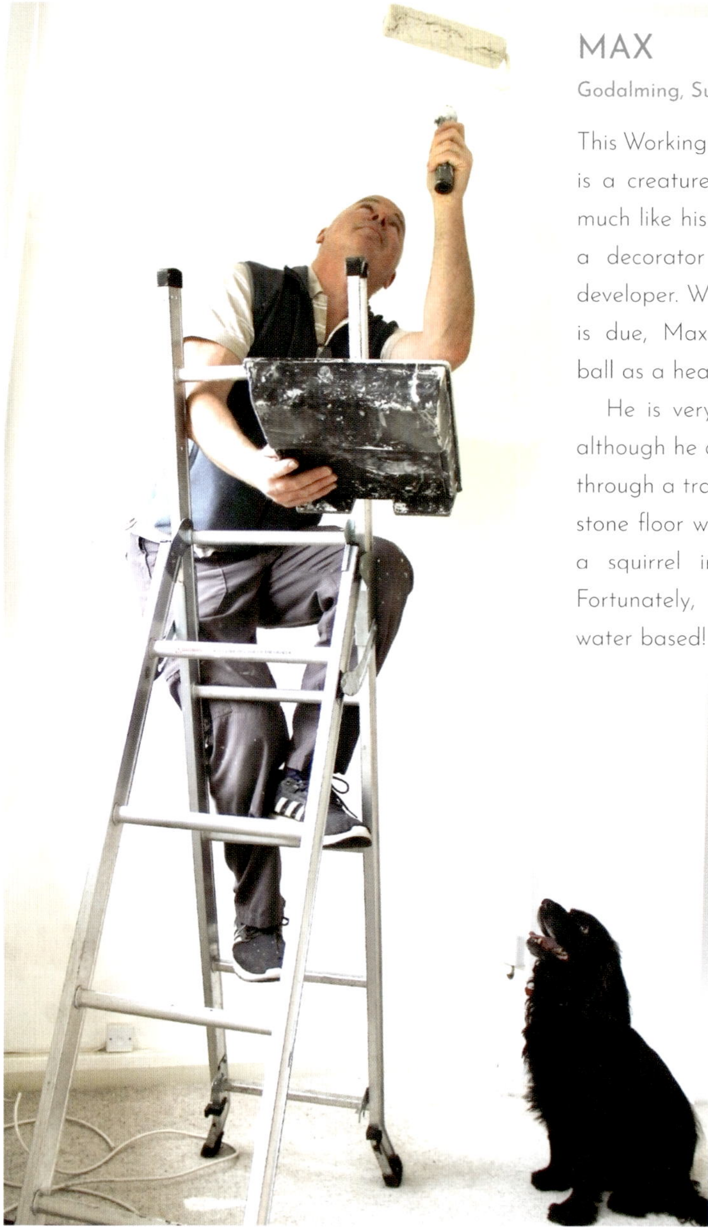

MAX

Godalming, Surrey, UK

This Working Cocker Spaniel is a creature of habit, very much like his master, David, a decorator and property developer. When break-time is due, Max will bring his ball as a heavy hint.

He is very well-behaved, although he did once bound through a tray of paint on a stone floor when he spotted a squirrel in the garden. Fortunately, the paint was water based!

BETSY & LUCKY Canals, London, UK

Betsy and Lucky are two dogs with very unusual life-work balances. They belong to two Polish narrowboat owners, Toma and Mika, who deliver coal, gas canisters and diesel fuel to narrowboats moored on the Regent's Canal and the Grand Union Canal in London. Toma, who has lived on the water for ten years, adopted Betsy, a British Bulldog, when a friend at the hostel where he was staying could no longer look after her. Mika decided he also needed a companion on his barge so he acquired Lucky, a large Turkish sheepdog.

The dogs have a very established routine. They have breakfast, are taken for a walk along the towpath, then jump back on board the barges. They wait for their beds to be laid out, listen out for the engines to start up, then lie down for the rest of the day. They act as PR but also have roles as guard dogs. They assist with the canal locks by barking at people or dogs who get in the way. Ironically, neither dog particularly likes water. Toma and Mika work solidly for two weeks at a stretch, then take a break. 'It's a hard life,' says Mika, 'but it is freedom.'

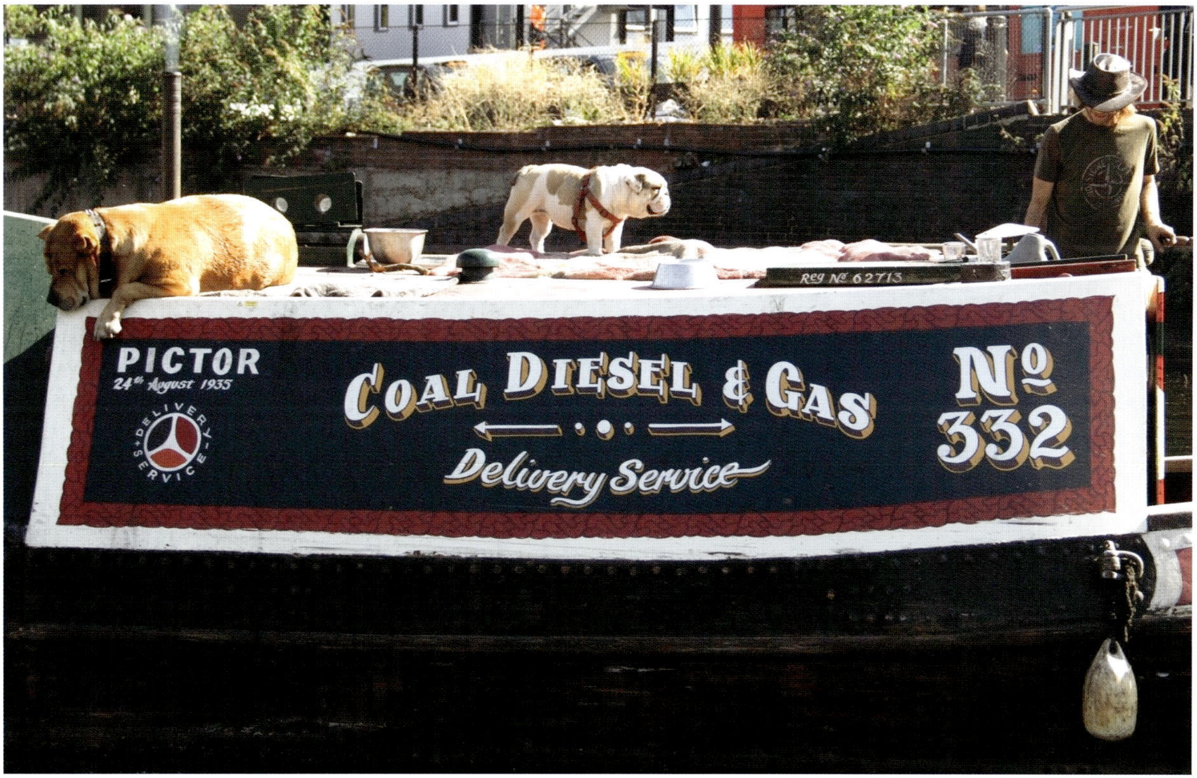

DUKE & BEAU

Ashton Keynes, Wiltshire, UK

Duke, a Beauceron, and Beau, a French Bulldog, have the run of the bus park and coach business founded by Barry's grandfather in the 1940s.

Duke was bred to be a French police dog, and once came third in his class at Crufts. He is the soppiest gentle giant and rarely leaves Barry's side, whereas Beau feels it is his duty to inspect every coach for crumbs. Barry's drivers have occasionally set off unwittingly with one of them on board.

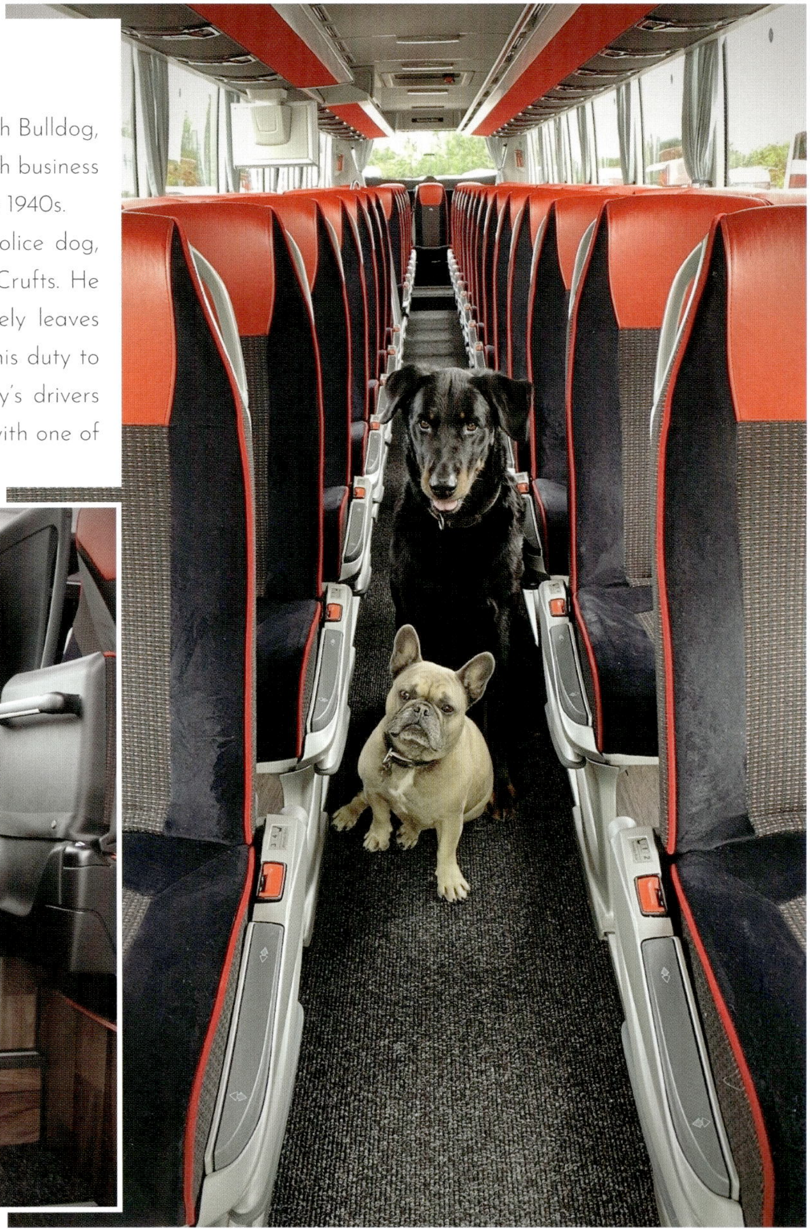

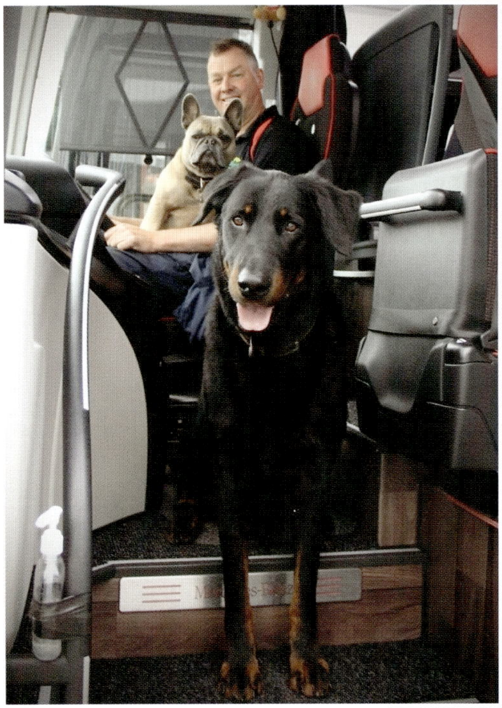

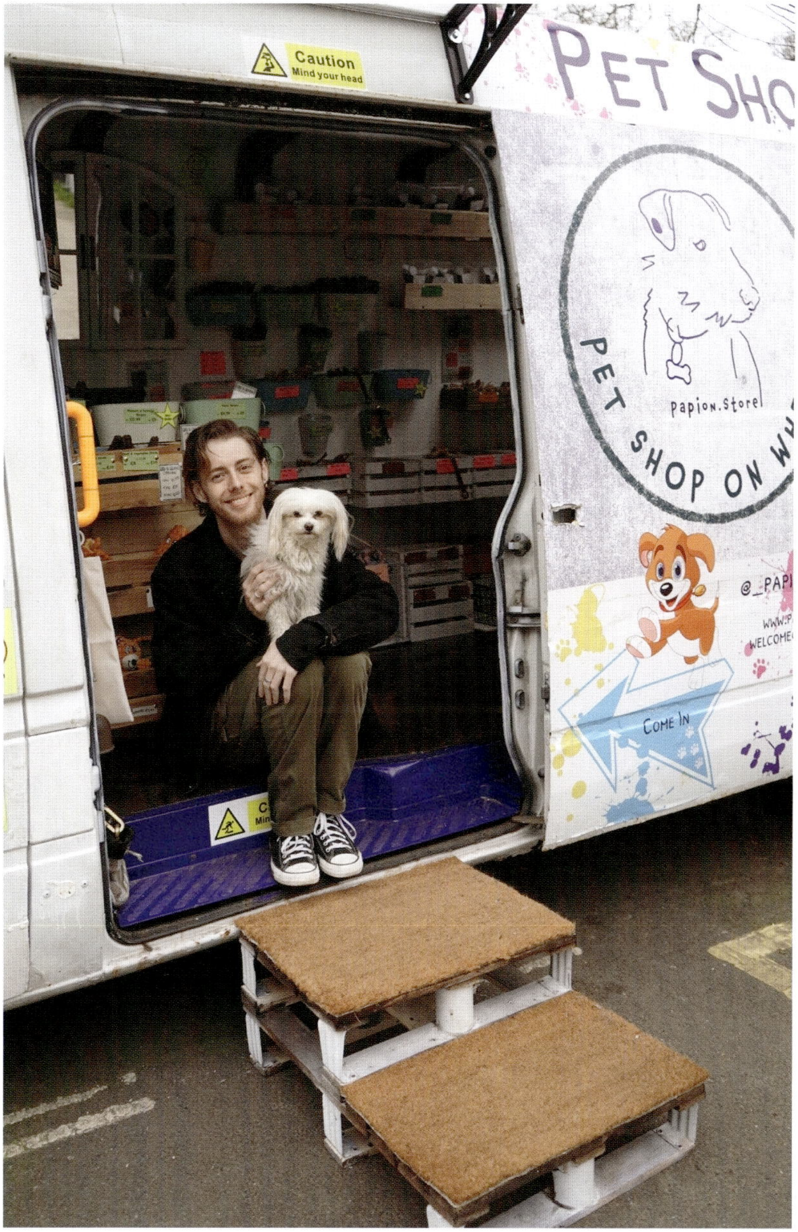

RILEY

Hackney, London, UK

Riley, one of three dogs, gives AJ a reason to get out of the house – not only to walk her but to take her to work. Having a dog brings AJ so much joy when he sees how they bring joy to others.

Named after a character in the Olsen twin movie *So Little Time*, Riley is only reactive towards other dogs if they come into the van too quickly.

She is very good around the treats on display in the pet shop on wheels that must smell like pure heaven to her. She can normally be found in her little bed next to the till or snoozing in AJ's lap.

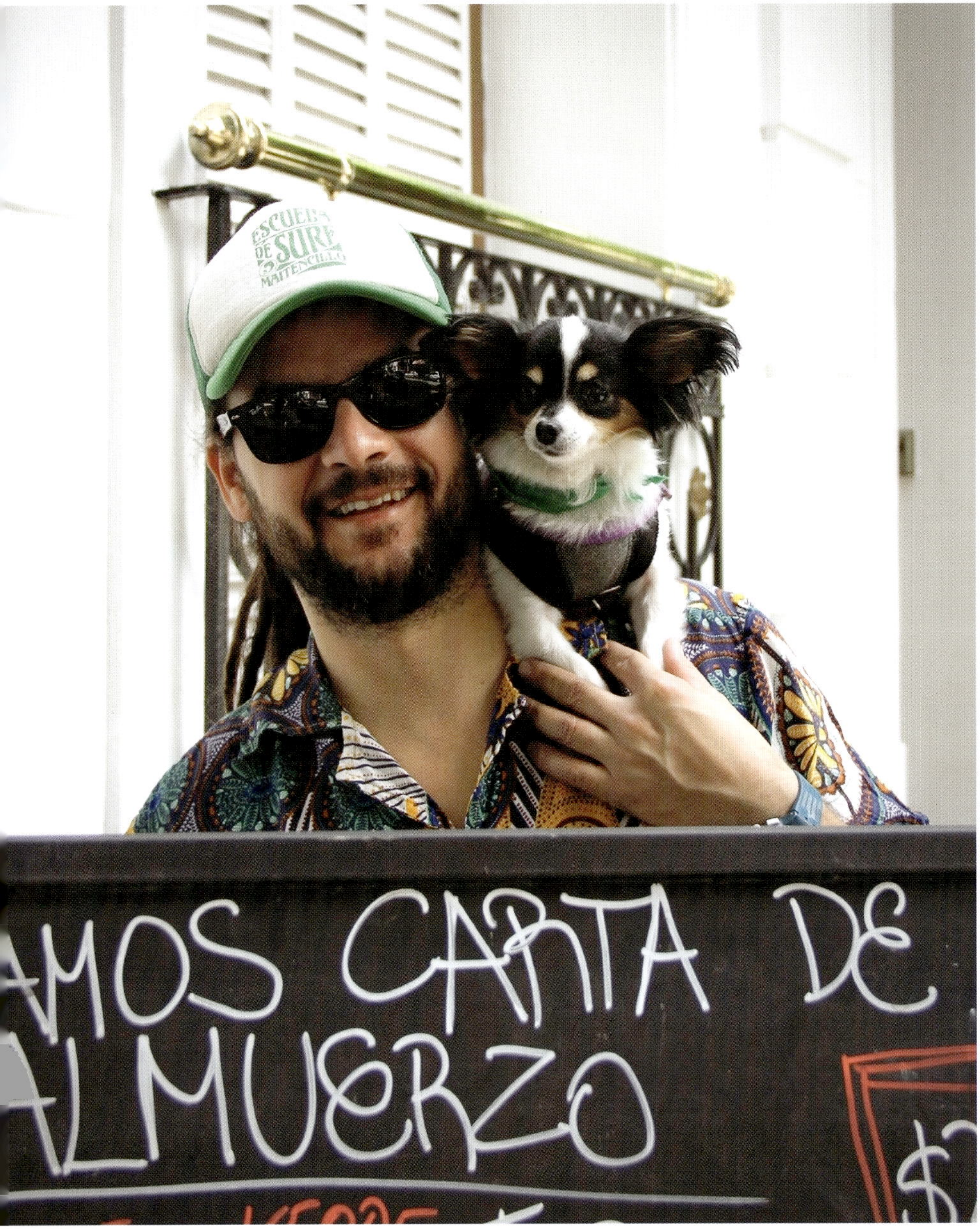

MOROTTA

Buenos Aires, Argentina

Morotta, a Papillon, is owned by Hernán, a Chilean tattoo artist, who works on signboards in Buenos Aires.

Morotta was rescued from a kill centre and now goes everywhere with Hernán, even to football training. She trembles a lot, and Hernán thinks it may be because she was mistreated before he got her. The green scarf she wears is in solidarity with the campaign to make abortion legal in Argentina.

Hernán plans to return to Chile to become a guide in the San Pedro de Atacama desert. Morotta will go too.

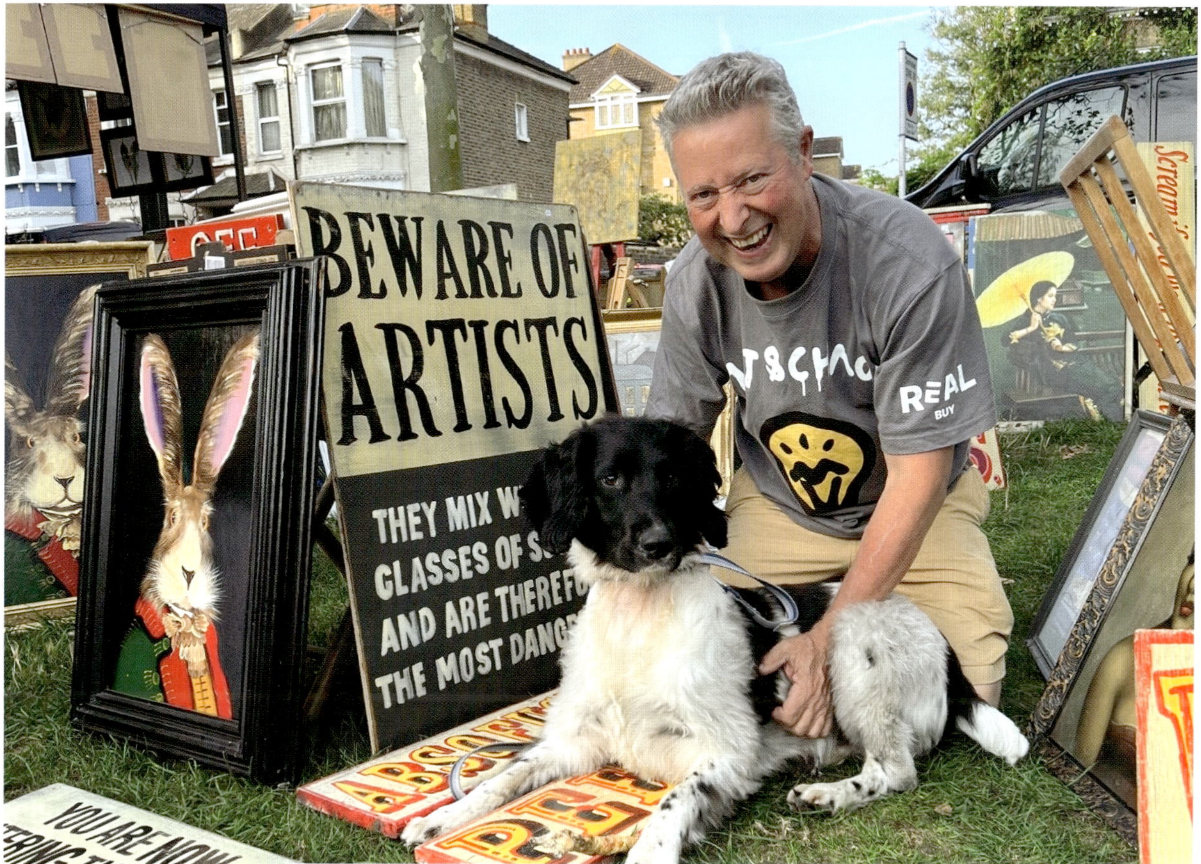

ERNIE

Barnes, London, UK

'He unwobbles me,' Richard says of Ernie, who has helped him cope after his wife died. This wonderful Springer Spaniel may not understand words, but he certainly understands moods. He saw Richard crying once and put a paw on him 'as if to say "sort yourself out" in dog language.'

Ernie travels with Richard to London bric-à-brac markets, where he lies among the home-made sign boards and artwork.

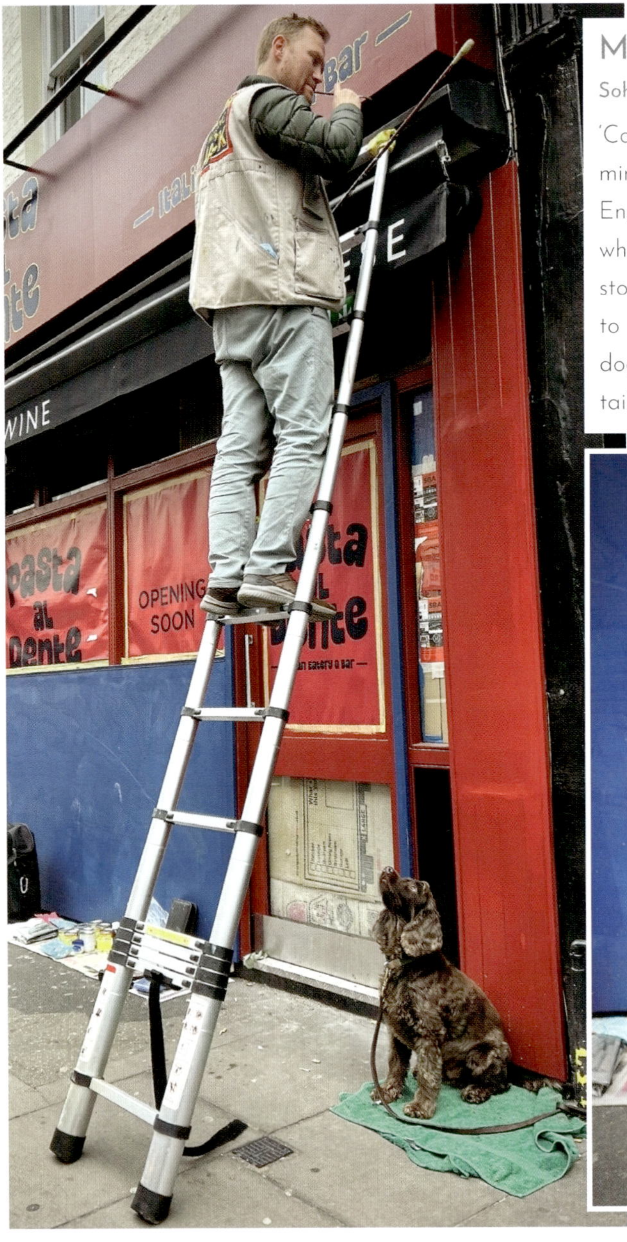

MARBLE

Soho, London, UK

'Calm when he needs to be – and bonkers every other minute' is how Jack, a signwriter, describes Marble, his English Working Cocker Spaniel. Marble lies on a blanket whilst Jack is up a ladder, painting. Passers-by invariably stop for a chat and a cuddle, and Marble is always happy to see people. He is one of a family of champion agility dogs and his flexibility becomes evident when he wags his tail so hard that his body bends in half.

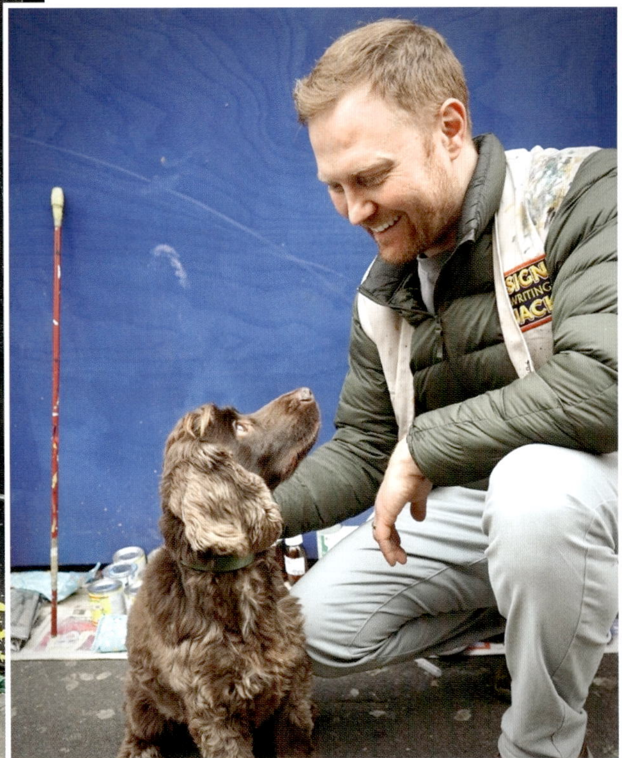

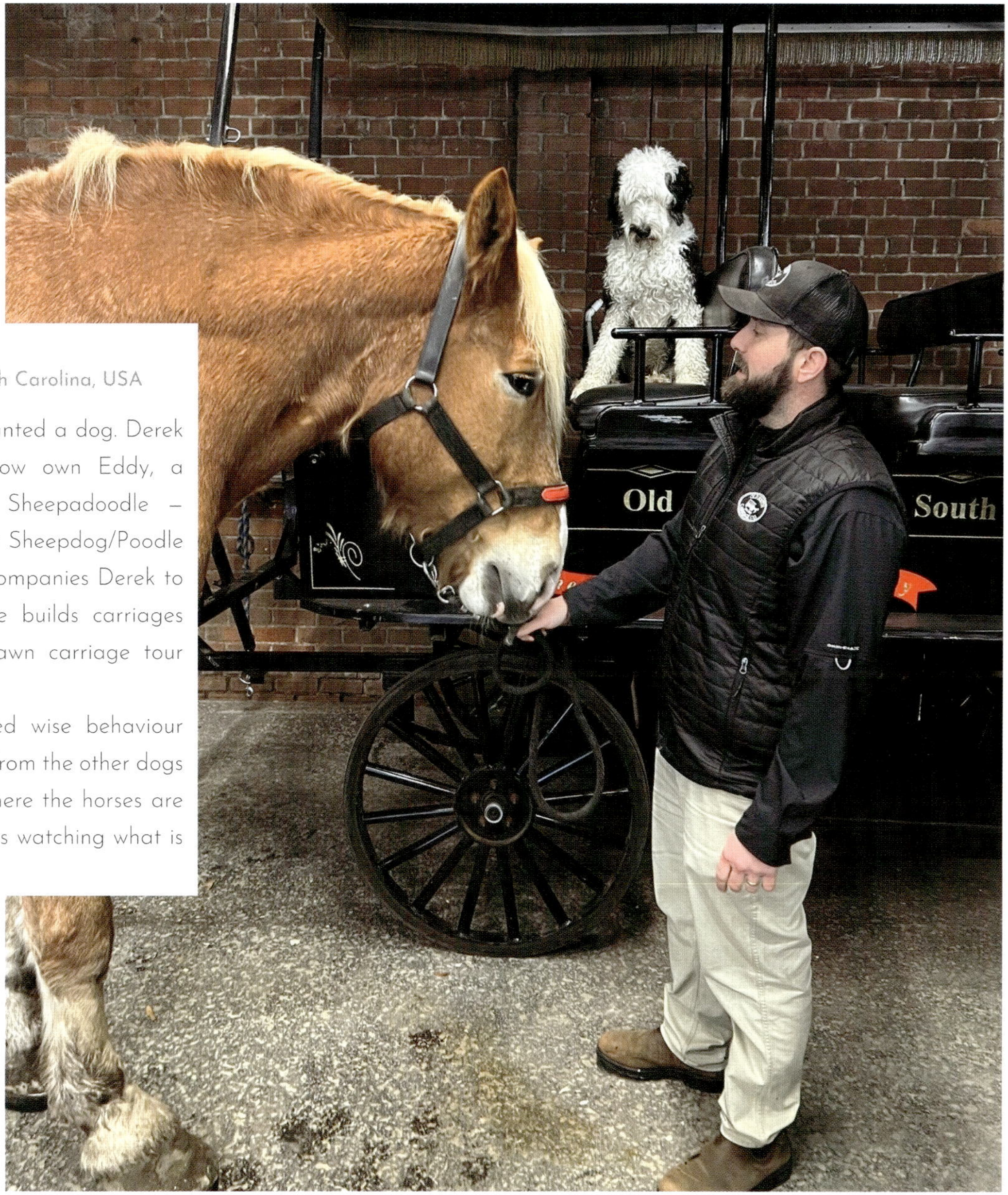

EDDY

Charleston, South Carolina, USA

Derek's wife wanted a dog. Derek didn't. They now own Eddy, a seven-year-old Sheepadoodle – an Old English Sheepdog/Poodle mix – who accompanies Derek to work, where he builds carriages for a horse-drawn carriage tour company.

Eddy learned wise behaviour around horses from the other dogs on the farm where the horses are kept, and enjoys watching what is going on.

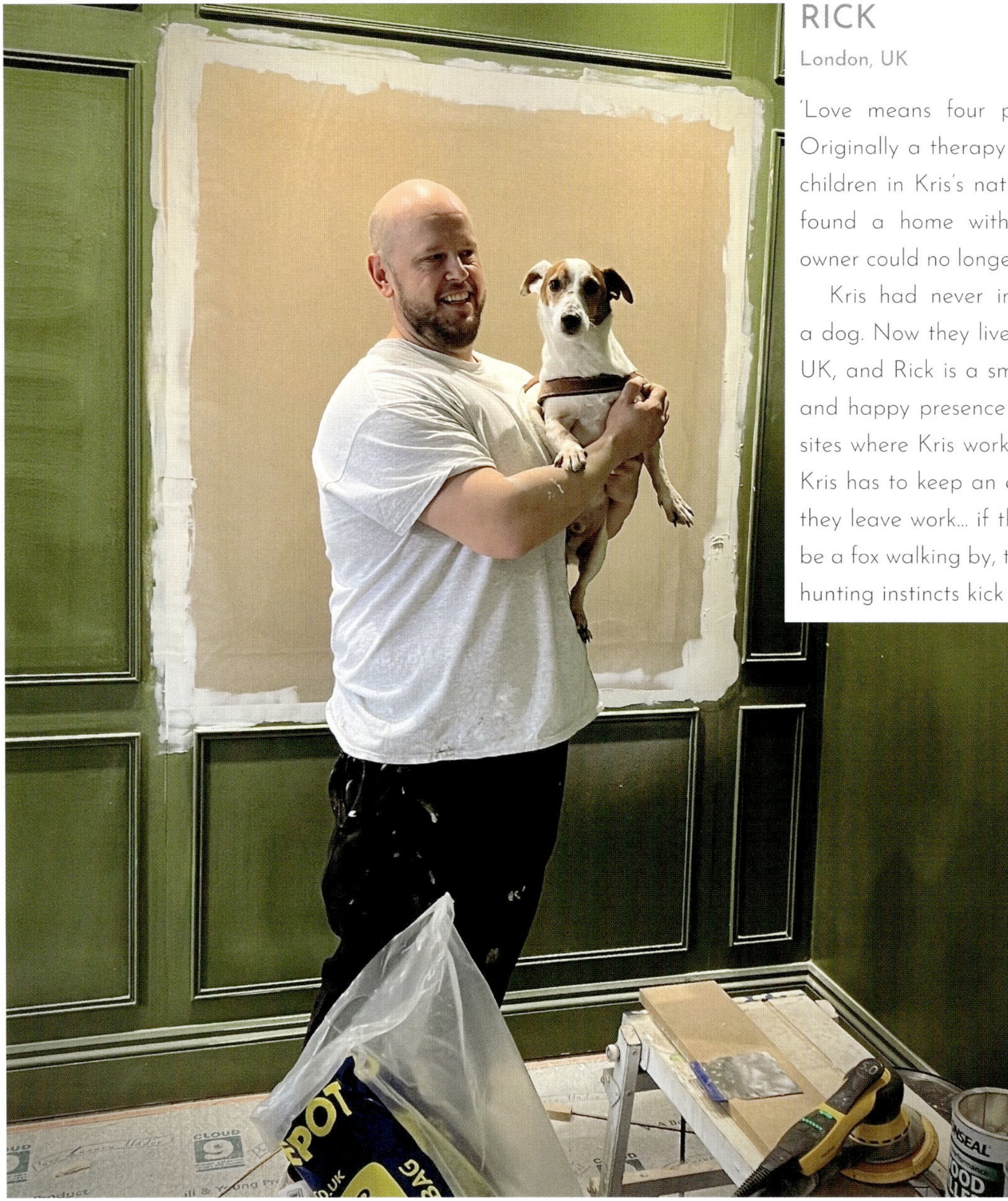

RICK

London, UK

'Love means four paws' says Kris. Originally a therapy dog for autistic children in Kris's native Poland, Rick found a home with Kris when his owner could no longer cope with him.

Kris had never intended to own a dog. Now they live together in the UK, and Rick is a small, well-trained and happy presence on the building sites where Kris works. The only time Kris has to keep an eye on him is as they leave work... if there happens to be a fox walking by, the Jack Russell's hunting instincts kick in.

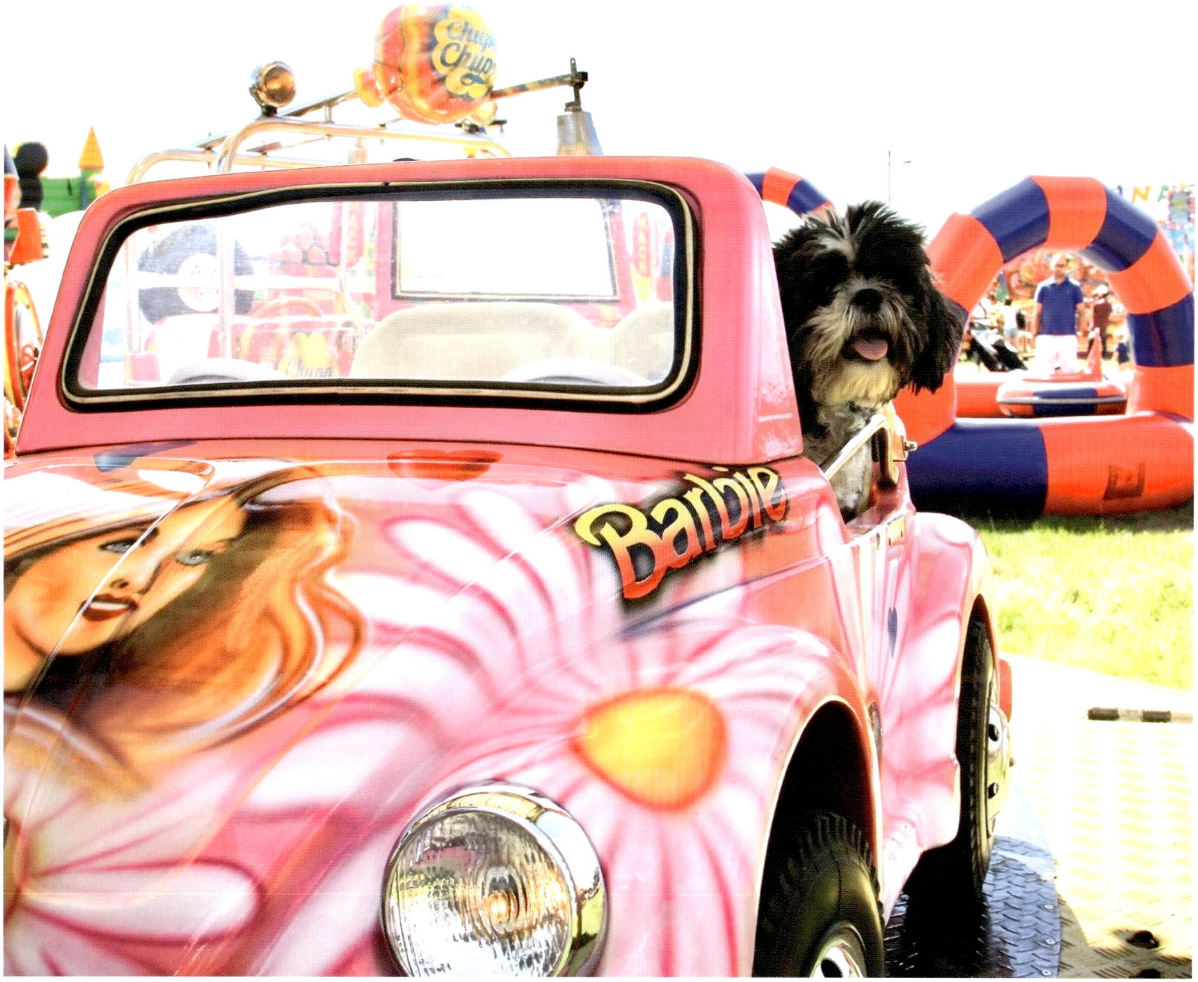

CLOUDY Wimbledon, London, UK

Seven-year-old Cloudy, a Shih Tzu, is a fairground dog. He once got hold of – and ate – a whole bag of raw sausages from the hot dog stall, hiding under the caravan and refusing to come out until he'd had his fill. He is always left off lead and generally lies next to the caravan belonging to his owner, Peggy. He only disappears when he smells cooking, and can often be found sharing someone's lunch in a neighbouring van. Cloudy loves chasing squirrels and bicycles.

BOGART

Naples, Florida, USA

One-eyed Bogart, a Boston Terrier, belongs to Bob, a carpenter from Ohio who started a charity to promote kindness and compassion towards children with disabilities and mental health issues, and to increase awareness around bullying. One Million Acts of Kindness was set up as a response to the Virginia Tech killing of 2007 and has become a lifetime mission for Bob.

Bogart and Bob have travelled the length and breadth of the USA in a blue bus painted with logos promoting kindness to others.

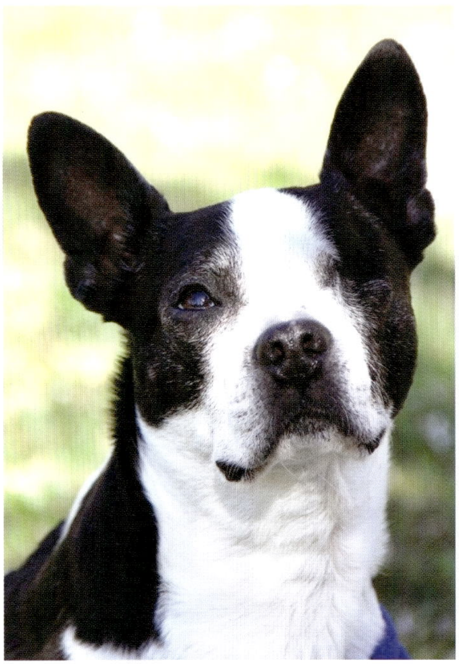

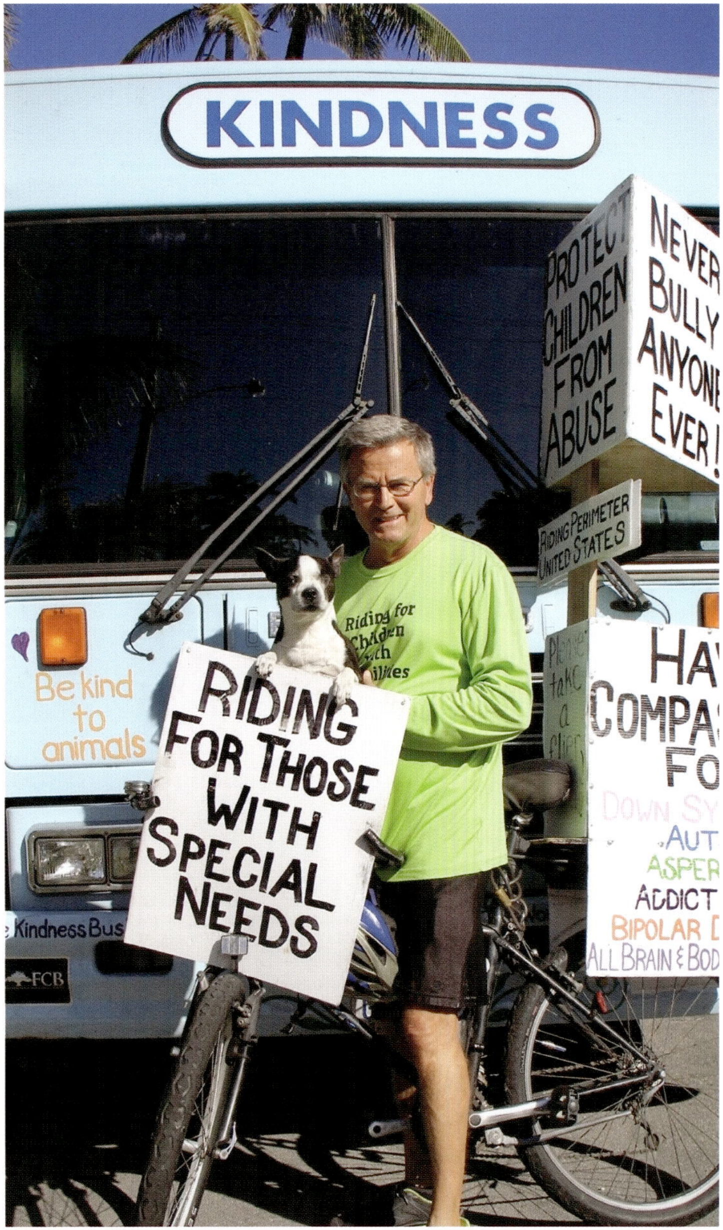

STAR Wimbledon, London, UK

Star is a thirteen-year-old rescue dog, who lives up to her name as she helps John with his depression. Her daily routine revolves round the water where she and John live on a narrowboat, taken up mostly by the book shop he runs on board.

Star loves lying in her favourite spot, duck watching from a porthole. She will bark near closing time if John is late shutting up. She has been a real confidence boost for John and is always cheerful and optimistic. He feels that Star has been put on earth to help him cope with life.

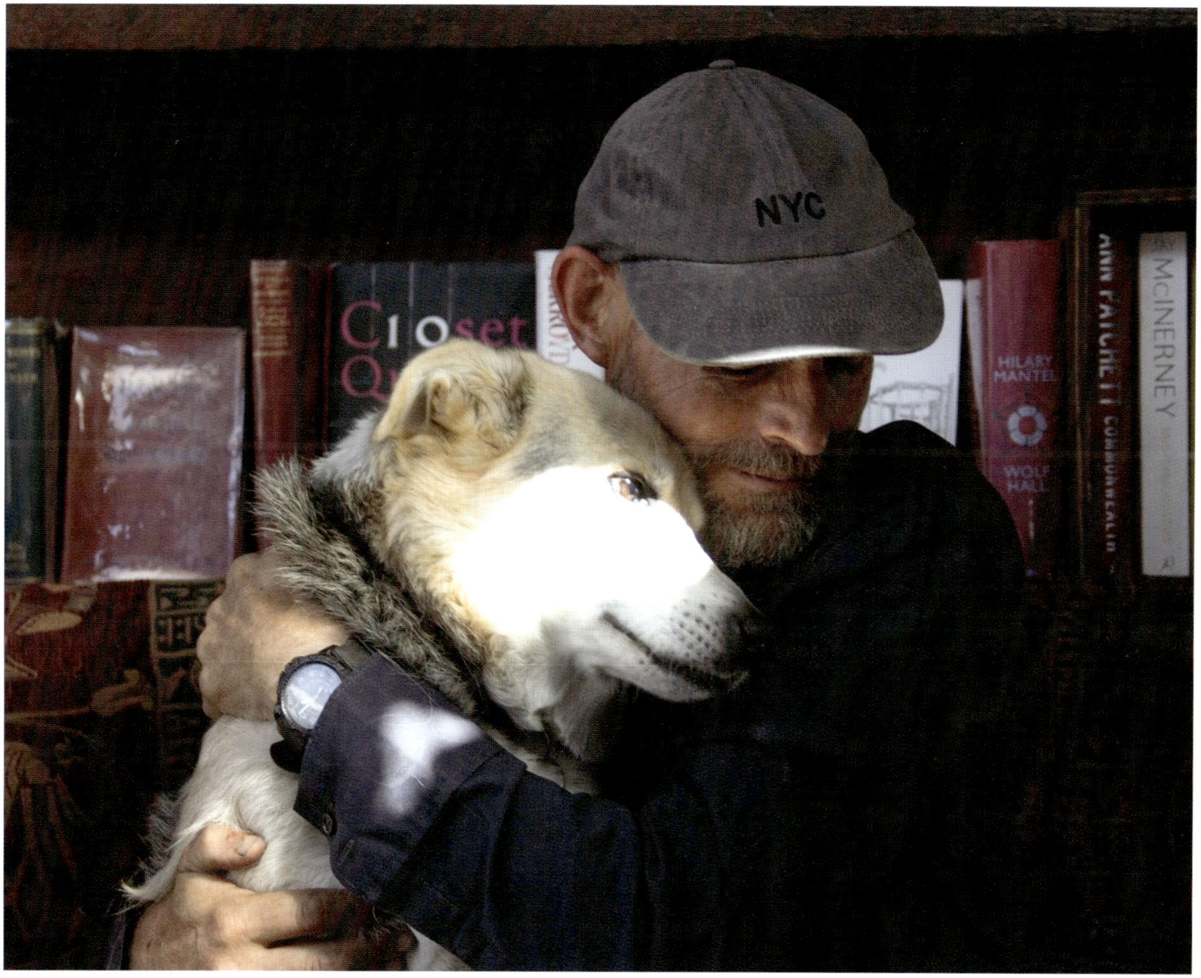

STUDIO DOGS

There is no question that studio dogs provide companionship during a long day of painting or pottery throwing – but more than that, they also appear to offer inspiration.

Studio dogs seem to sense when it's appropriate to be still and when it's the right time to nudge for a bit of attention.

On my studio visits, I am filled with a sense of calm, as if the dog and its aura dictate a meditative pace. Who could fail to feel artistically stimulated in these wonderful workspaces?

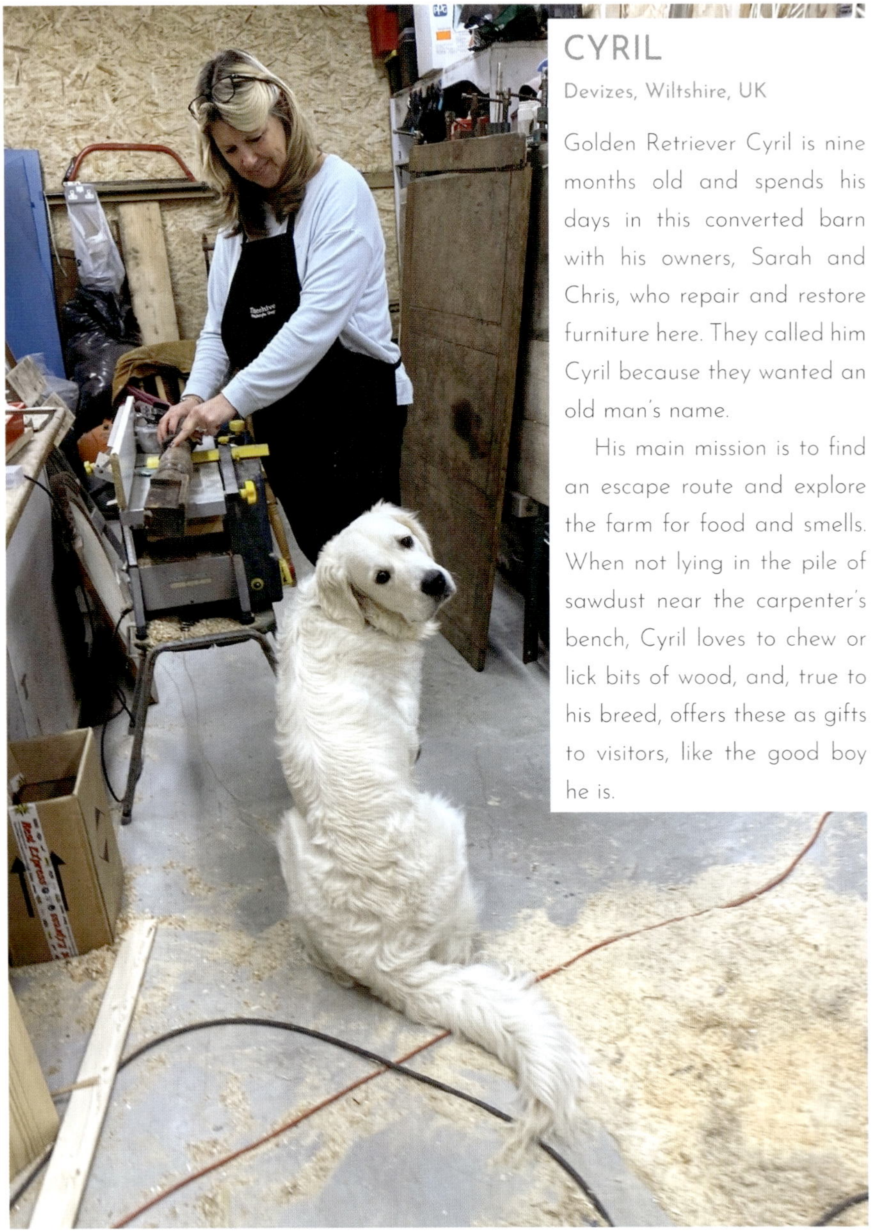

CYRIL

Devizes, Wiltshire, UK

Golden Retriever Cyril is nine months old and spends his days in this converted barn with his owners, Sarah and Chris, who repair and restore furniture here. They called him Cyril because they wanted an old man's name.

His main mission is to find an escape route and explore the farm for food and smells. When not lying in the pile of sawdust near the carpenter's bench, Cyril loves to chew or lick bits of wood, and, true to his breed, offers these as gifts to visitors, like the good boy he is.

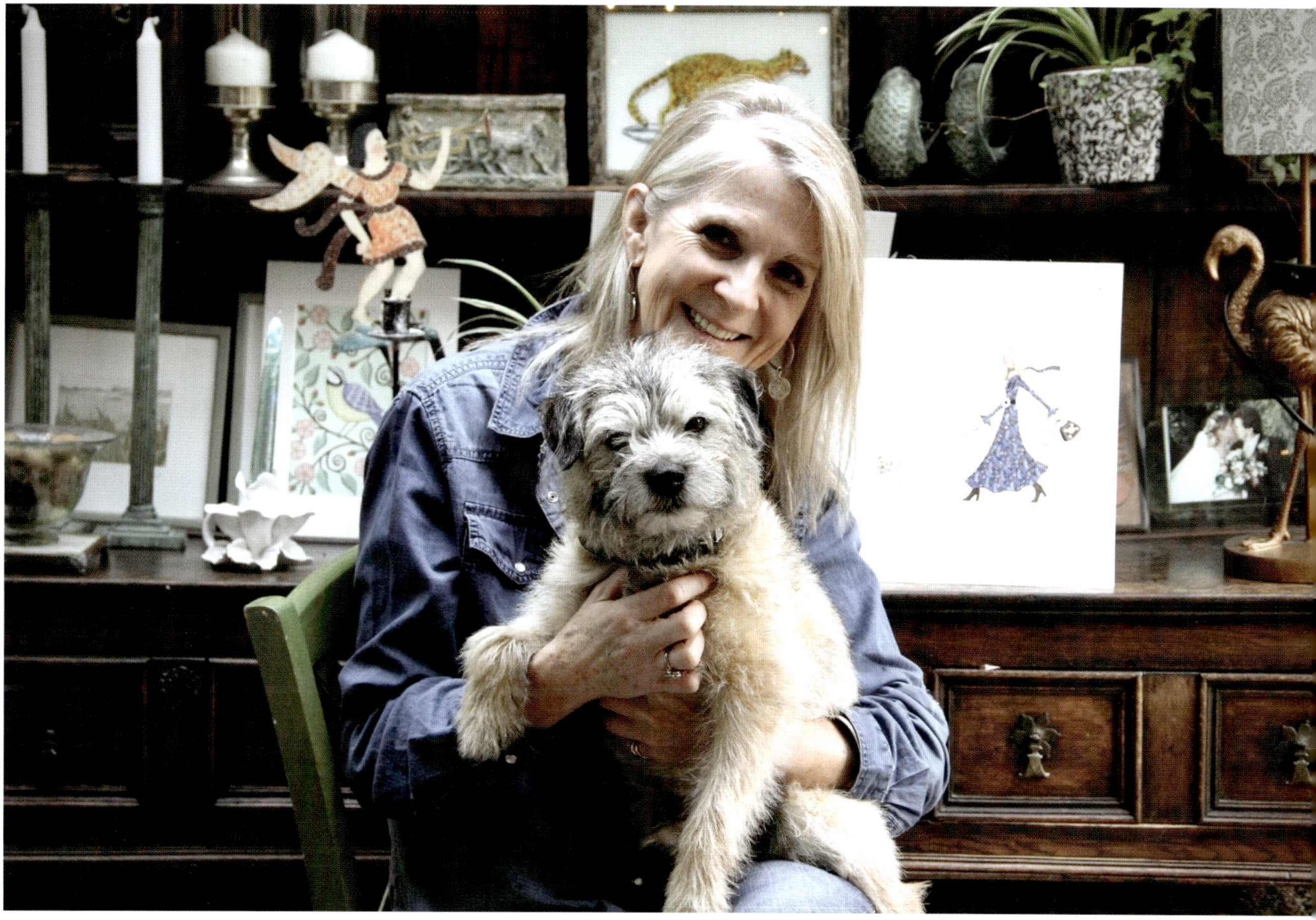

JUMBLE

Wandsworth, London, UK

Camilla is an artist, who paints personalised maps, and Jumble, a ten-year-old Border Terrier, is her 'little soulmate'. He's the inspiration for many of her paintings; indeed, he features in every single map she produces.

Jumble's routine revolves around sleep. He has a bed in Camilla's room and, after breakfast, takes himself off there again. He also has the choice of a bed in Camilla's studio or in the kitchen. When the working day is over, Jumble loves lying on the back of the sofa as the family watches television.

BERNIE Barnes, London, UK

Bernie is a Bernese Mountain dog, whose only desire is to be with her own 'pack' – and she will squeeze herself into the smallest of spaces in order to be near Charlotte and her family. Bernie came into their lives after Charlotte suffered a serious brain injury during a lacrosse match. She feels she recovered much faster thanks to Bernie's calm presence.

Charlotte is a milliner, who works from a studio in her back garden where Bernie provides companionship and comfort. In the winter, the dog becomes a 3D rug and keeps Charlotte's feet beautifully warm as she assembles her wonderful creations.

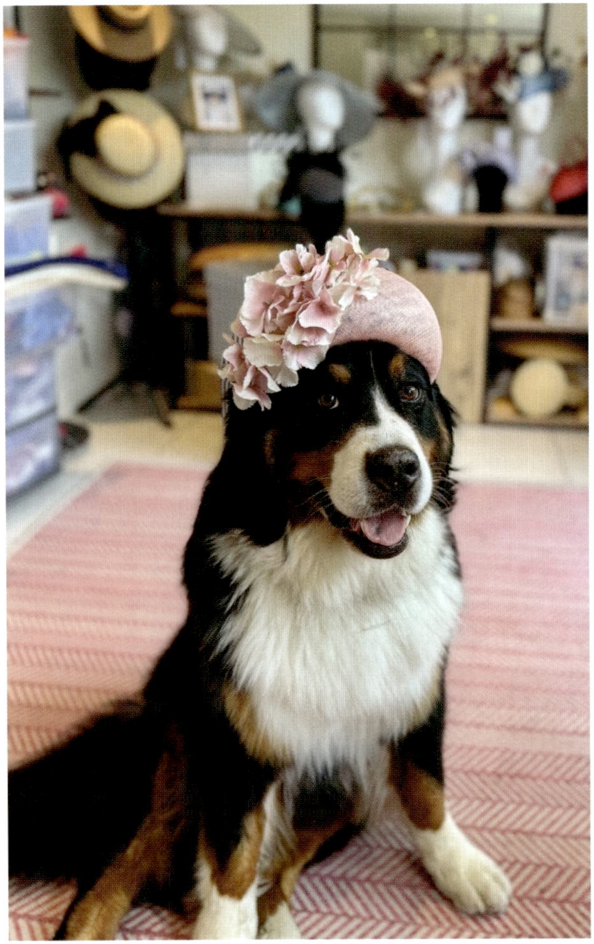

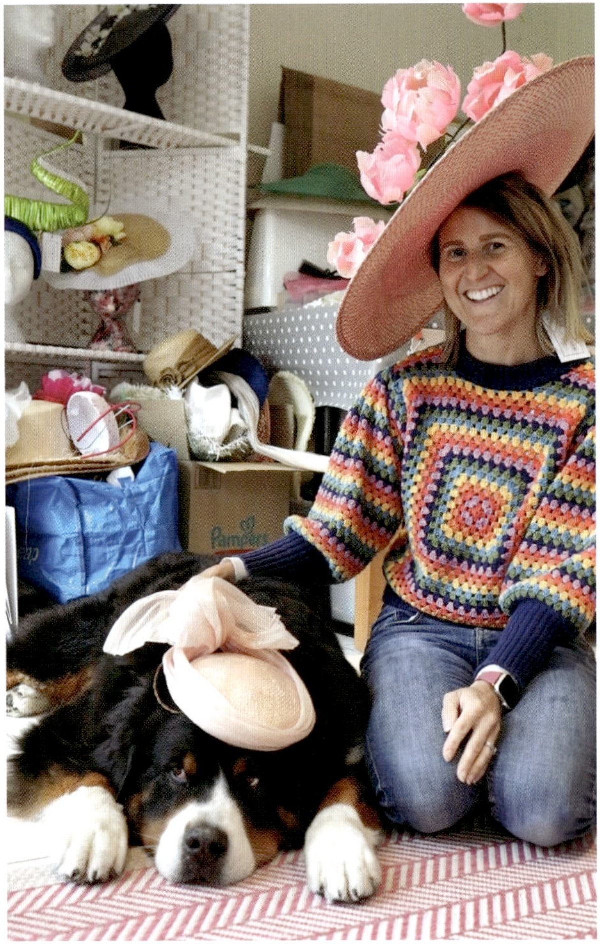

ARCHIE West Horsley, Surrey, UK

Ten-year-old Archie, a blue roan Cocker Spaniel, keeps Adam company in his glass-blowing studio. Archie loves people and interacting with them. He is careful around glass and keeps away from the kilns. He is also happy in the office trailer, where he sneaks onto the large swivel chair and helps himself to crumbs on the table after tea breaks.

He is proficient at rollovers and other commands but, equally, can whine for England, according to Adam. Archie whines for his treat at 3pm every afternoon and often whines during his two-hour grooming session, although his groomer says she is just 'listening to his stories'. His bedtime treat is a raw carrot.

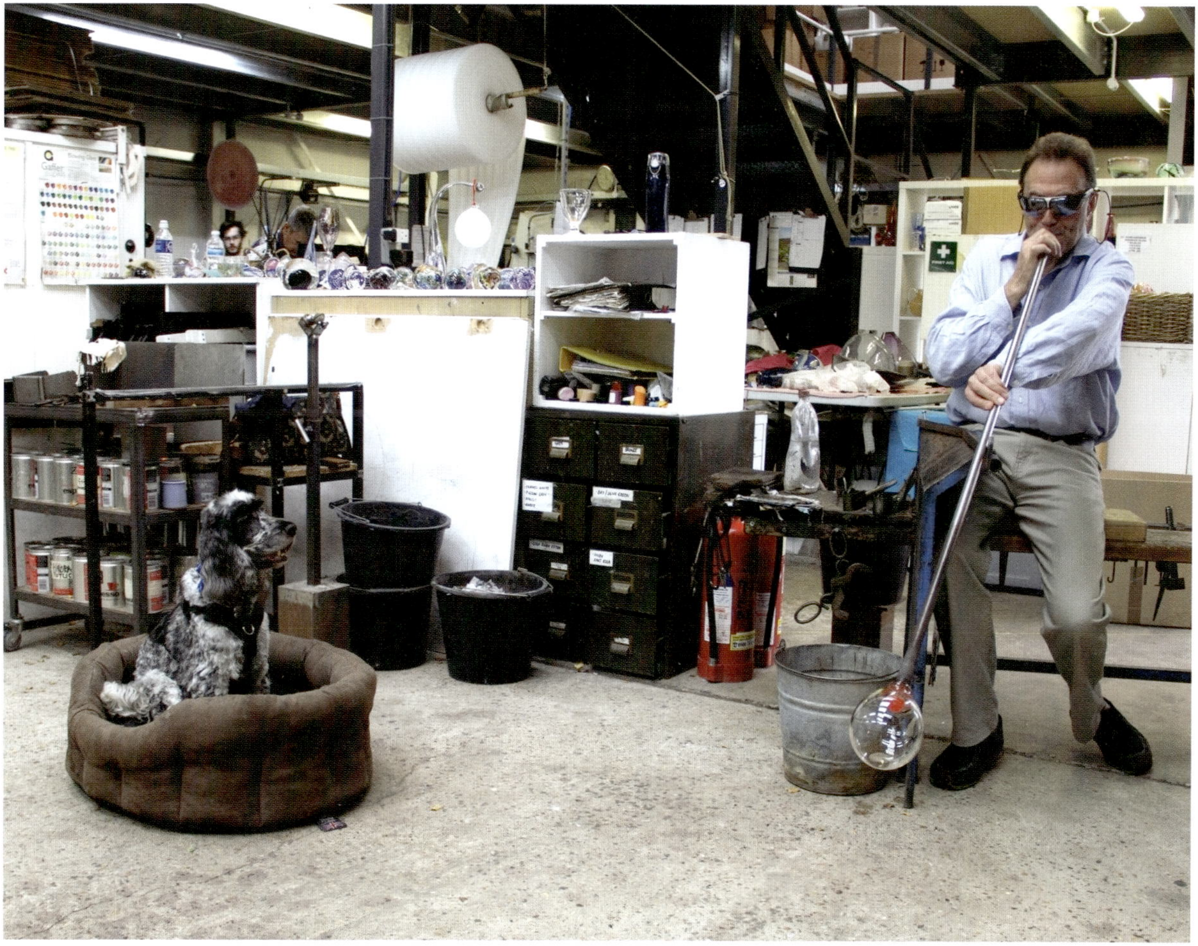

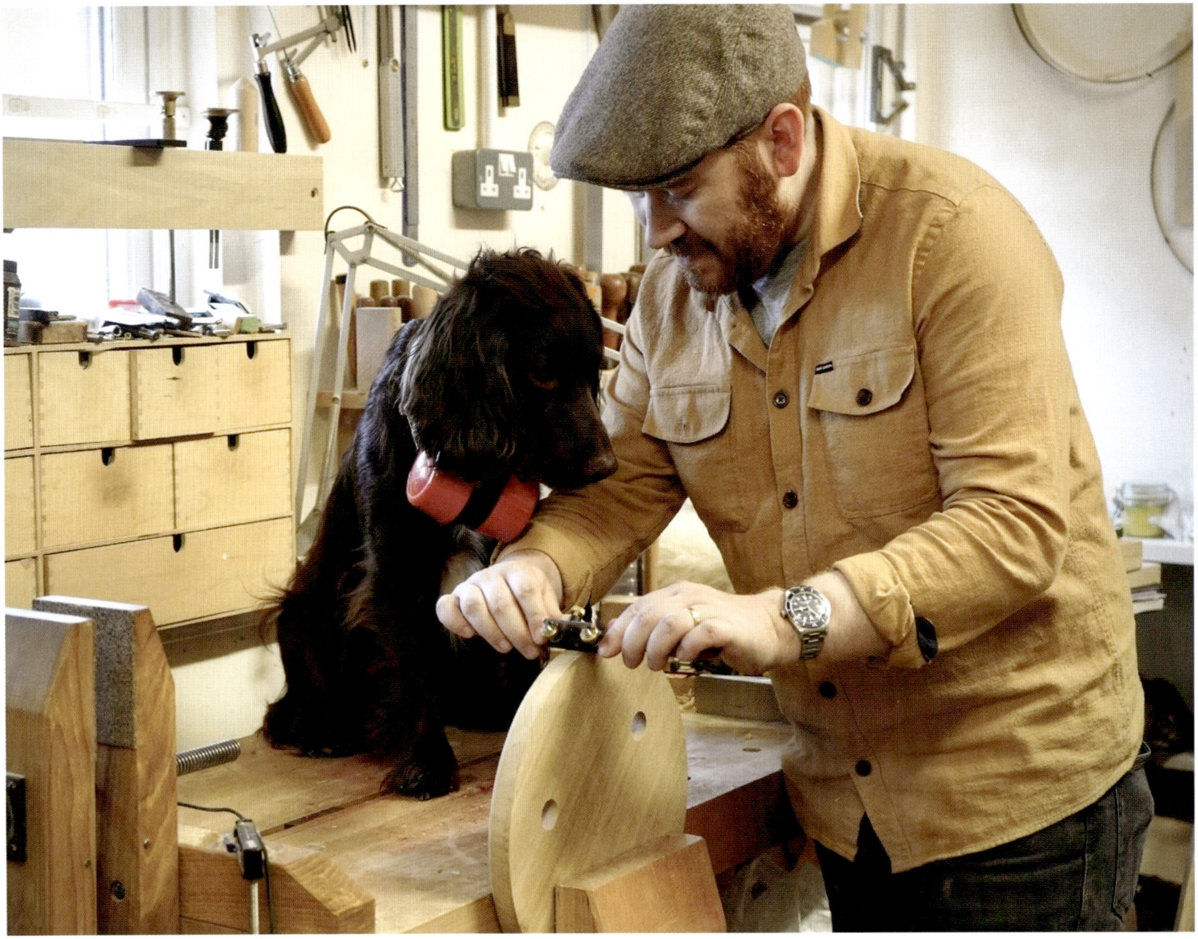

MONTY Andover, Hampshire, UK

Monty, a Sprocker, is five, and David's constant companion at the studio workshop where he makes bespoke wooden furniture and gives classes. During lockdown, Monty became very vocal, as visitors were few and far between. In fact, according to David, he has now turned into a doorbell.

Monty's routine includes greeting the students, including two autistic boys who are learning wood-working skills. They particularly love having Monty around.

Monty enjoys being involved in any work done at ground level, and quite often comes away covered in shavings.

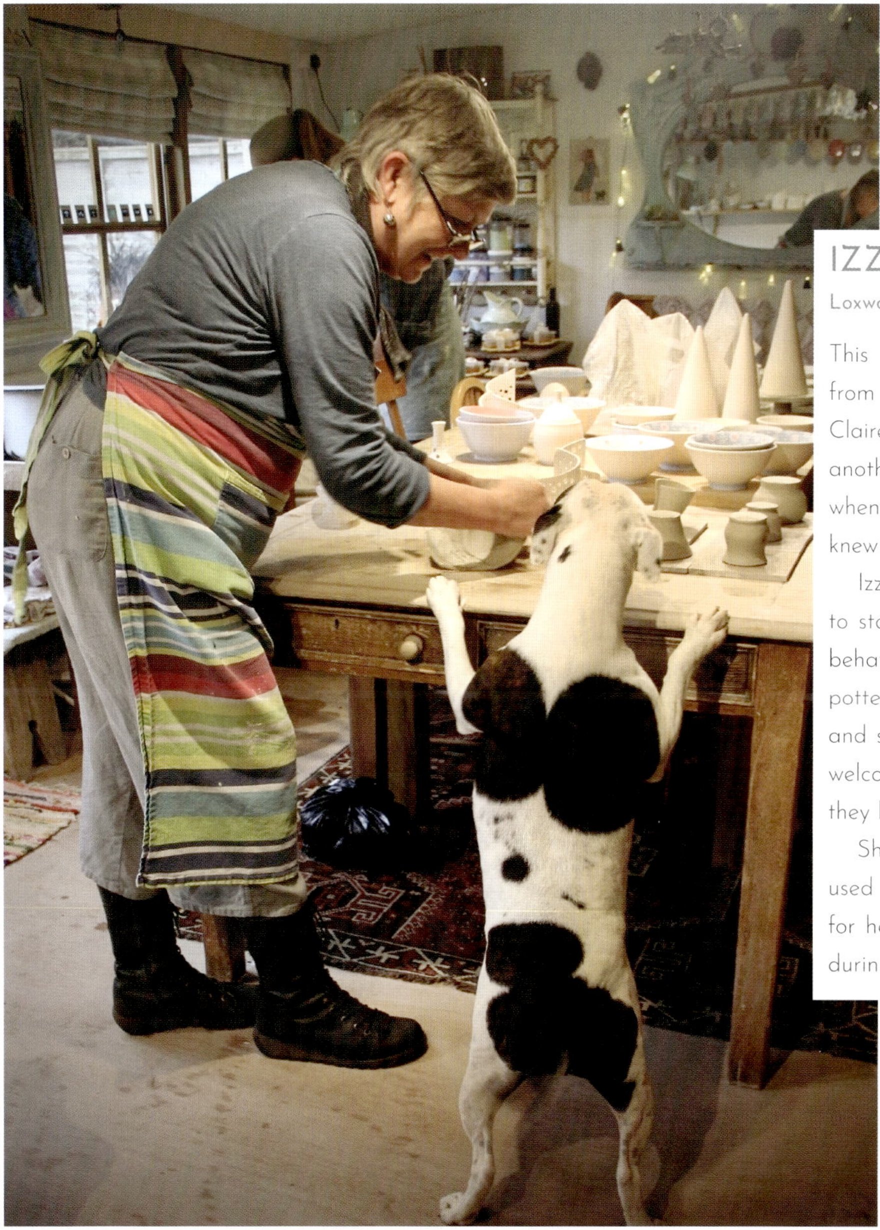

IZZY

Loxwood, West Sussex, UK

This Staffordshire Bull Terrier came from Battersea Dogs & Cats Home. Claire, a potter, had previously owned another Staffie, also called Izzy – so when this one was advertised, she knew that it was meant to be.

Izzy Mark Two was uncontrollable to start with, but now is beautifully behaved. She has never broken any pottery, is extremely affectionate, and stands at the door of the shed welcoming students, thinking that they have just come to visit her.

She's also very beguiling. Claire used up all the chicken intended for her own lunch as treats for Izzy during the photo session.

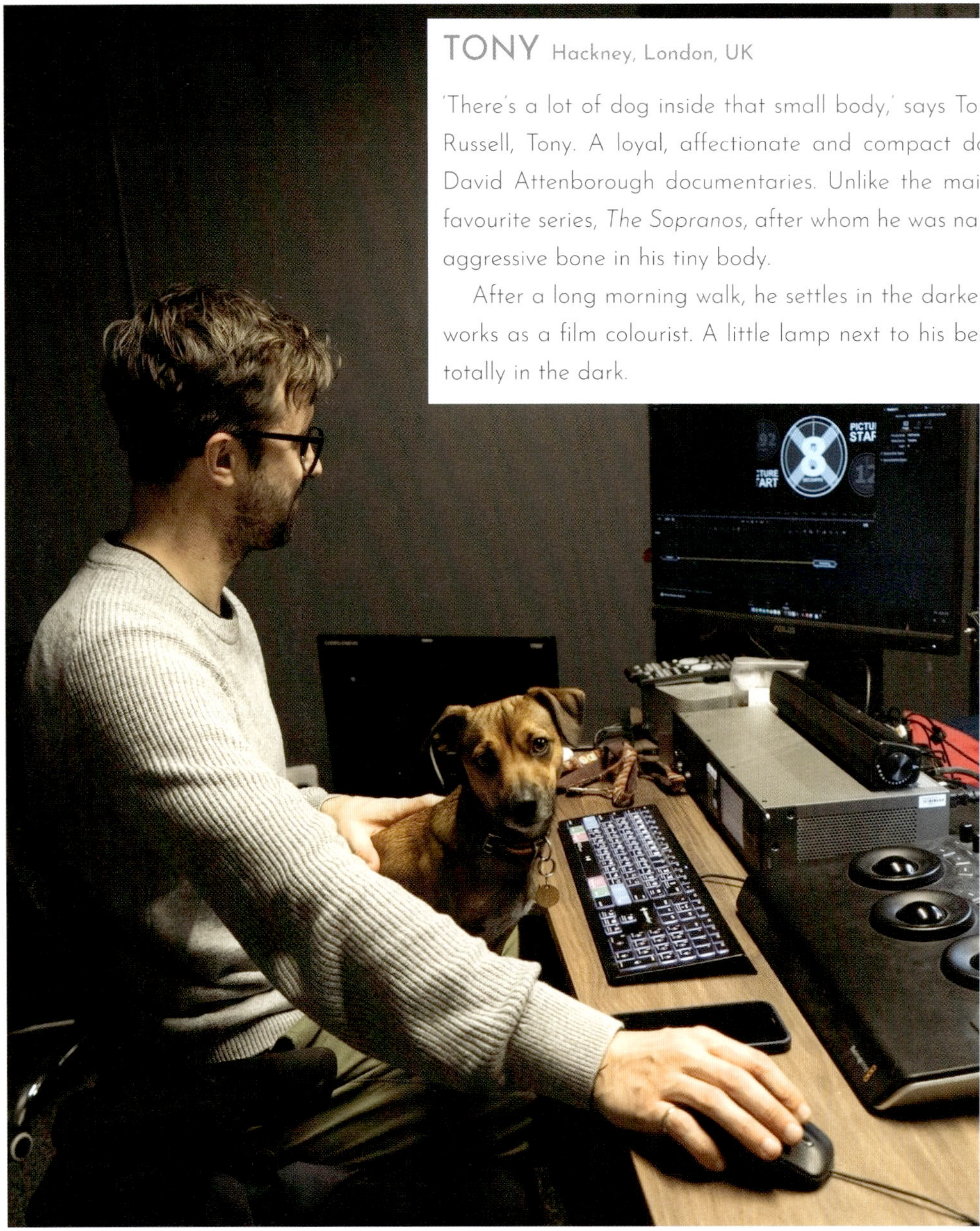

TONY Hackney, London, UK

'There's a lot of dog inside that small body,' says Tom's wife of their Jack Russell, Tony. A loyal, affectionate and compact dog, he only barks at David Attenborough documentaries. Unlike the main character in Tom's favourite series, *The Sopranos*, after whom he was named, Tony has not an aggressive bone in his tiny body.

After a long morning walk, he settles in the darkened room where Tom works as a film colourist. A little lamp next to his bed ensures Tony is not totally in the dark.

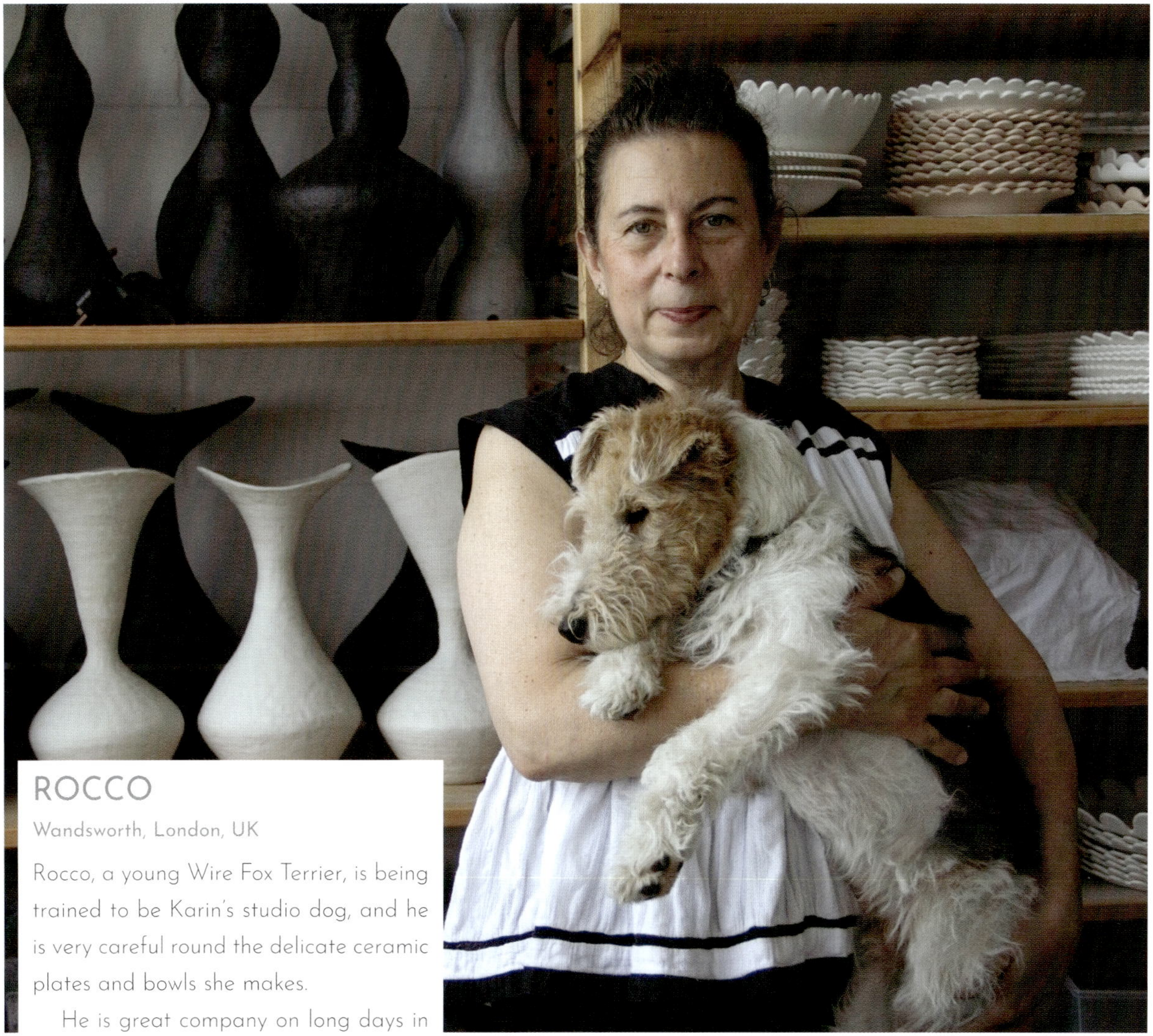

ROCCO

Wandsworth, London, UK

Rocco, a young Wire Fox Terrier, is being trained to be Karin's studio dog, and he is very careful round the delicate ceramic plates and bowls she makes.

He is great company on long days in the studio, and likes to lie in the corridor, secured by an extra-long lead, so that anyone who walks past can make a fuss of him.

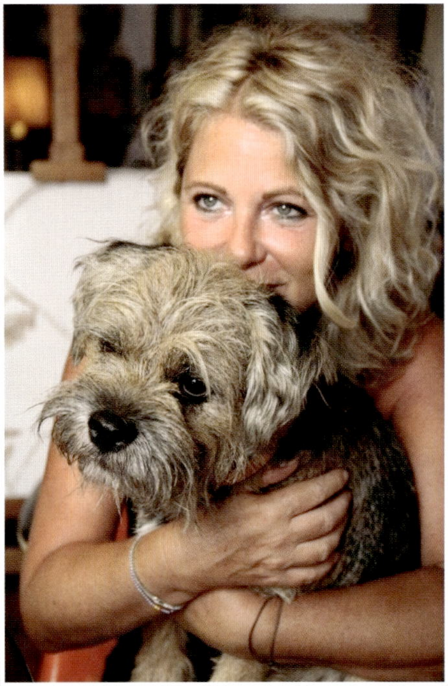

GINO Grimaud, Var, France

Gino is something of a celebrity, who has advertised for jewellery designers and dog clothes collections. He has also posed for his sculpture. His artist owner, Ariane, has studios in Grimaud and Paris.

Gino is a type of terrier formerly bred to kill wild boars. He is rather a Jekyll and Hyde character and once bit Ariane's husband on the buttock when he raised his voice.

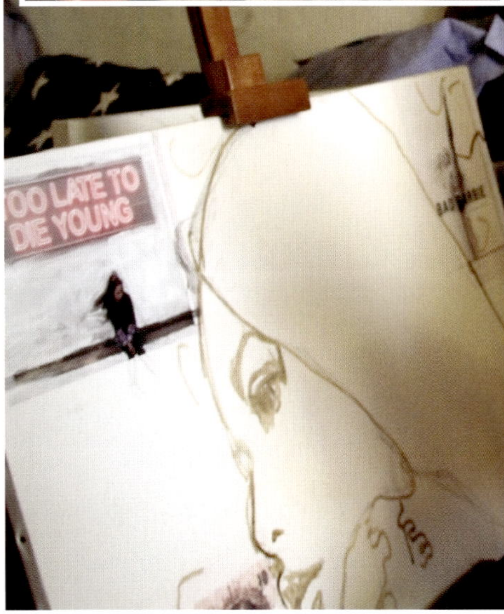

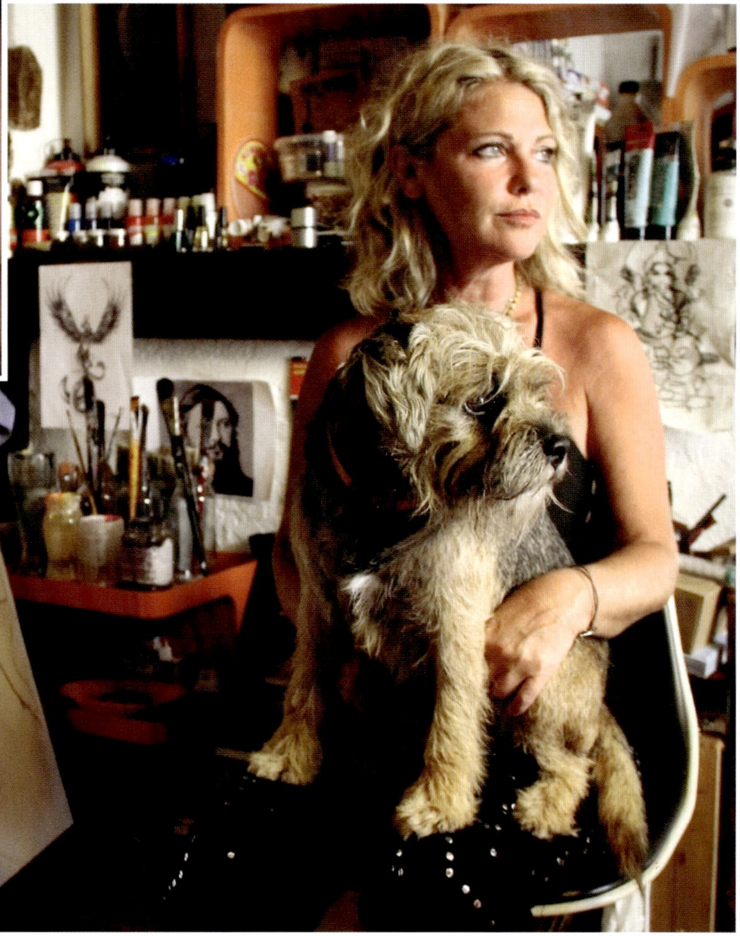

RUFUS Kingston upon Thames, London, UK

This resident gym dog is Rufus, a three-year-old Irish rescue: part-Bernese Mountain Dog, part-Border Collie. He can normally be found lying on his bed under the desk or on the carpet (he is not allowed on the gym mat) fast asleep while the music blares out during classes. He wakes when the music stops and is always on the scrounge for a treat.

Rufus is generally a very settled boy, but becomes very excited when his owner, Jim, puts on his jacket and earphones, as he knows there will be a walk involved. Rufus likes all types of water except for bathwater, and is an enthusiastic swan-chaser.

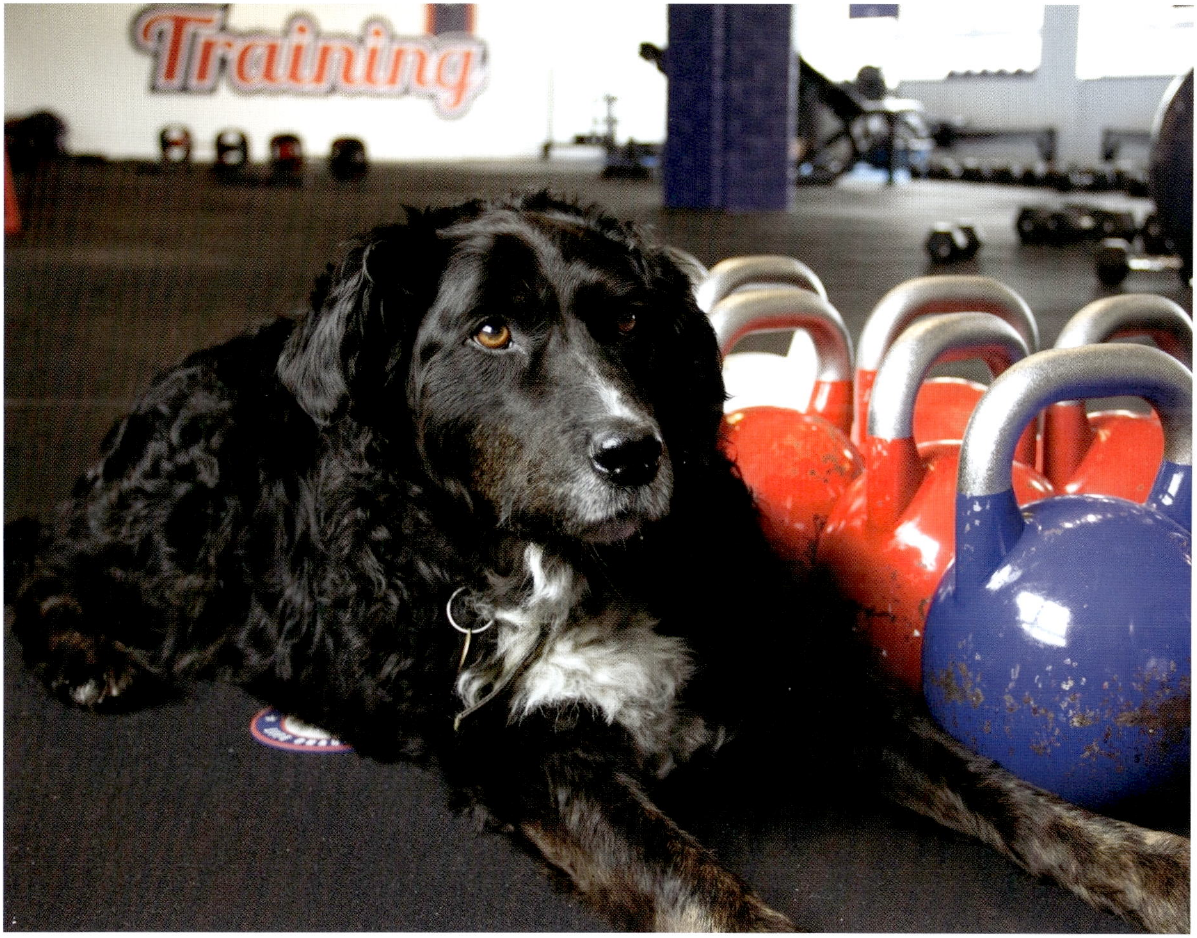

BUDAI Montevideo, Uruguay

Budai, a British Bulldog pup, named after Buddha, is smothered with love by her owners in their tattoo parlour in the Old City of Montevideo. When not perched on the counter next to an old cash register, Budai plays with children's toys on the shop floor. The tattoo artists specifically chose the breed because British Bulldogs are known to be calm.

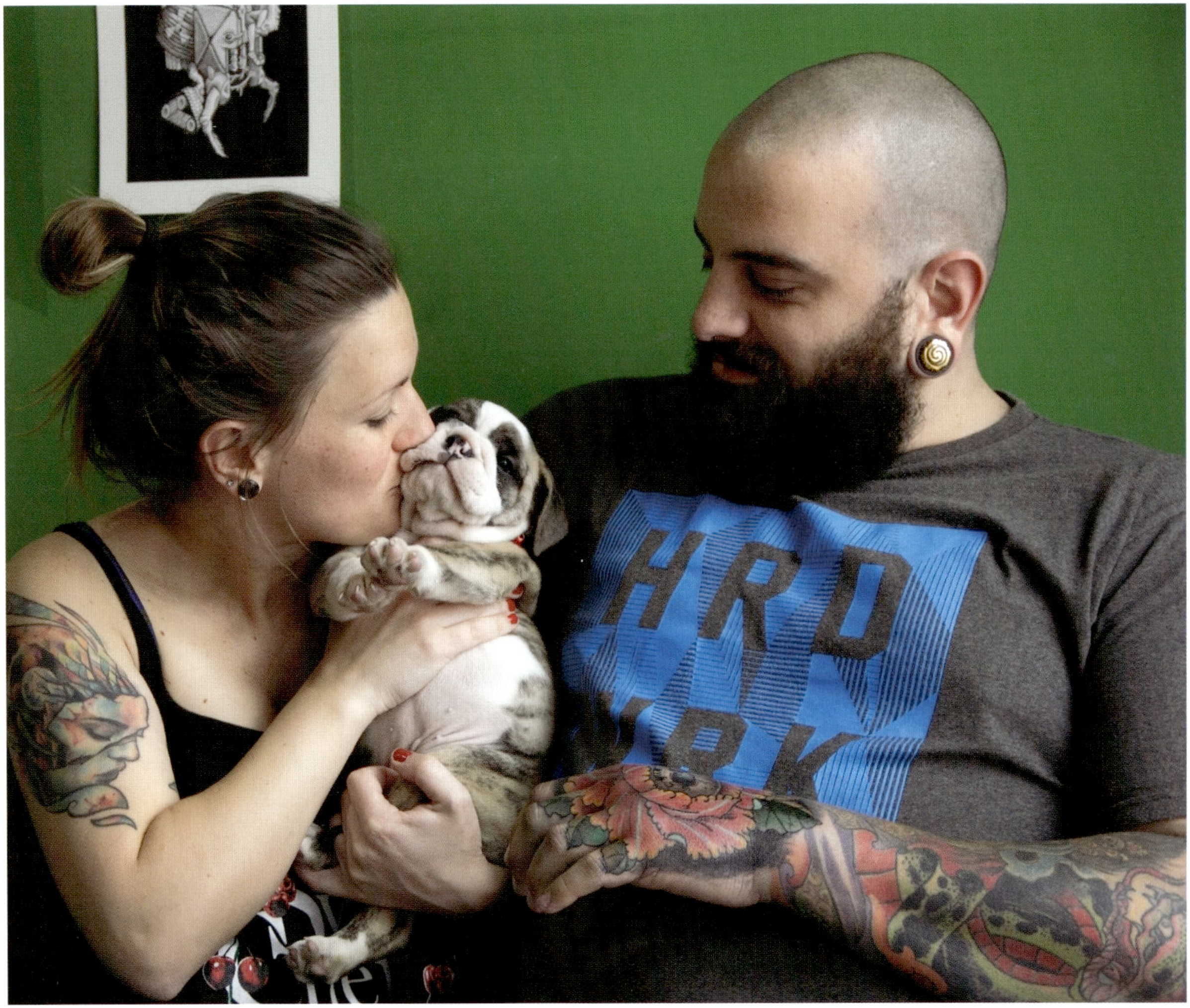

MARCEL Saint-Tropez, Var, France

Marcel is a one-and-a-half-year-old Whippet, whose French artist owner, Corinne, claims he is like a flying dog. Thankfully, this is only on walks; in the studio, he moves around like a cat – although he does have a tendency to drink the water out of the flower vases.

He grew up alongside a little girl whose parents own a nearby shop. She will feed him and play with him during the day. Like a good French dog, he loves eating baguette crusts.

Marcel often features in Corinne's paintings, and one of them hangs in the local council office.

Corinne says they have a great connection – 'we are both better for being together all the time.'

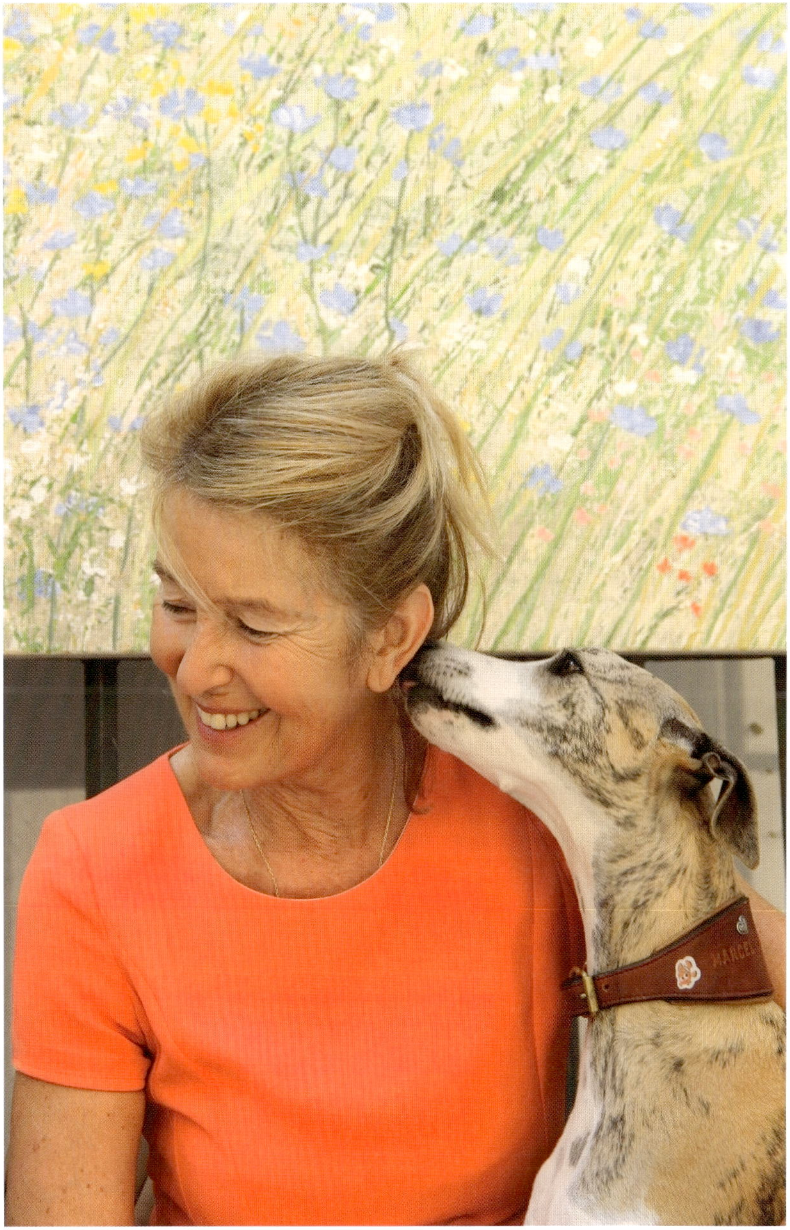

ACKNOWLEDGEMENTS

To my three sons, Toffer, Mikey and Nic – and to our much-adored Golden Retriever, Benjy, who for sixteen years was instrumental in showing us unconditional love, through good times and bad.

My siblings – Cath, Dave and Sharon – for encouraging me and always being there for me.

Andrew Wilson, fellow photographer and dog lover, who over the years motivated me to persevere.

Anne Tudor for her guidance and help in contacting Peter Egan who, on behalf of All Dogs Matter, kindly wrote the foreword. Thank you also to Ira Moss and Philly Stock from ADM for their kind co-operation.

My favourite humans – dog lovers all – who have supported me over the years. And especially Michael, who has tolerated endless hours of disrupted walking as I dive into shops on yet another photographic 'dog hunt'.

Finally, but not least, Jill Glenn and Claire Steele, my lovely, thoughtful publishers, whose belief in my project, along with their guidance, visuals and wordsmithery, helped make this a lovely book.

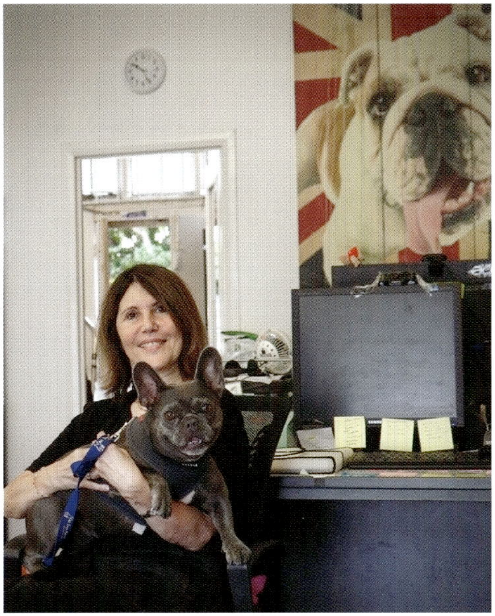

Ira Moss with her rescue Frenchie, Mimi (in charge of security), at the offices of All Dogs Matter, the London rehoming charity she set up over a decade ago with actor and patron Peter Egan. The charity now rehomes around 350 dogs a year.

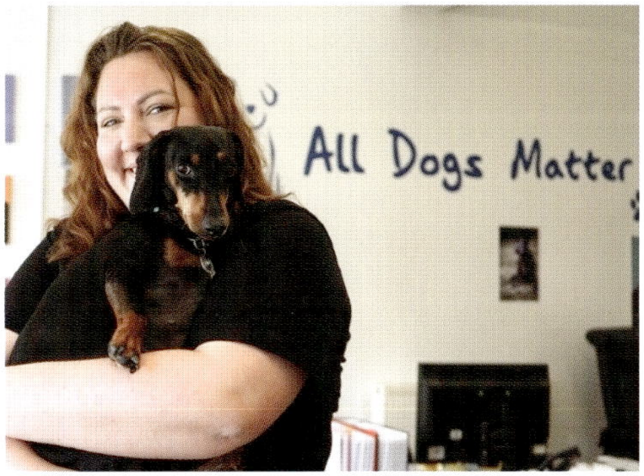

Philly Stock, who is in charge of marketing, communications and events at All Dogs Matter, with her Dachshund, Molly, the office 'ambassadog'.

Thank you for purchasing this book. All Dogs Matter directly benefits from every copy sold.

ABOUT THE AUTHOR

Jackie Richards was born in Montevideo, Uruguay, and has lived in London since her early twenties. After many years as a presenter and producer for the BBC's Latin American service, she turned her creative focus to photography – a passion that began at the age of eleven with a Box Brownie, and continued through darkroom studies at Richmond Adult Community College.

Dogs have always played a central role in Jackie's life. Following the loss of her family's Golden Retriever, she began photographing the dogs she encountered in work environments as she travelled throughout the UK and abroad, in locations from barbers to barracks, cafés to campsites, gift shops to golf courses – a project that grew into *Dogs in the Workplace*.

She is the mother of three sons and enjoys travel, bridge, tennis, and working (persistently) on her golf handicap – ideally with a dog or two close by.

The age of the dogs in this book relates to the day they were photographed.
Some have sadly passed on, and are fondly remembered.